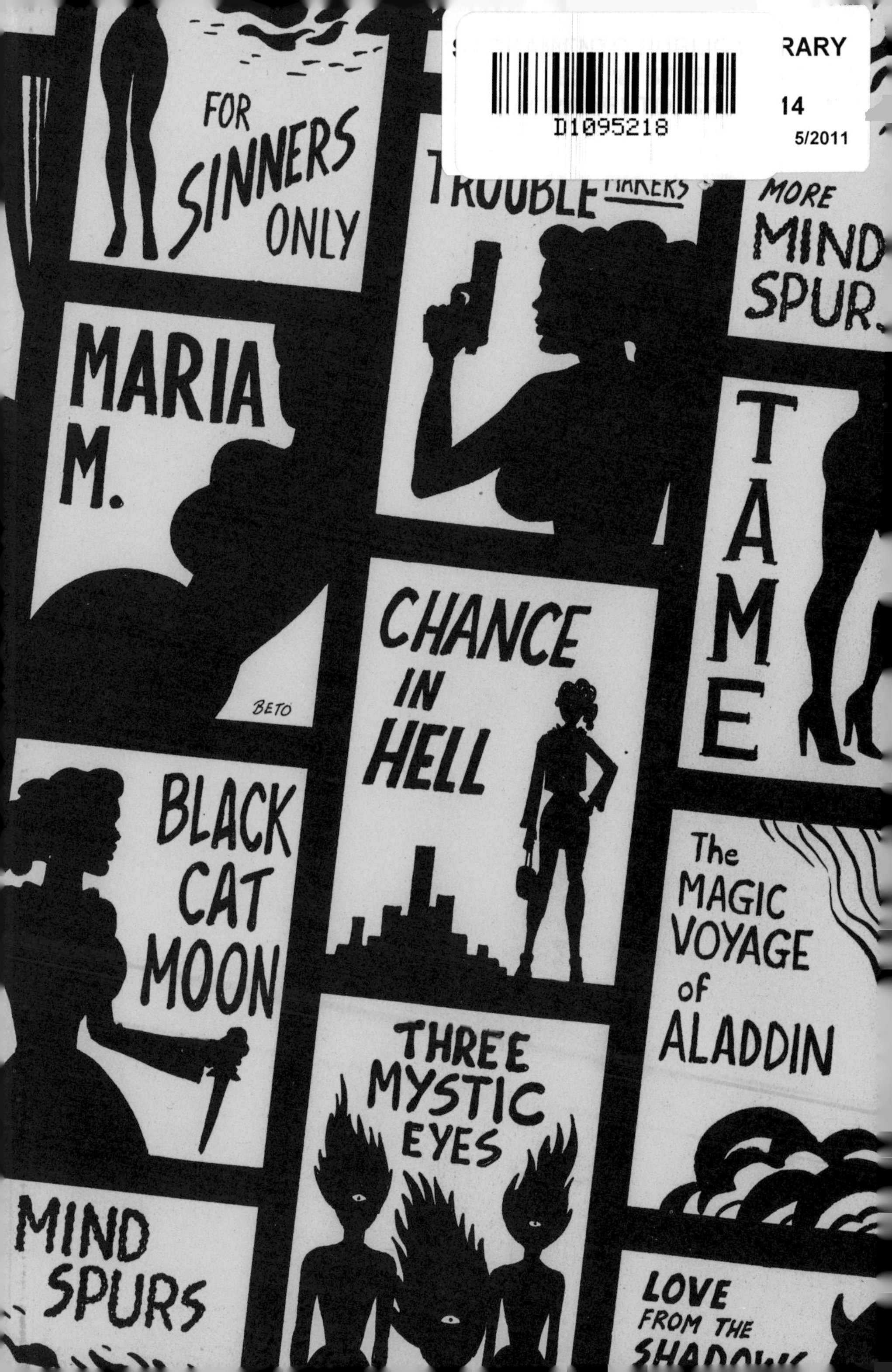
FOR SINNERS ONLY
TROUBLE MAKERS
MORE MIND SPUR
MARIA M.
BETO
TAME
CHANCE IN HELL
BLACK CAT MOON
The MAGIC VOYAGE of ALADDIN
THREE MYSTIC EYES
MIND SPURS
LOVE FROM THE

BY GILBERT HERNANDEZ

LOVE FROM THE SHADOWS

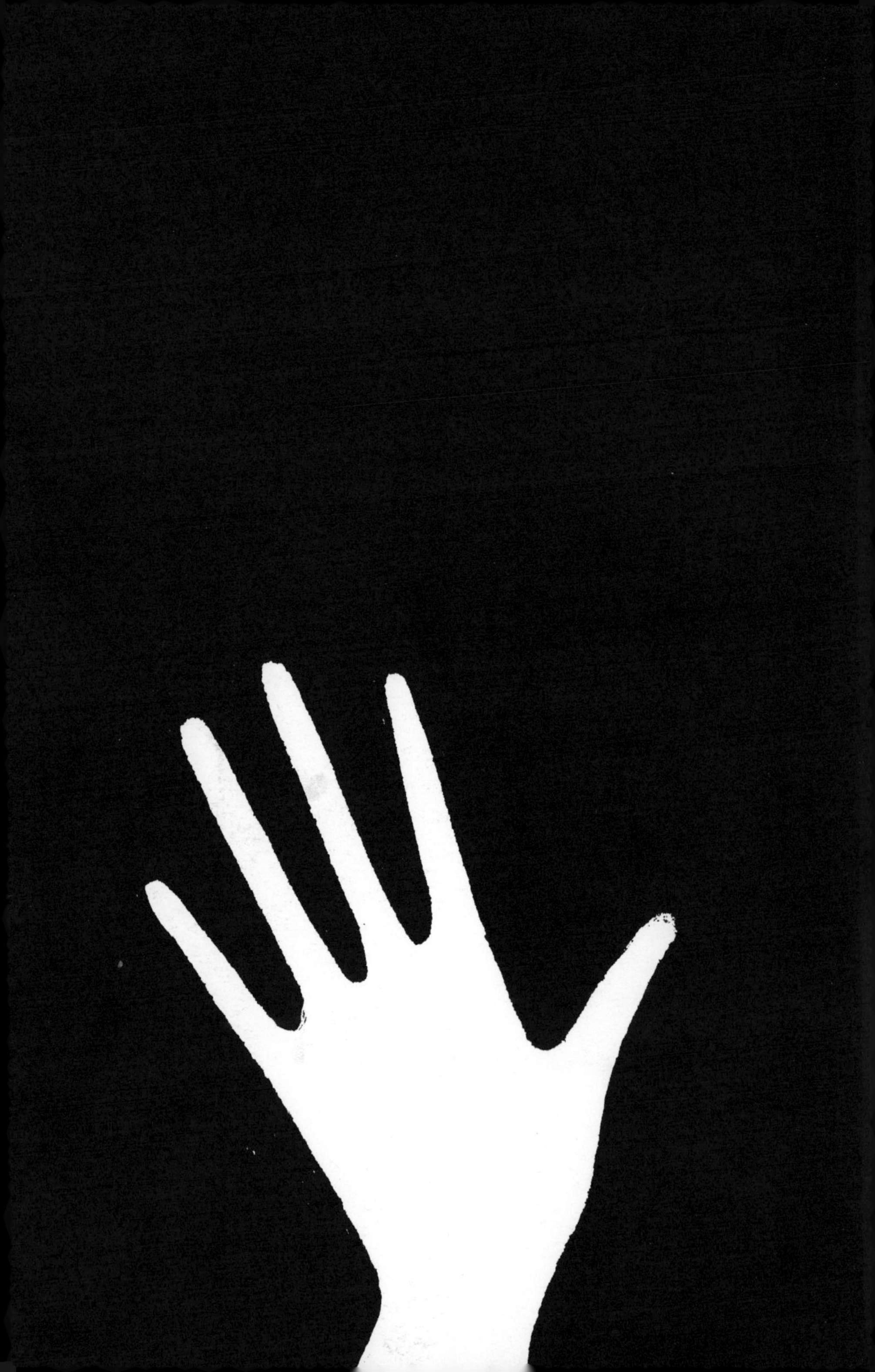

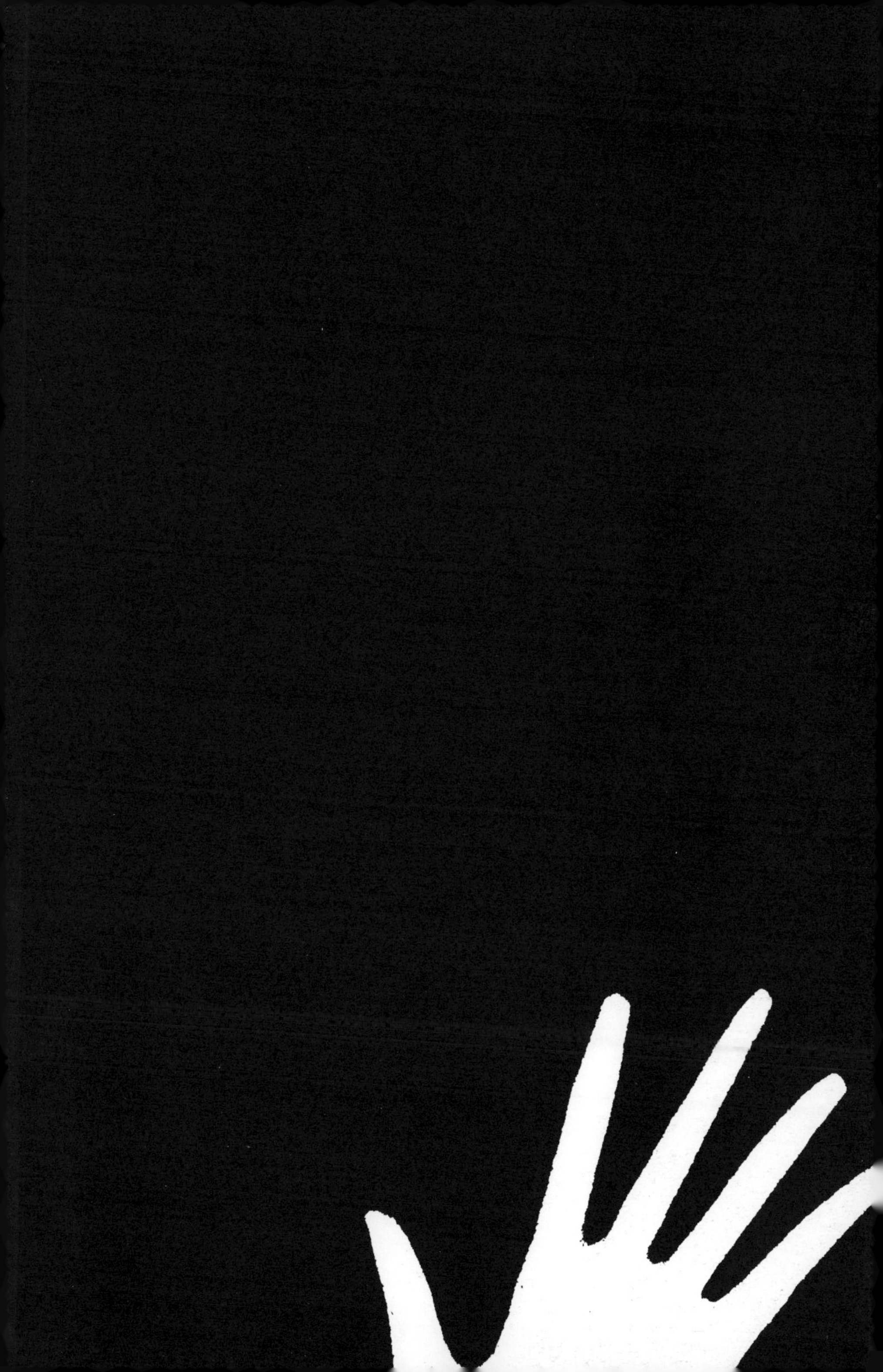

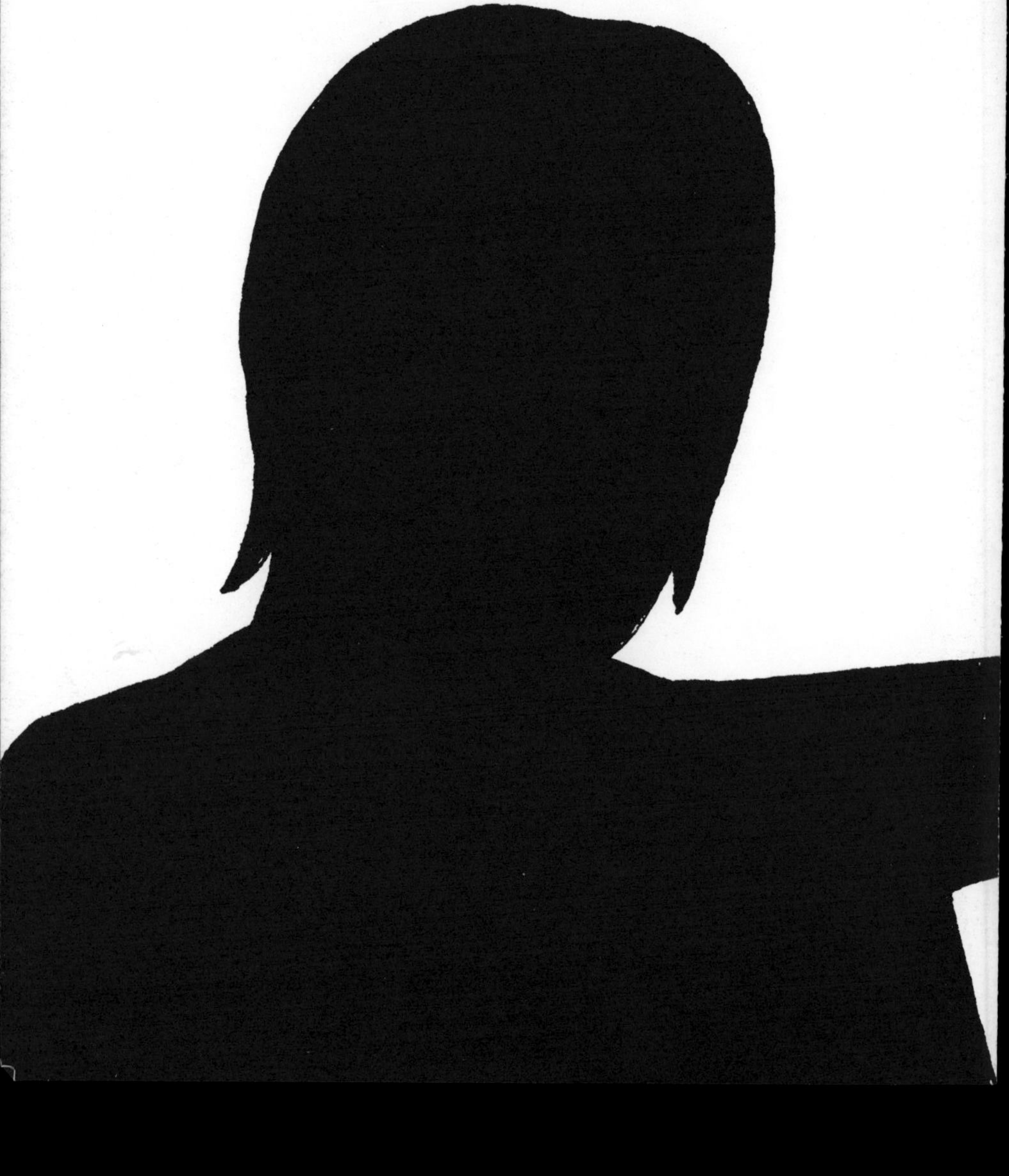

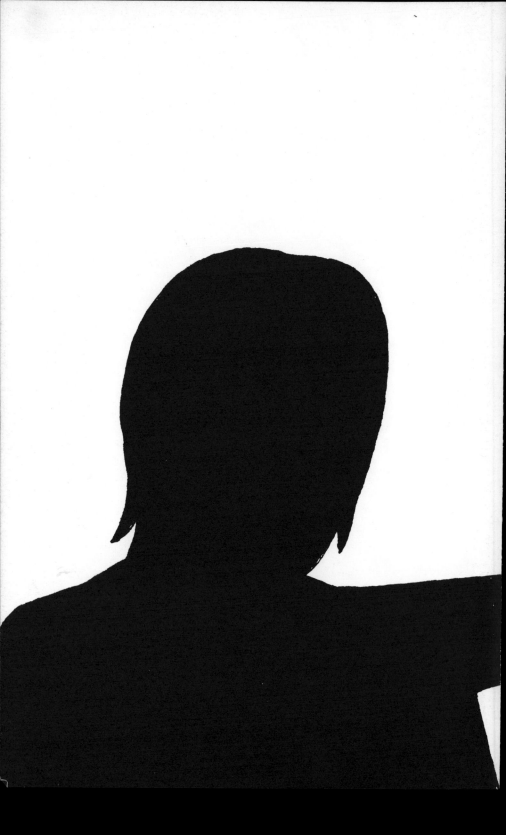

FANTAGRAPHICS BOOKS
7563 Lake City Way
Seattle, Washington 98115

EDITOR . . . . Gary Groth
DESIGN . . . . Alexa Koenings
PRODUCTION . . . . Paul Baresh
ASSOCIATE PUBLISHER . . . . Eric Reynolds
PUBLISHERS . . . . Gary Groth & Kim Thompson

LOVE
FROM THE
SHADOWS

BETO
2010

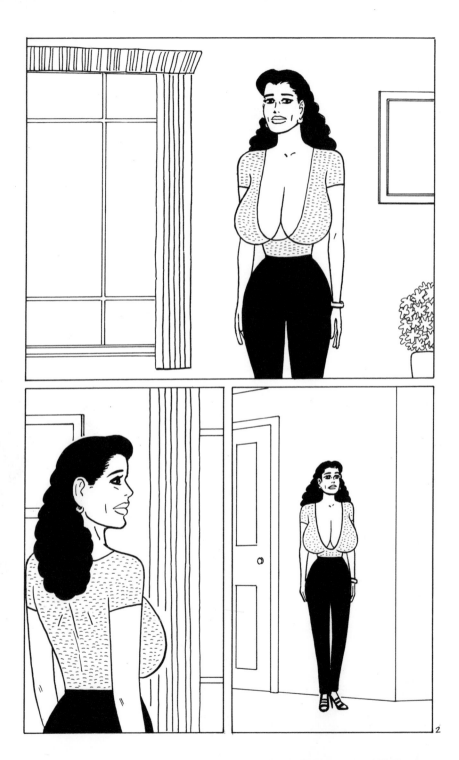

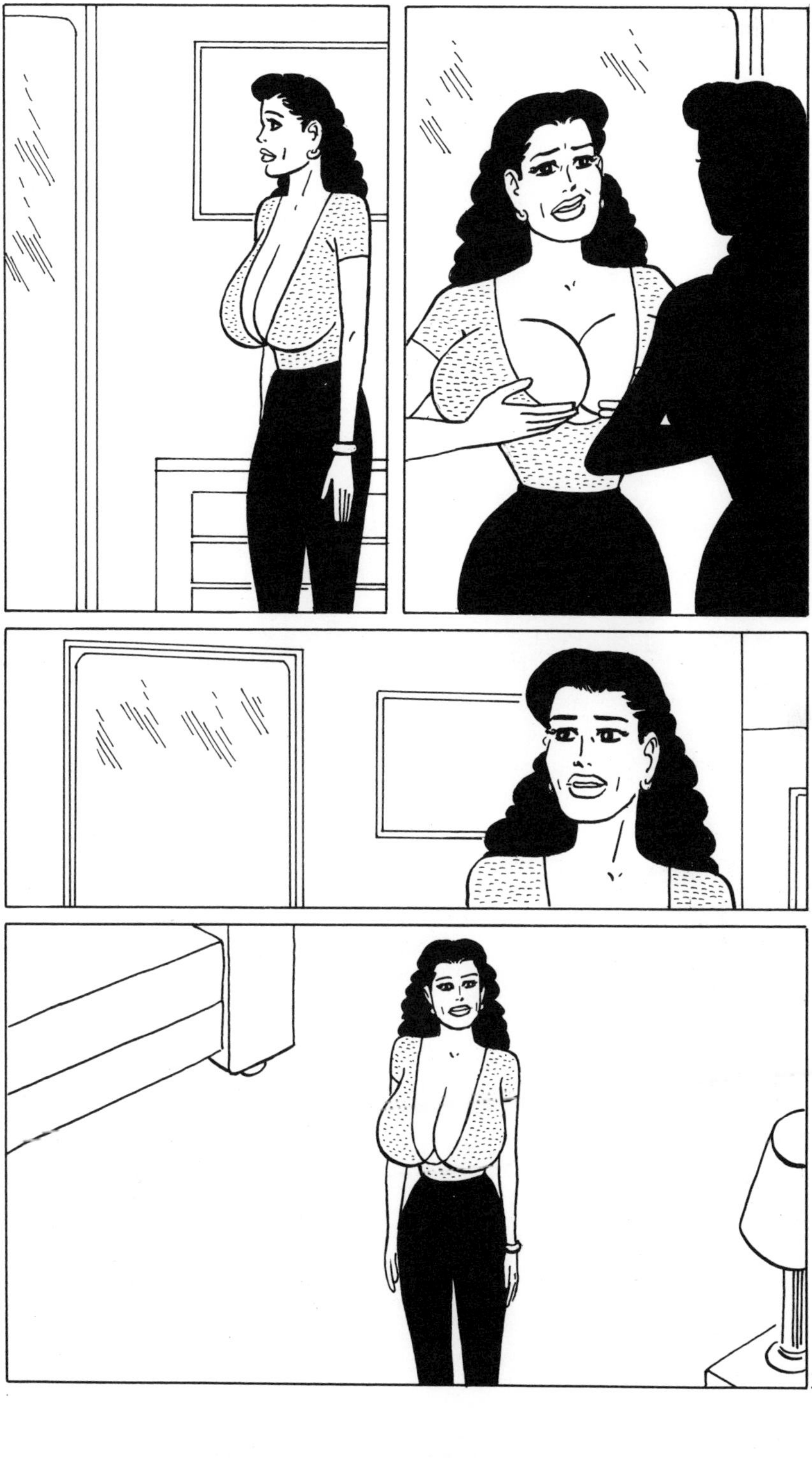

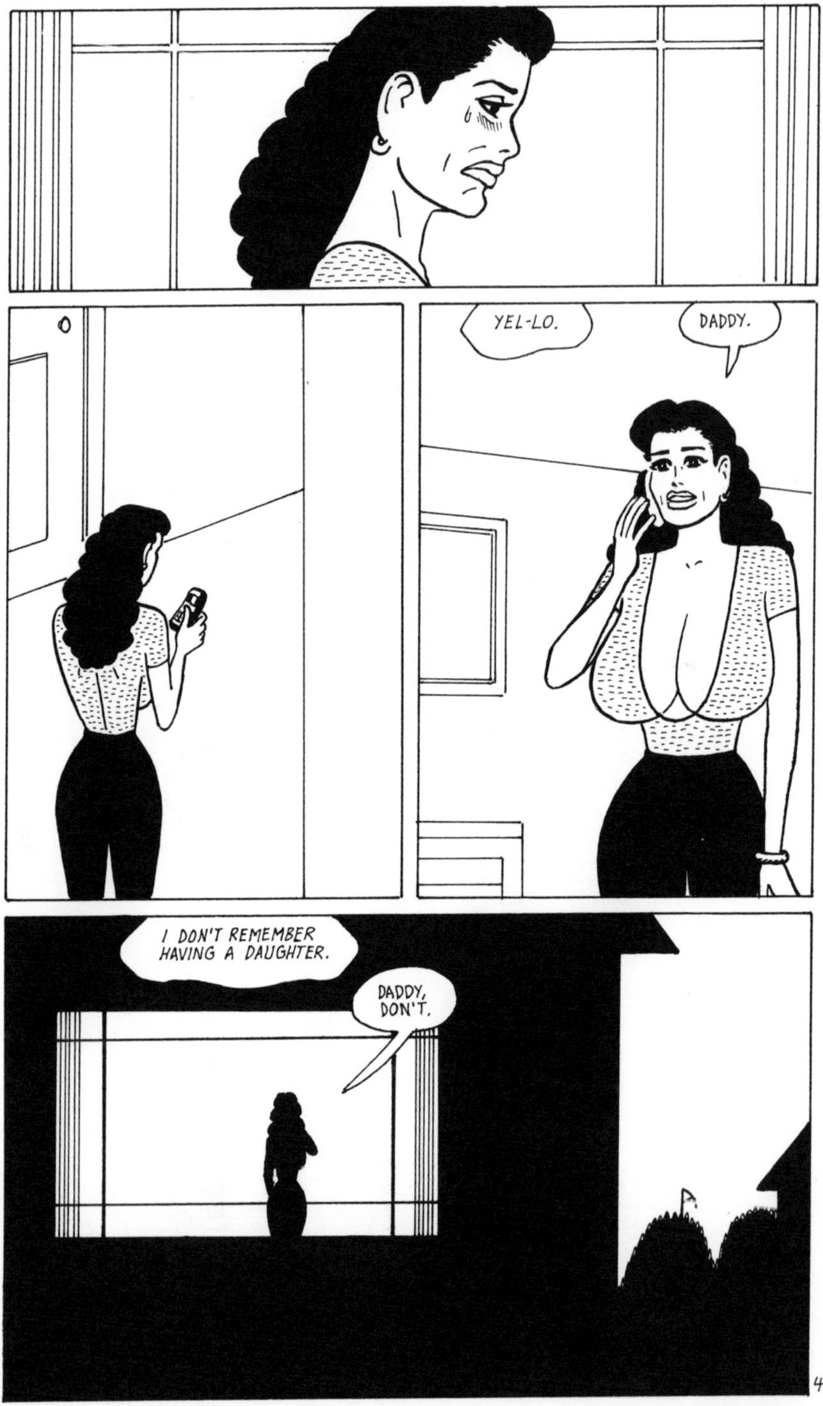
YEL-LO.
DADDY.
I DON'T REMEMBER HAVING A DAUGHTER.
DADDY, DON'T.

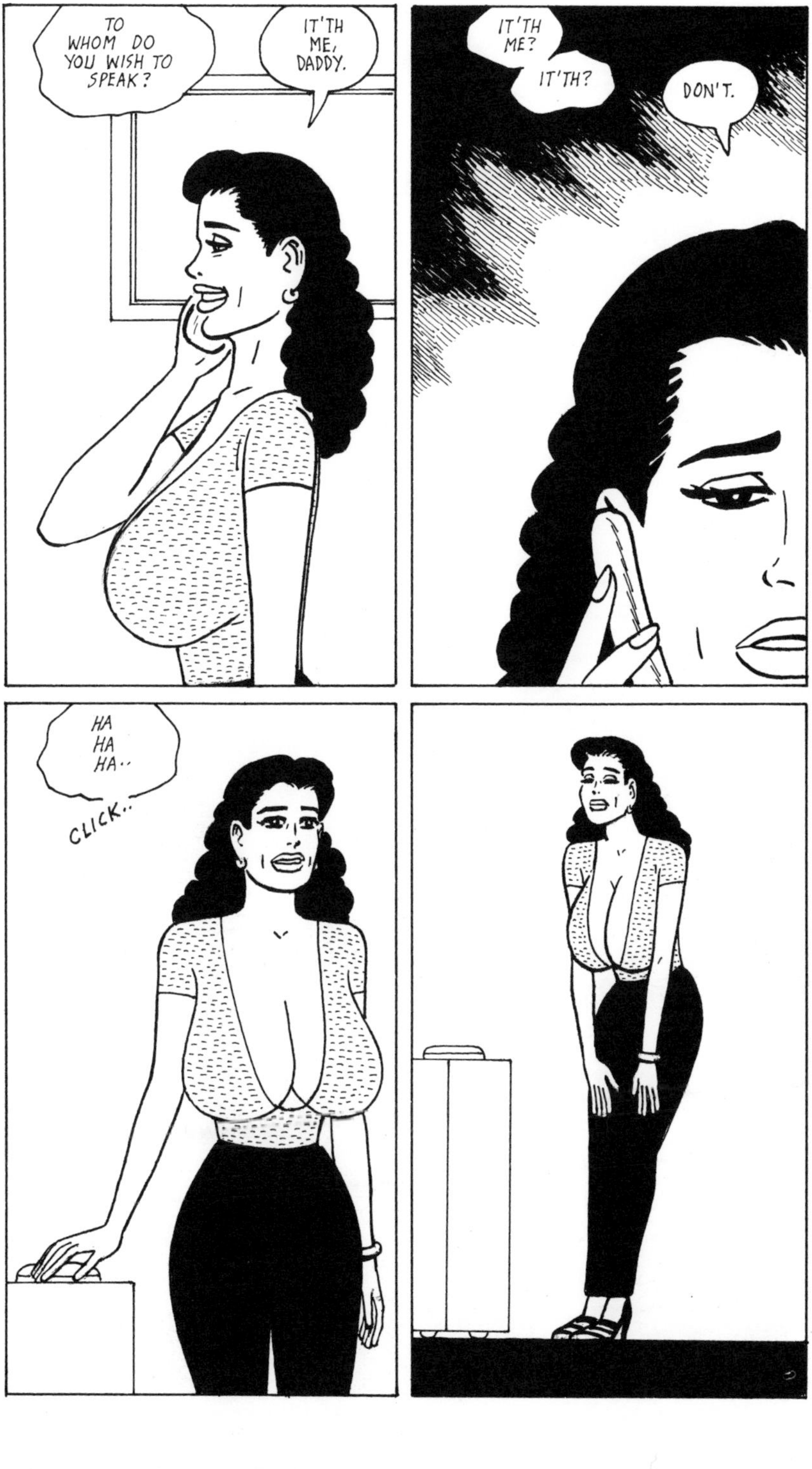
TO WHOM DO YOU WISH TO SPEAK?
IT'TH ME, DADDY.
IT'TH ME?
IT'TH?
DON'T.
HA HA HA..
CLICK..

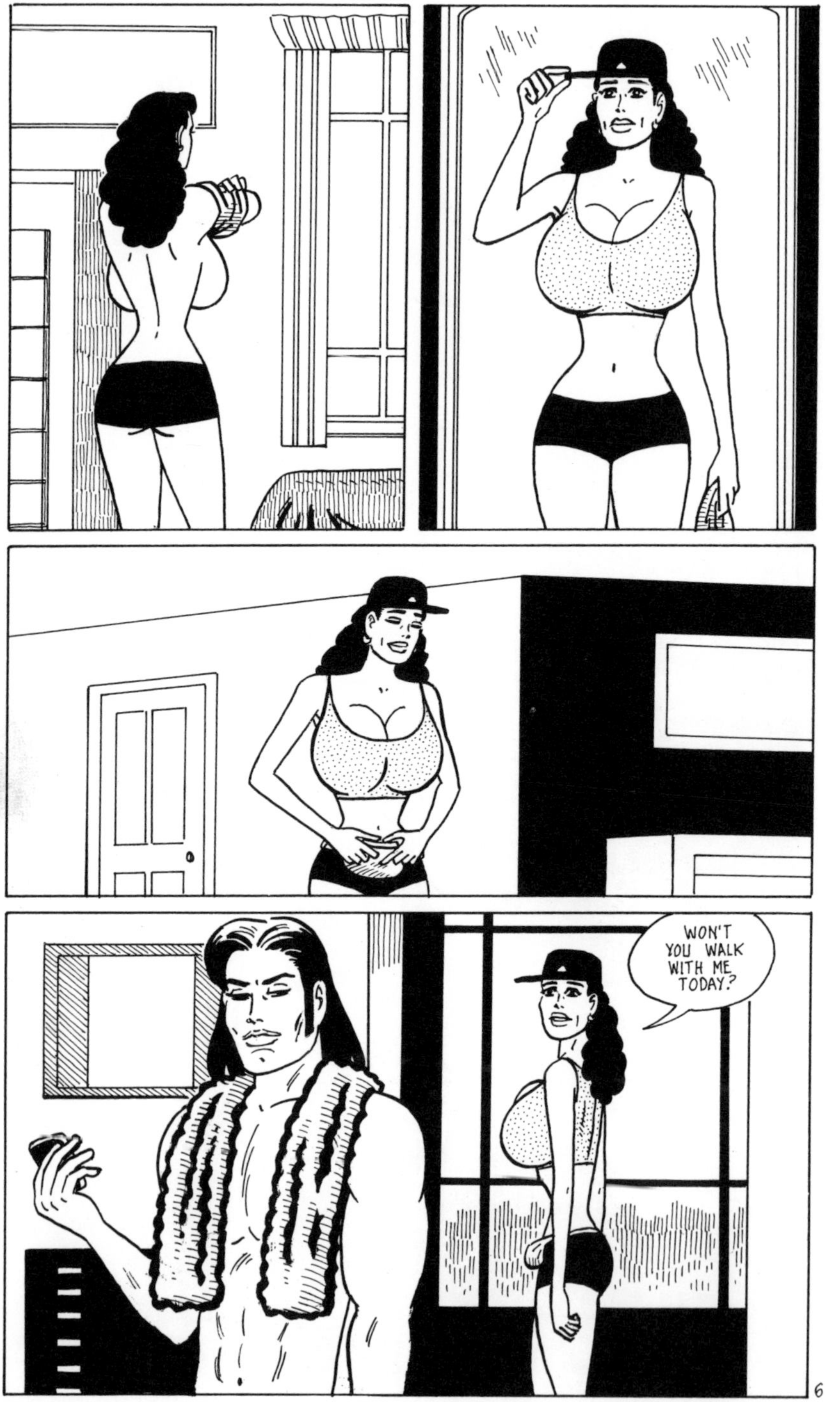
WON'T YOU WALK WITH ME TODAY?

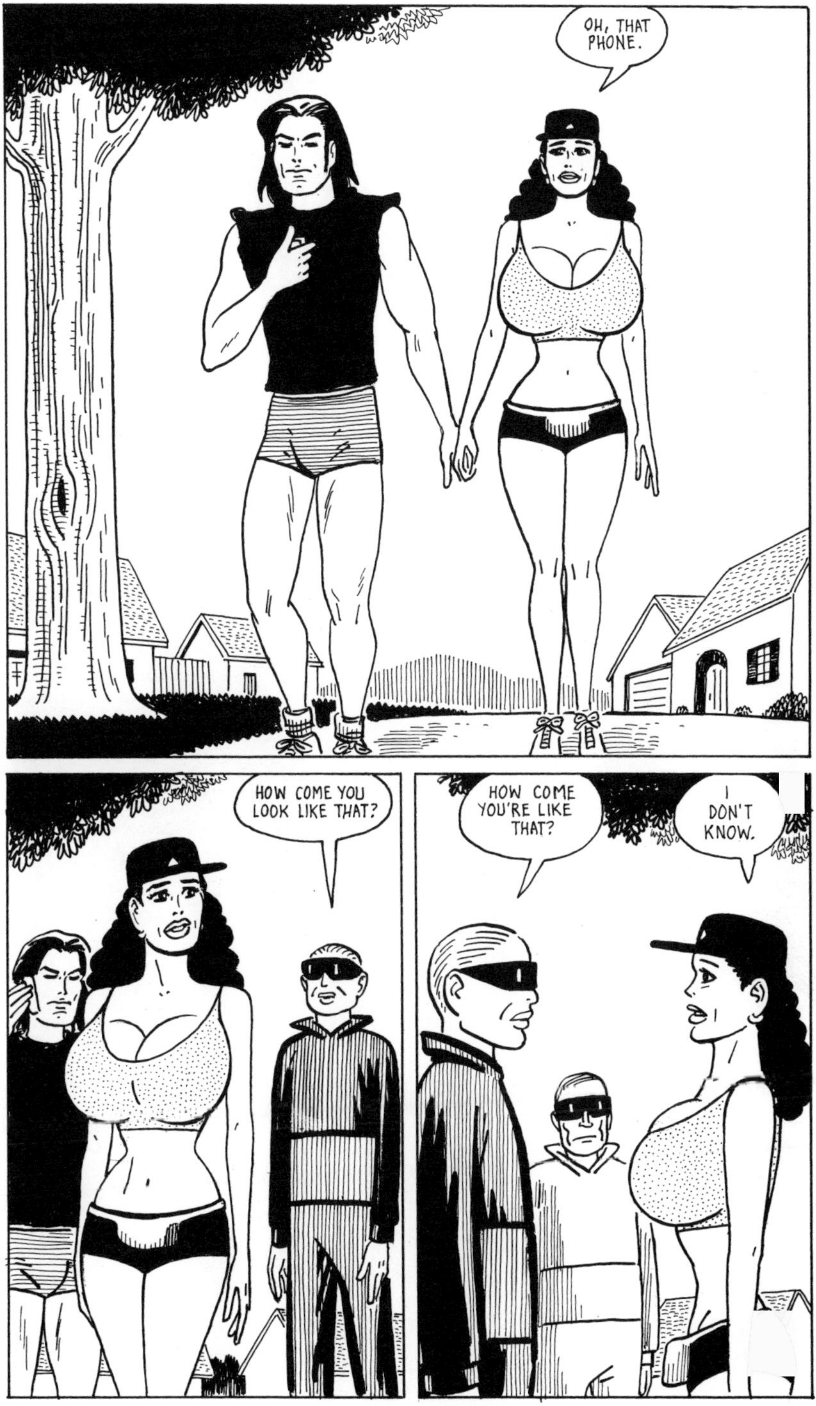
OH, THAT PHONE.
HOW COME YOU LOOK LIKE THAT?
HOW COME YOU'RE LIKE THAT?
I DON'T KNOW.

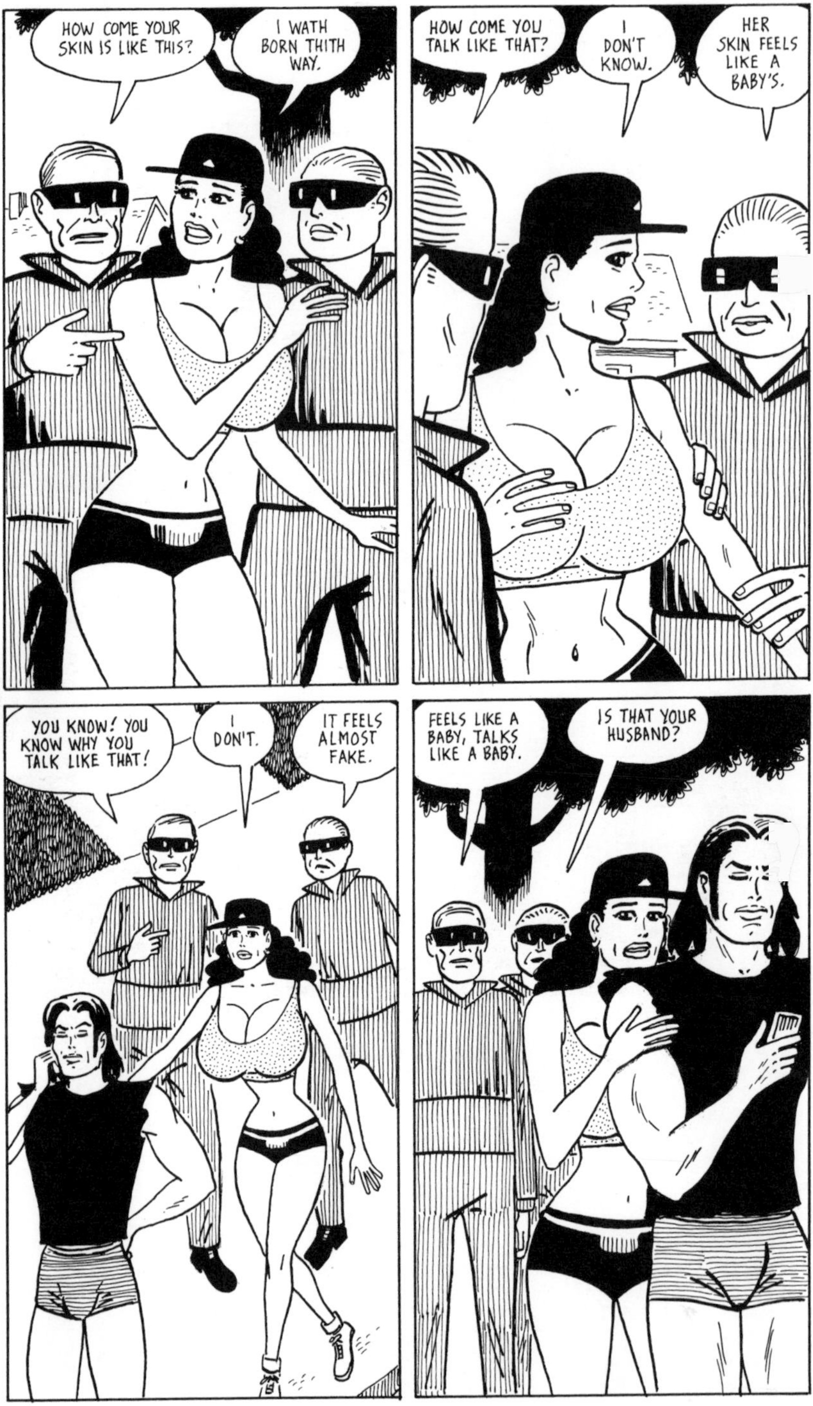
HOW COME YOUR SKIN IS LIKE THIS?
I WATH BORN THITH WAY.
HOW COME YOU TALK LIKE THAT?
I DON'T KNOW.
HER SKIN FEELS LIKE A BABY'S.
YOU KNOW! YOU KNOW WHY YOU TALK LIKE THAT!
I DON'T.
IT FEELS ALMOST FAKE.
FEELS LIKE A BABY, TALKS LIKE A BABY.
IS THAT YOUR HUSBAND?

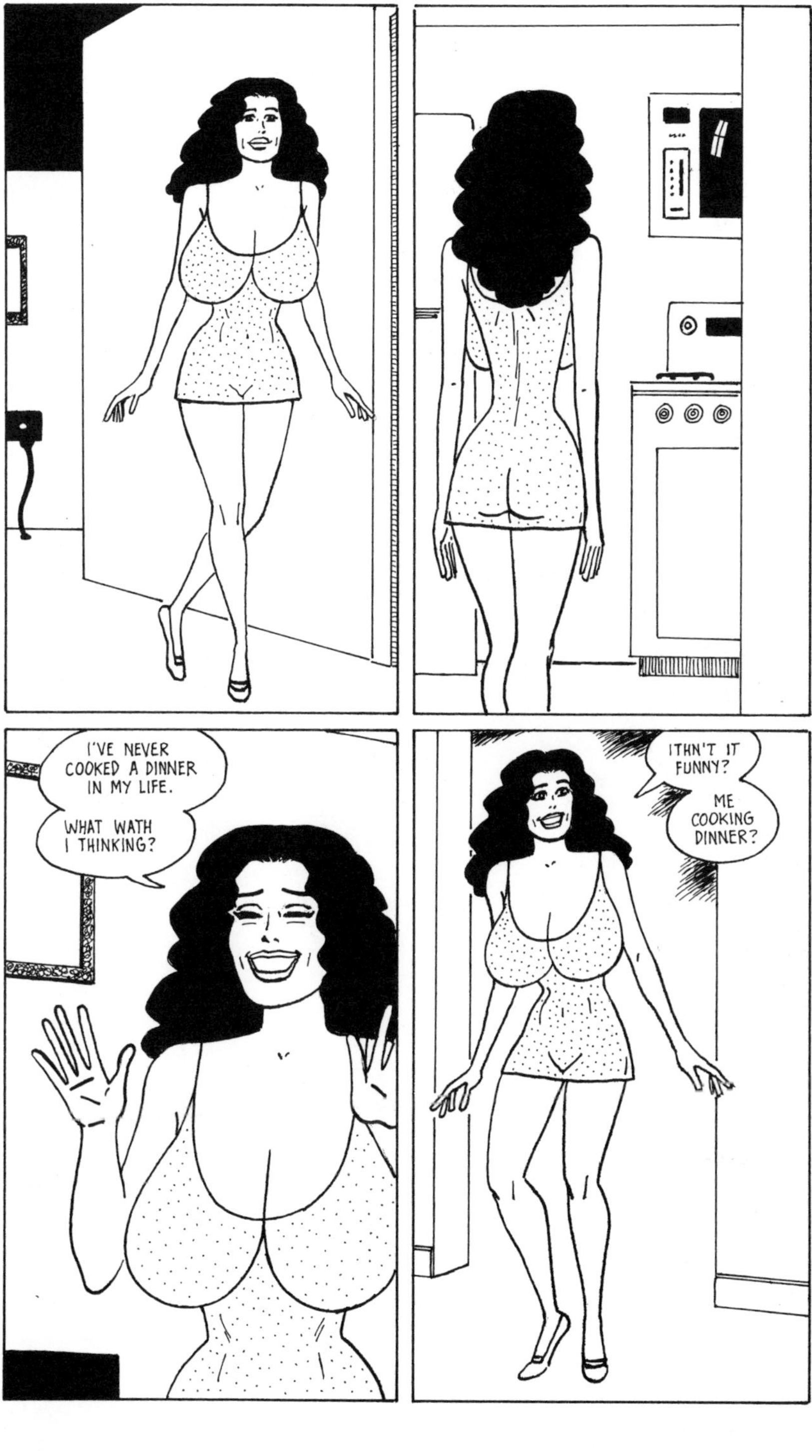
I'VE NEVER COOKED A DINNER IN MY LIFE.
WHAT WATH I THINKING?
ITHN'T IT FUNNY?
ME COOKING DINNER?

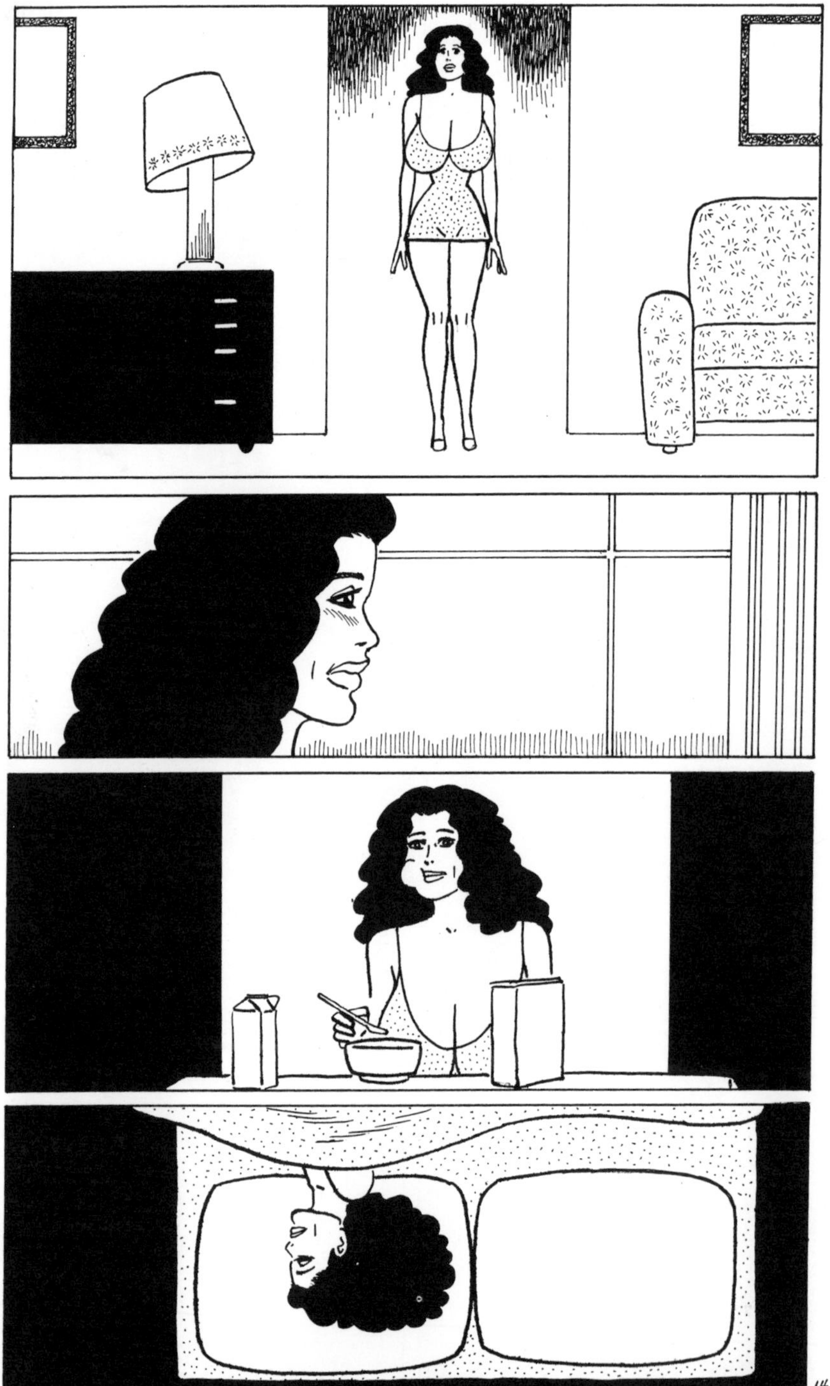

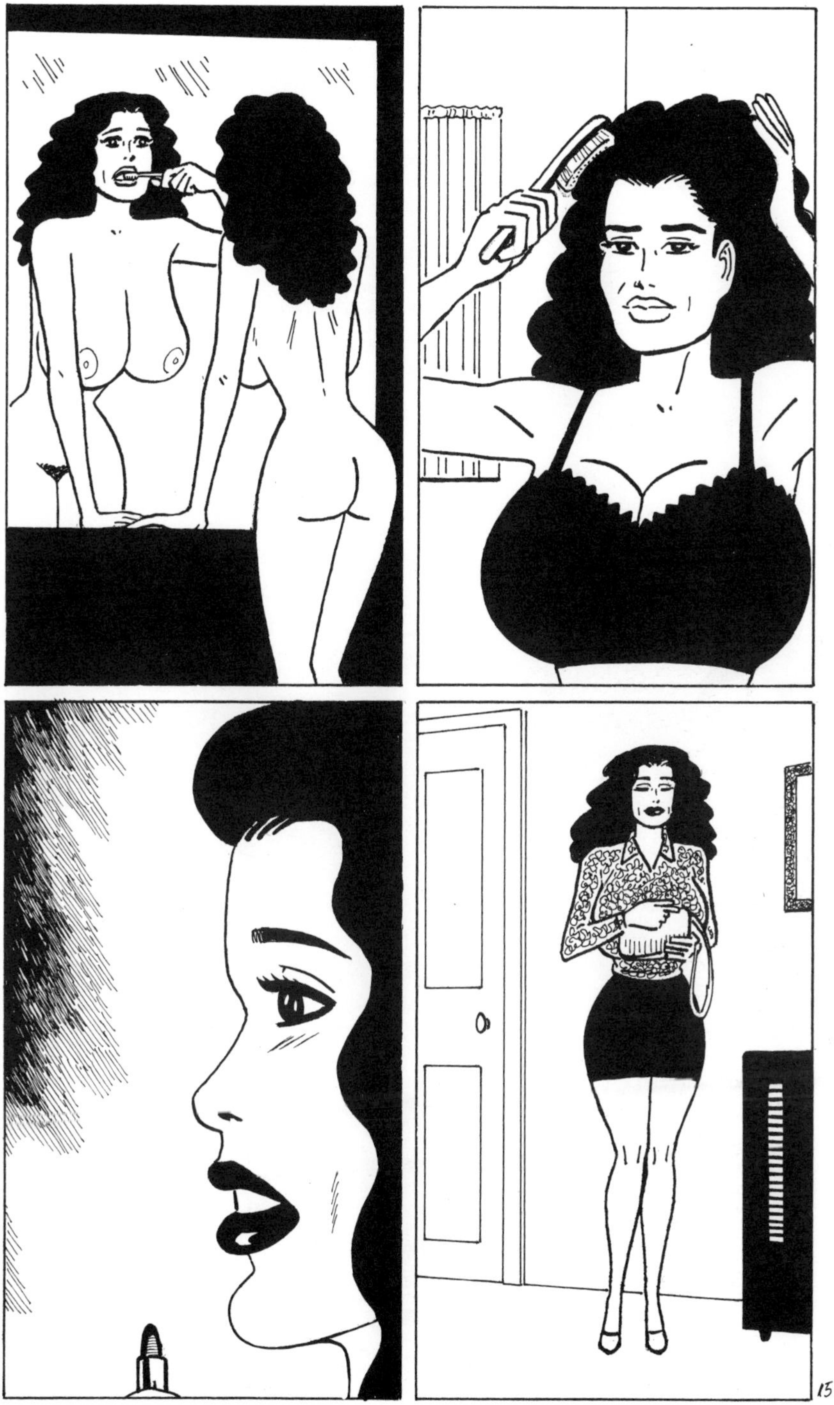

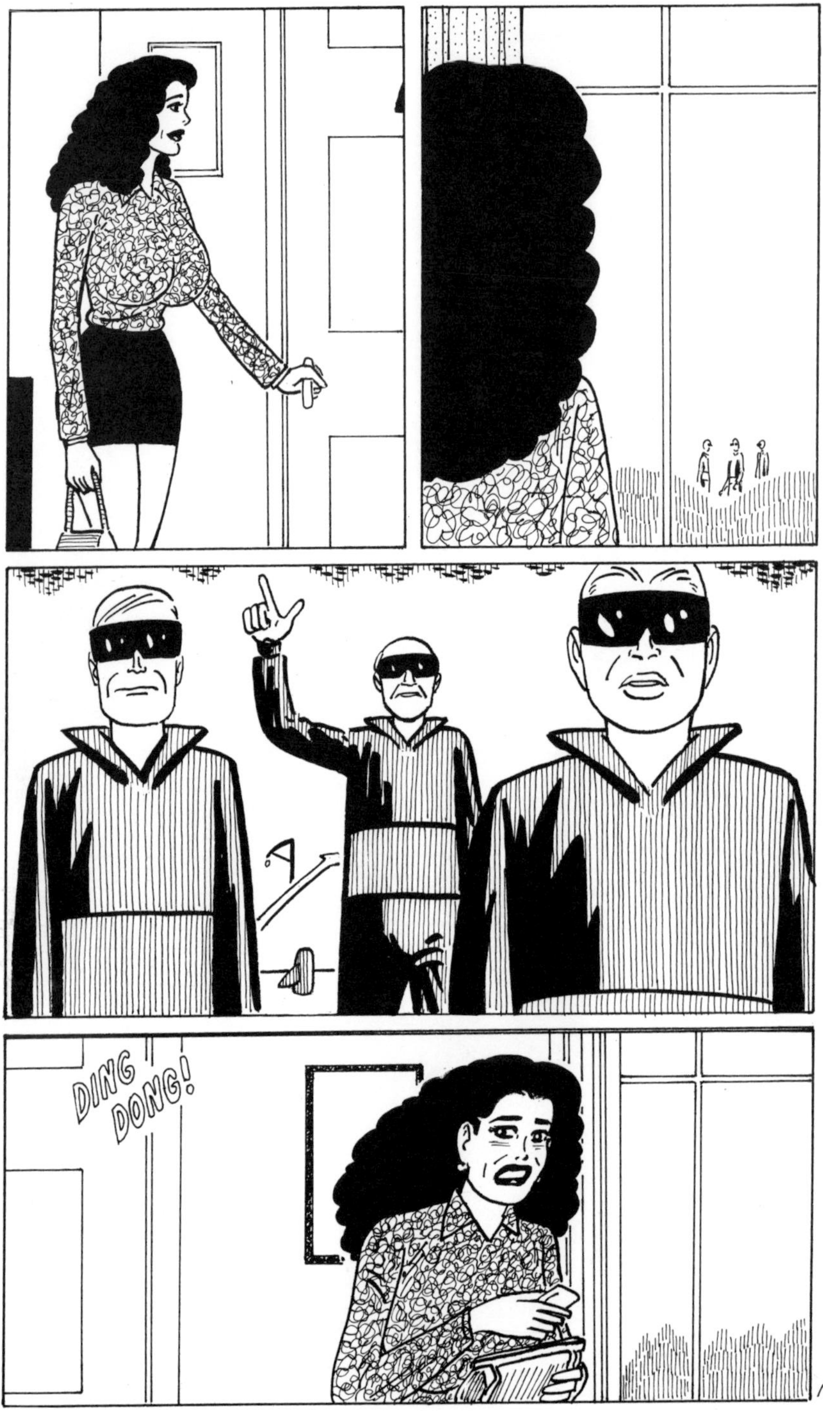
DING DONG!

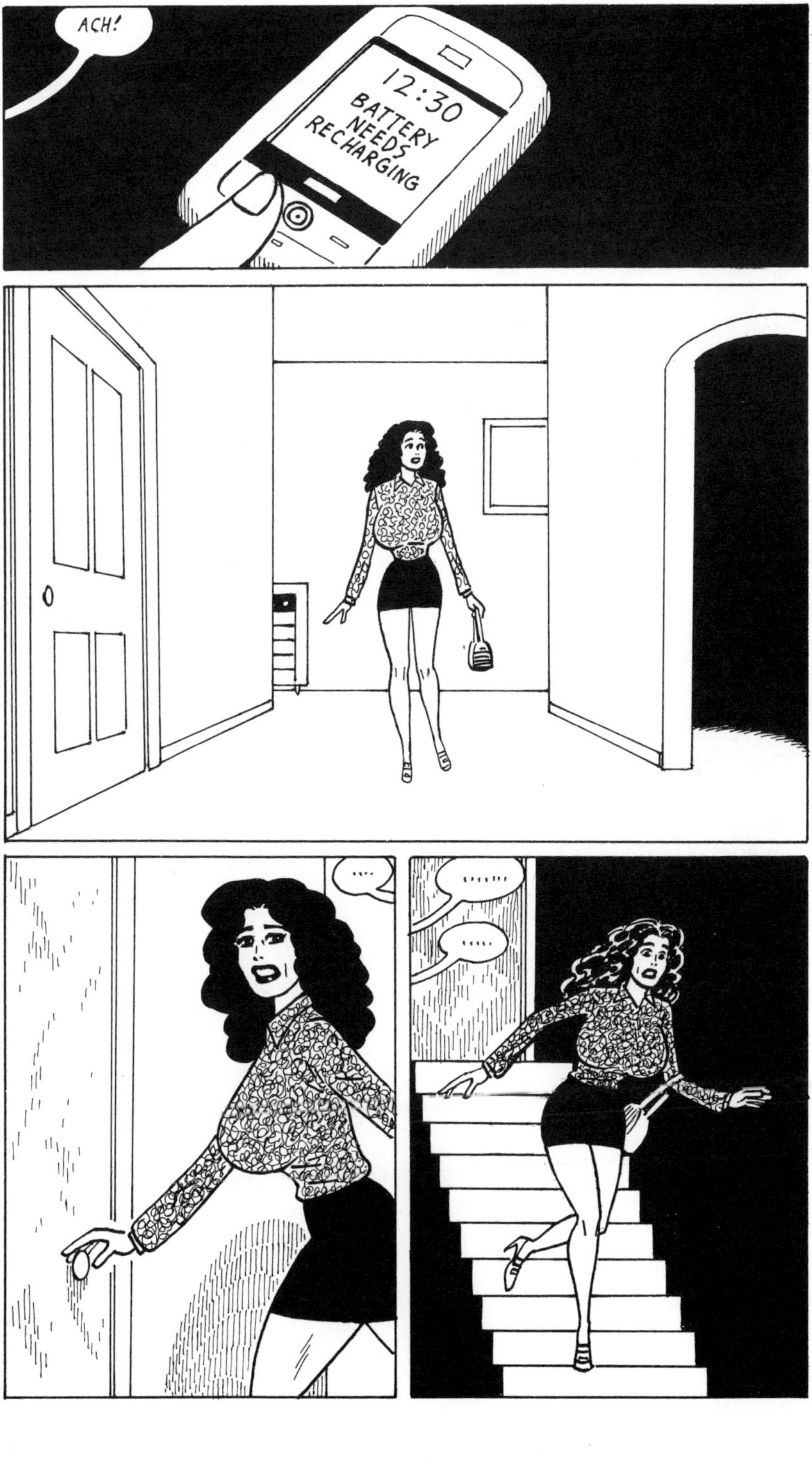
ACH!
12:30
BATTERY NEEDS RECHARGING

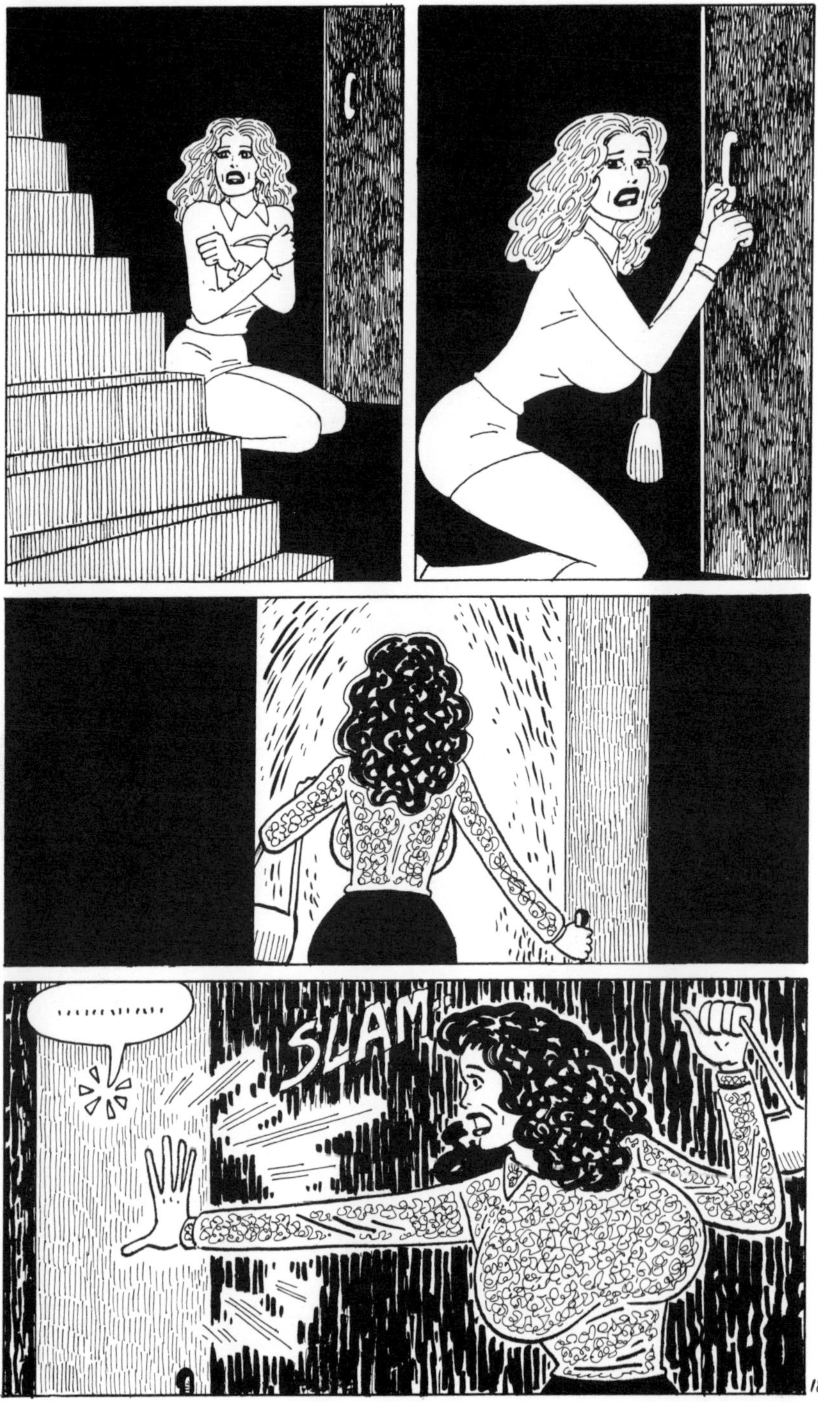
SLAM

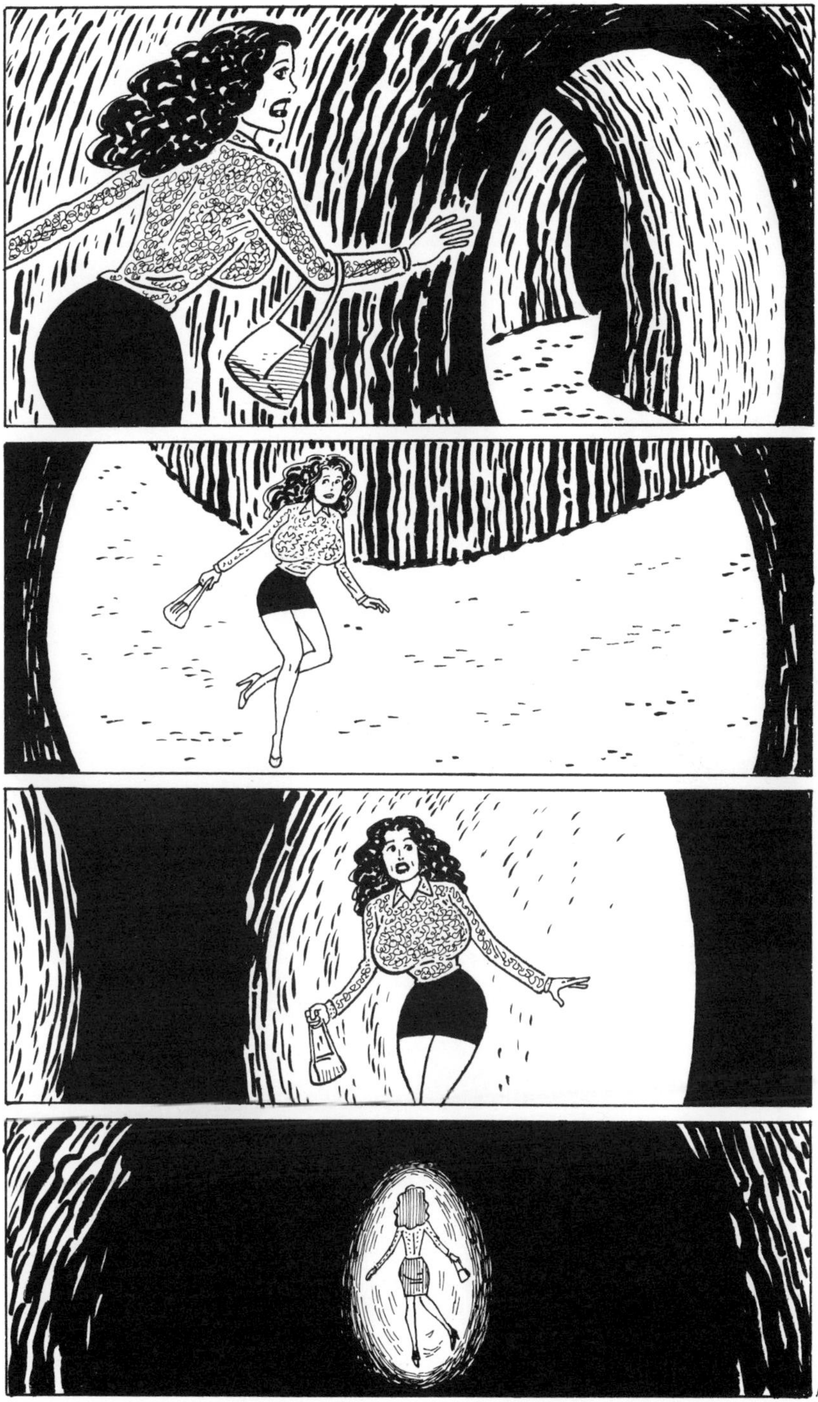

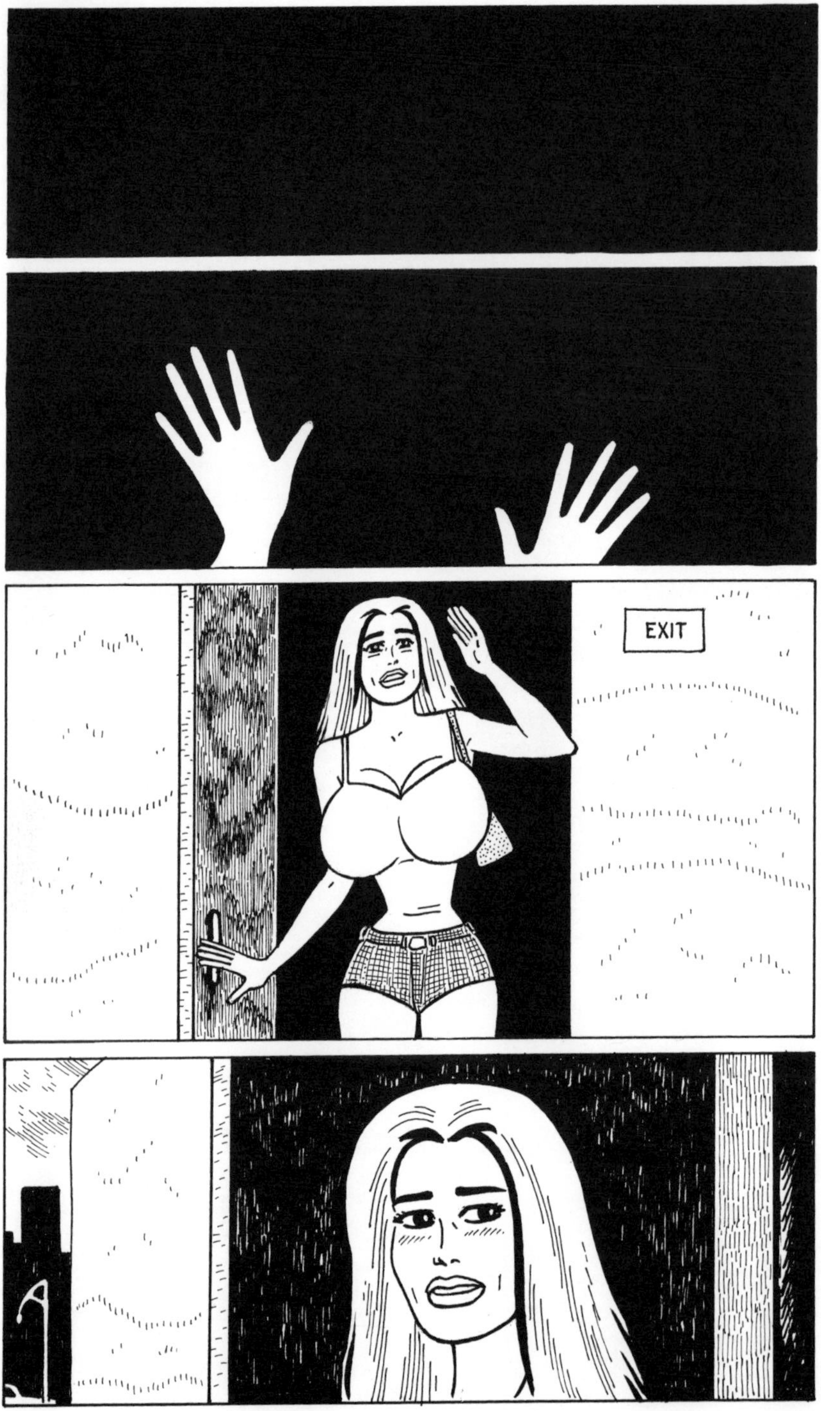
EXIT

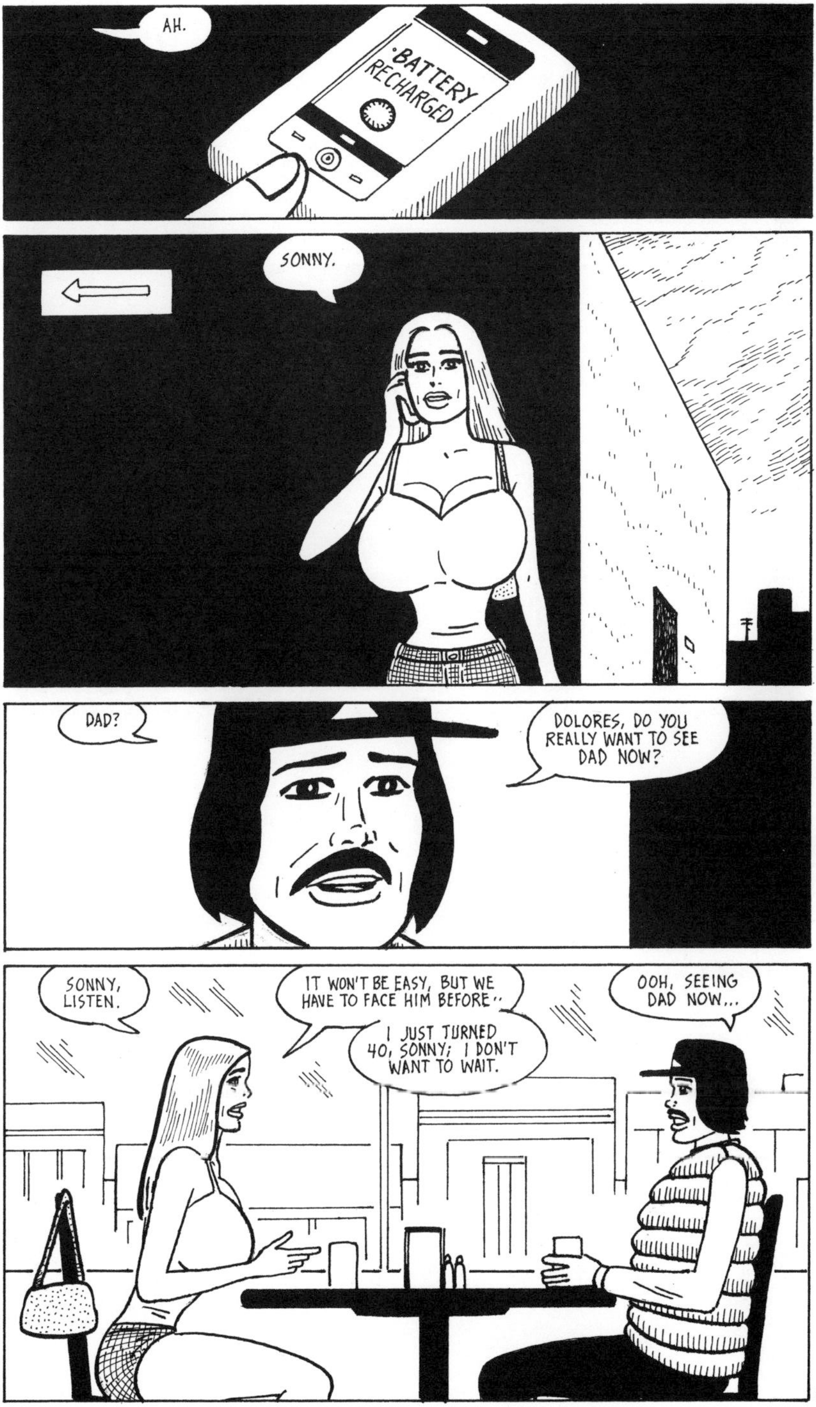

AH.
BATTERY RECHARGED
SONNY.
DAD?
DOLORES, DO YOU REALLY WANT TO SEE DAD NOW?
SONNY, LISTEN.
IT WON'T BE EASY, BUT WE HAVE TO FACE HIM BEFORE..
I JUST TURNED 40, SONNY; I DON'T WANT TO WAIT.
OOH, SEEING DAD NOW...

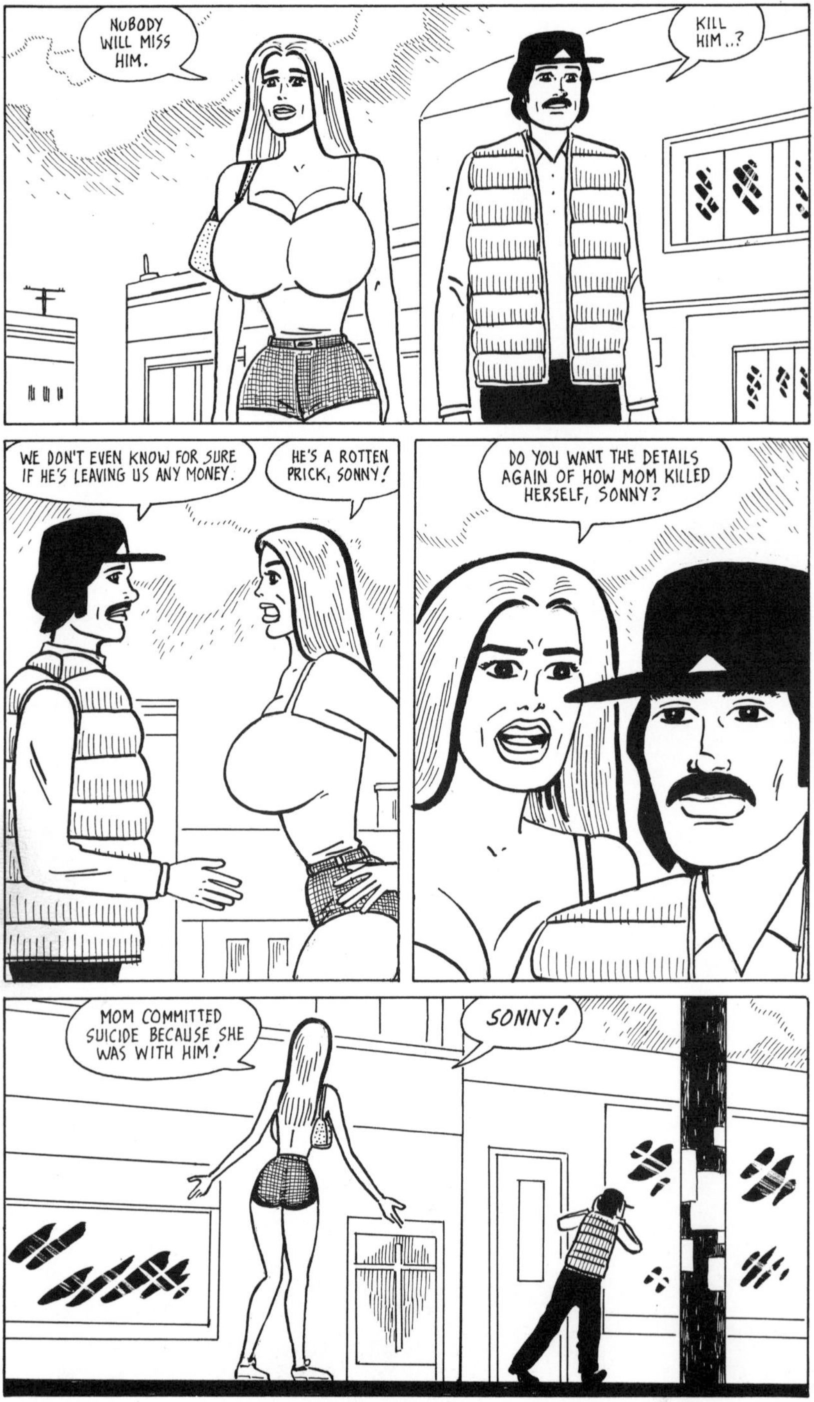
NOBODY WILL MISS HIM.
KILL HIM..?
WE DON'T EVEN KNOW FOR SURE IF HE'S LEAVING US ANY MONEY.
HE'S A ROTTEN PRICK, SONNY!
DO YOU WANT THE DETAILS AGAIN OF HOW MOM KILLED HERSELF, SONNY?
MOM COMMITTED SUICIDE BECAUSE SHE WAS WITH HIM!
SONNY!

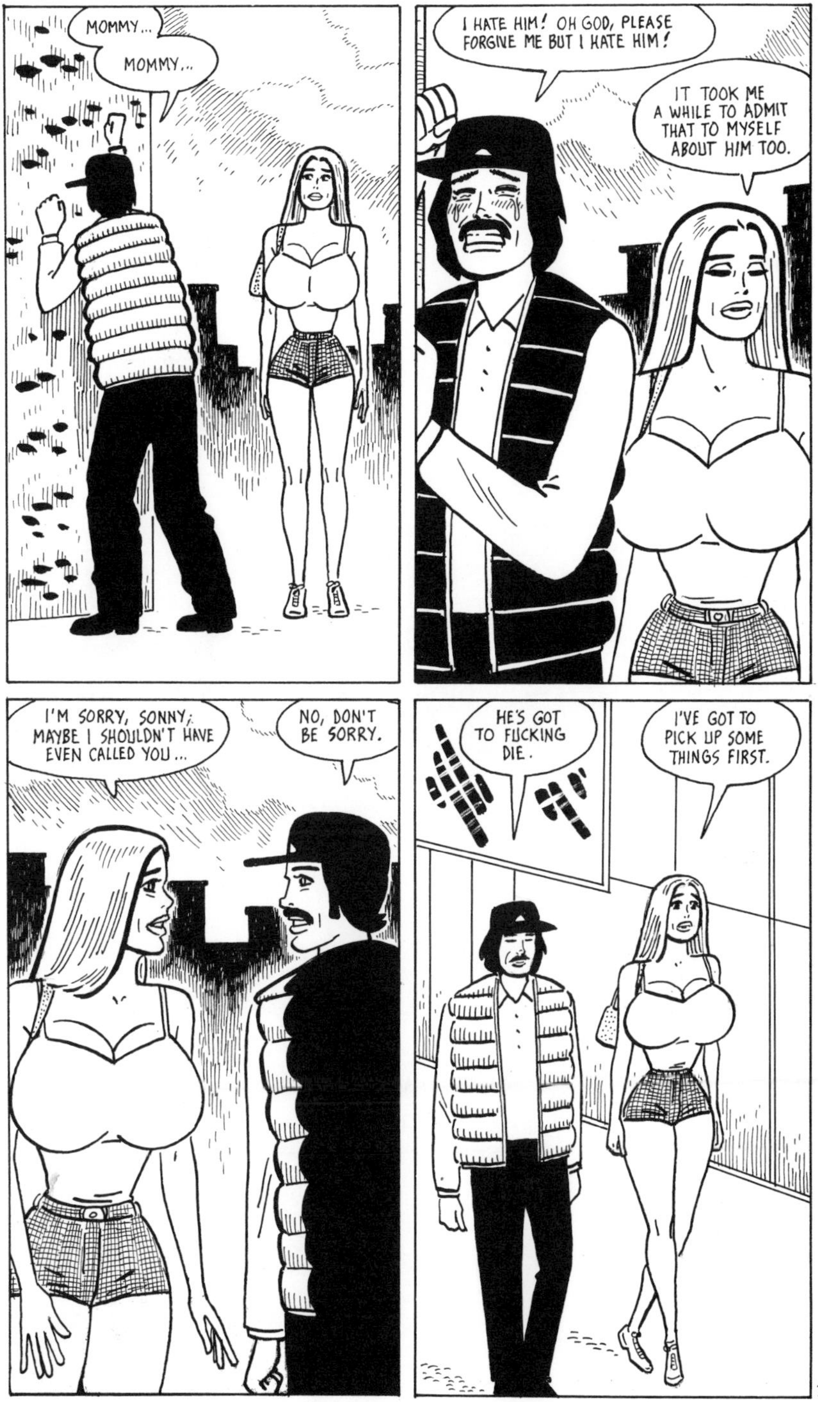
MOMMY...
MOMMY...
I HATE HIM! OH GOD, PLEASE FORGIVE ME BUT I HATE HIM!
IT TOOK ME A WHILE TO ADMIT THAT TO MYSELF ABOUT HIM TOO.
I'M SORRY, SONNY; MAYBE I SHOULDN'T HAVE EVEN CALLED YOU...
NO, DON'T BE SORRY.
HE'S GOT TO FUCKING DIE.
I'VE GOT TO PICK UP SOME THINGS FIRST.

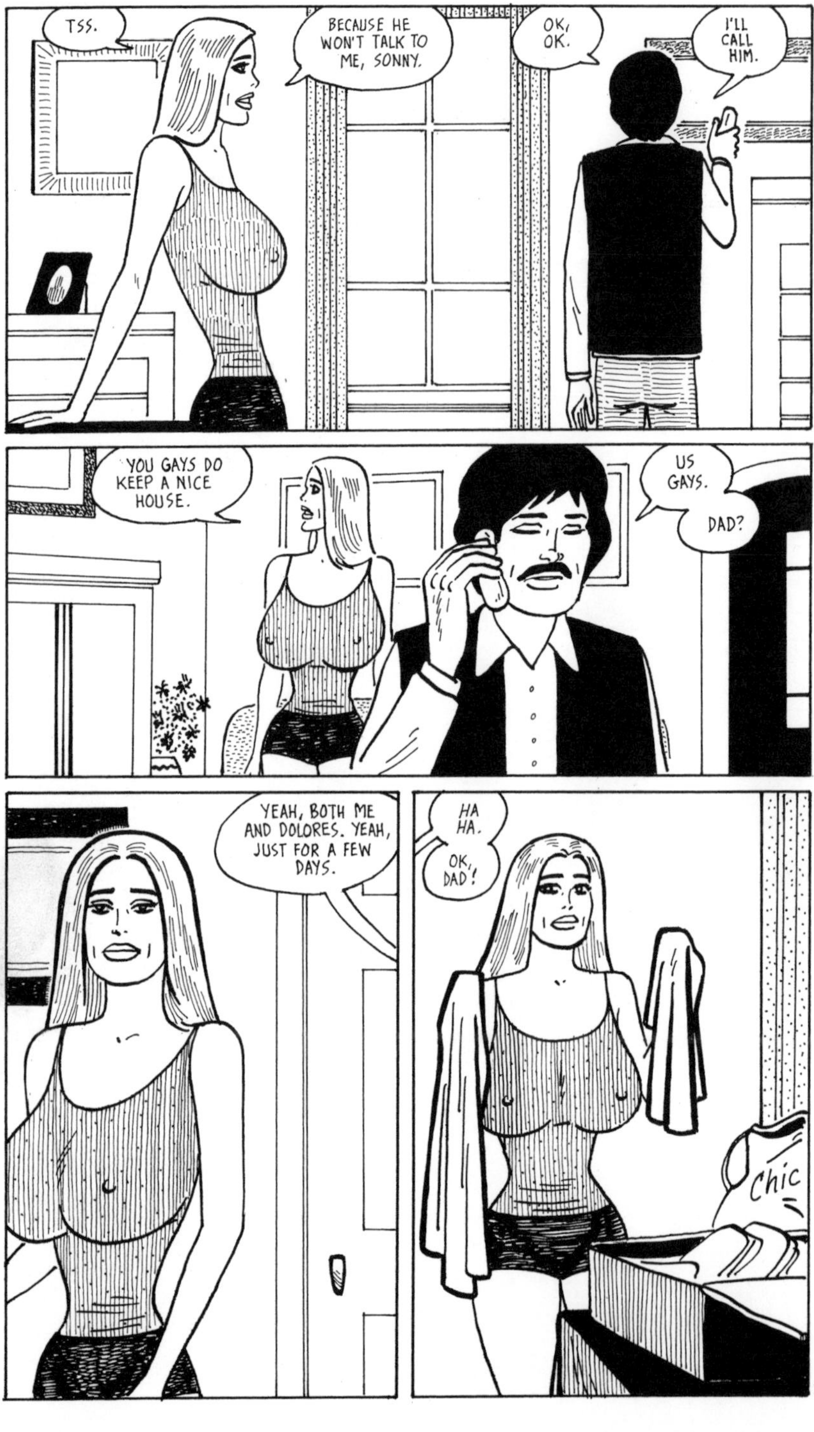
TSS.
BECAUSE HE WON'T TALK TO ME, SONNY.
OK, OK.
I'LL CALL HIM.
YOU GAYS DO KEEP A NICE HOUSE.
US GAYS.
DAD?
YEAH, BOTH ME AND DOLORES. YEAH, JUST FOR A FEW DAYS.
HA HA.
OK, DAD!
Chic

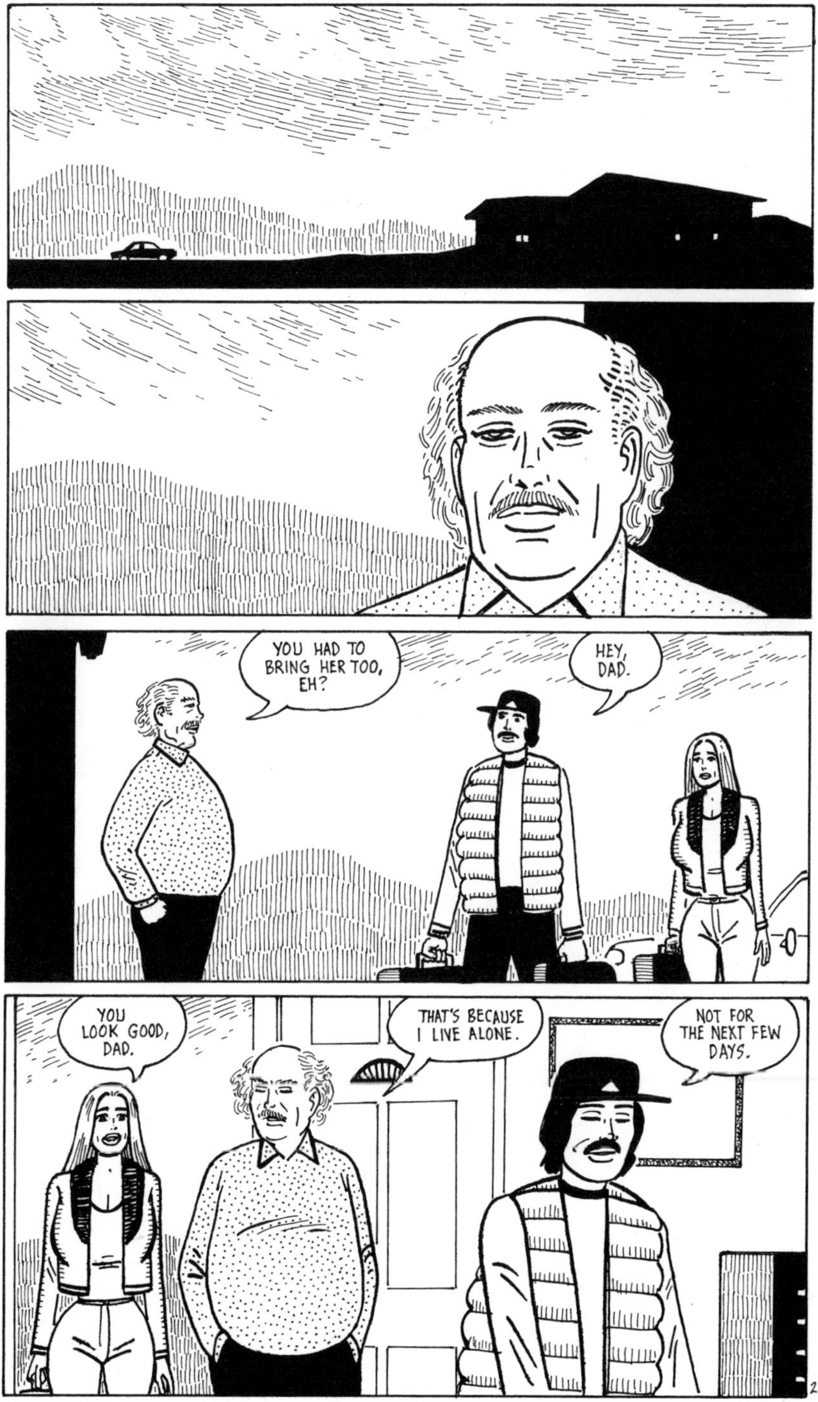
YOU HAD TO BRING HER TOO, EH?
HEY, DAD.
YOU LOOK GOOD, DAD.
THAT'S BECAUSE I LIVE ALONE.
NOT FOR THE NEXT FEW DAYS.

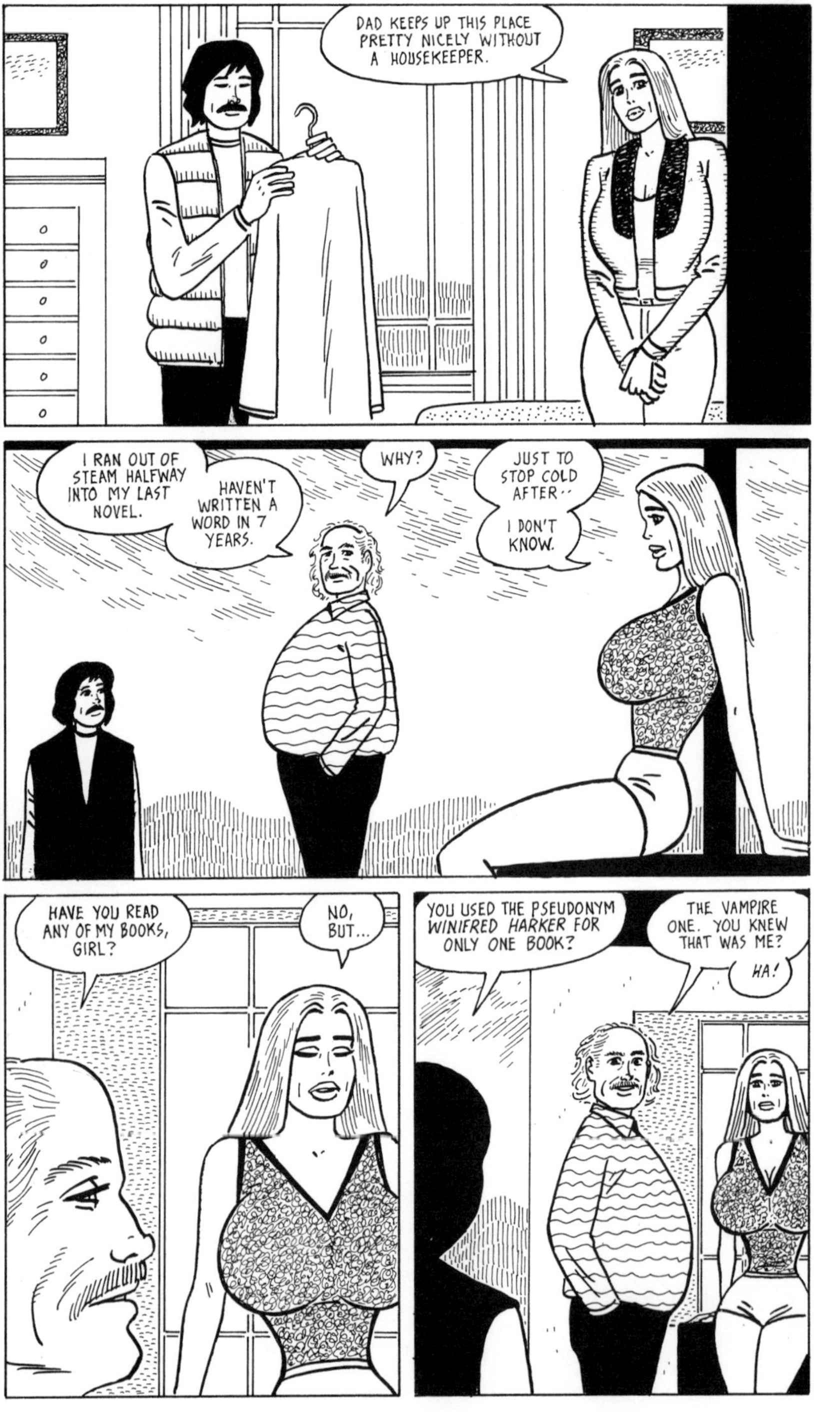
DAD KEEPS UP THIS PLACE PRETTY NICELY WITHOUT A HOUSEKEEPER.
I RAN OUT OF STEAM HALFWAY INTO MY LAST NOVEL.
HAVEN'T WRITTEN A WORD IN 7 YEARS.
WHY?
JUST TO STOP COLD AFTER··
I DON'T KNOW.
HAVE YOU READ ANY OF MY BOOKS, GIRL?
NO, BUT...
YOU USED THE PSEUDONYM *WINIFRED HARKER* FOR ONLY ONE BOOK?
THE VAMPIRE ONE. YOU KNEW THAT WAS ME?
HA!

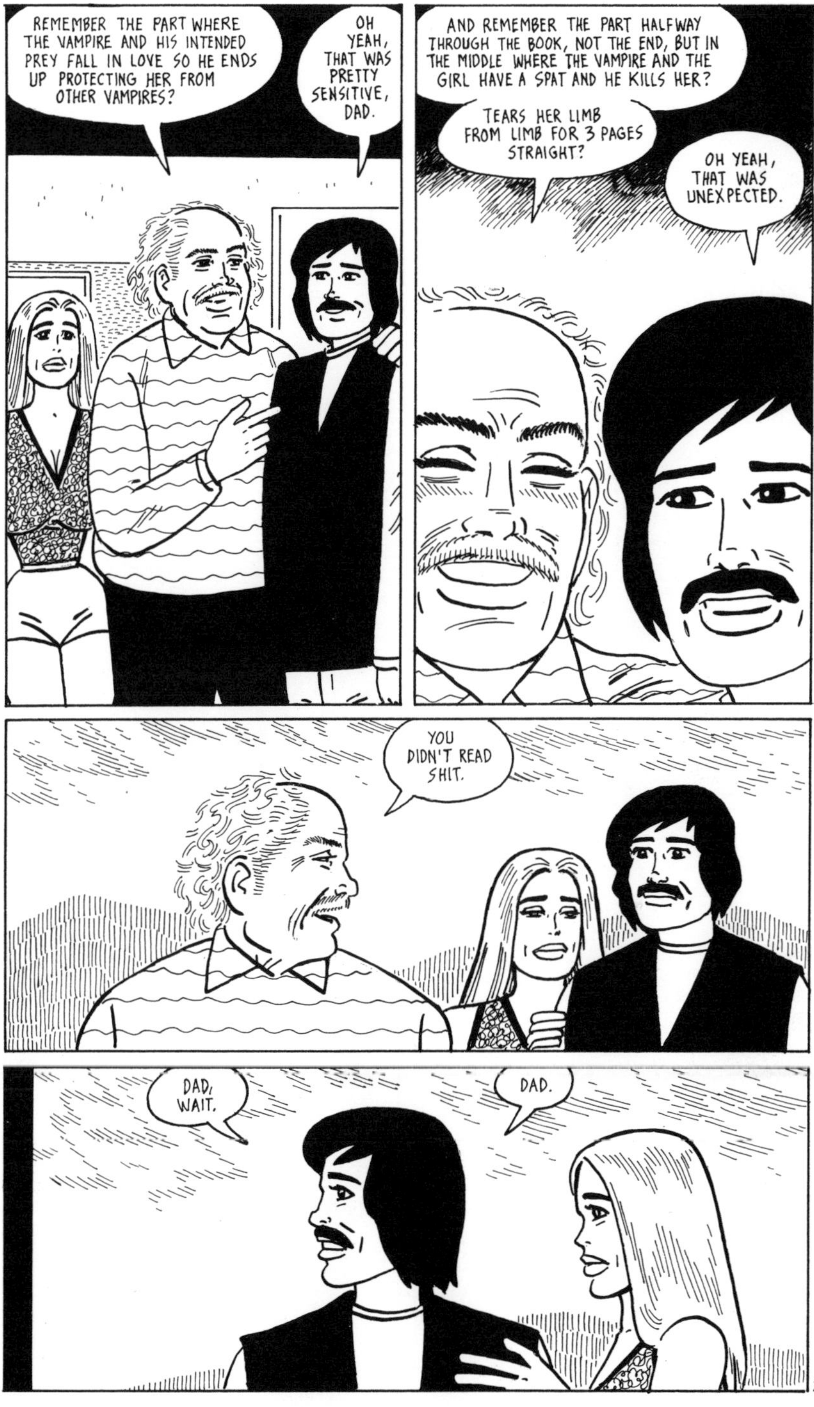
REMEMBER THE PART WHERE THE VAMPIRE AND HIS INTENDED PREY FALL IN LOVE SO HE ENDS UP PROTECTING HER FROM OTHER VAMPIRES?
OH YEAH, THAT WAS PRETTY SENSITIVE, DAD.
AND REMEMBER THE PART HALFWAY THROUGH THE BOOK, NOT THE END, BUT IN THE MIDDLE WHERE THE VAMPIRE AND THE GIRL HAVE A SPAT AND HE KILLS HER?
TEARS HER LIMB FROM LIMB FOR 3 PAGES STRAIGHT?
OH YEAH, THAT WAS UNEXPECTED.
YOU DIDN'T READ SHIT.
DAD, WAIT.
DAD.

OH, WILL YOU TURN OUT THE LIGHT AND FINISH THAT TOMORROW?
THIS ACTUALLY ISN'T BAD.
DAD'S UNFINISHED NOVEL IS CALLED *WOMANDRAKE*.
KING VAMPIRE
MOST VAMPIRE STORIES ARE THINLY VEILED RAPE FANTASIES FOR WOMEN.
HE'S HOT, HE'S A KILLING MACHINE BUT HE'S OH SO SENSITIVE WITH ME.
NOT IN MY STORIES.
WHAT'S *WOMANDRAKE*?
MY UPDATE ON THE GERMAN STORY OF A PROSTITUTE INSEMINATED WITH A HANGED MAN'S SEMEN.
THE UNHOLY OFFSPRING GROWS UP TO BE *ALRAUNE* AND IS UNABLE TO LOVE, THEREFORE TAKES HER REVENGE ON MANKIND; EMPHASIZE *MAN*.
A REAL CASTRATING BITCH, THAT *ALRAUNE*.
TO SEEK OUT LOVE BY DESTROYING MEN.
SOUNDS LIKE YOUR MOTHER.

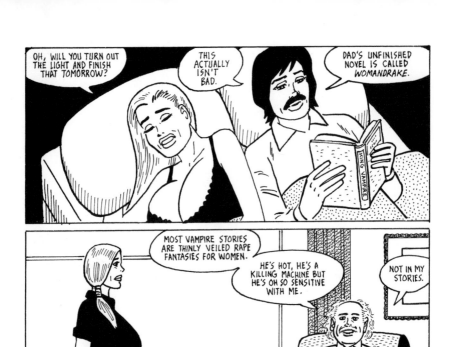

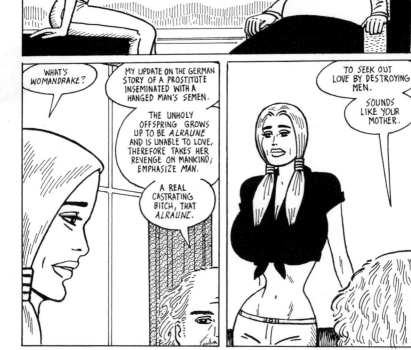

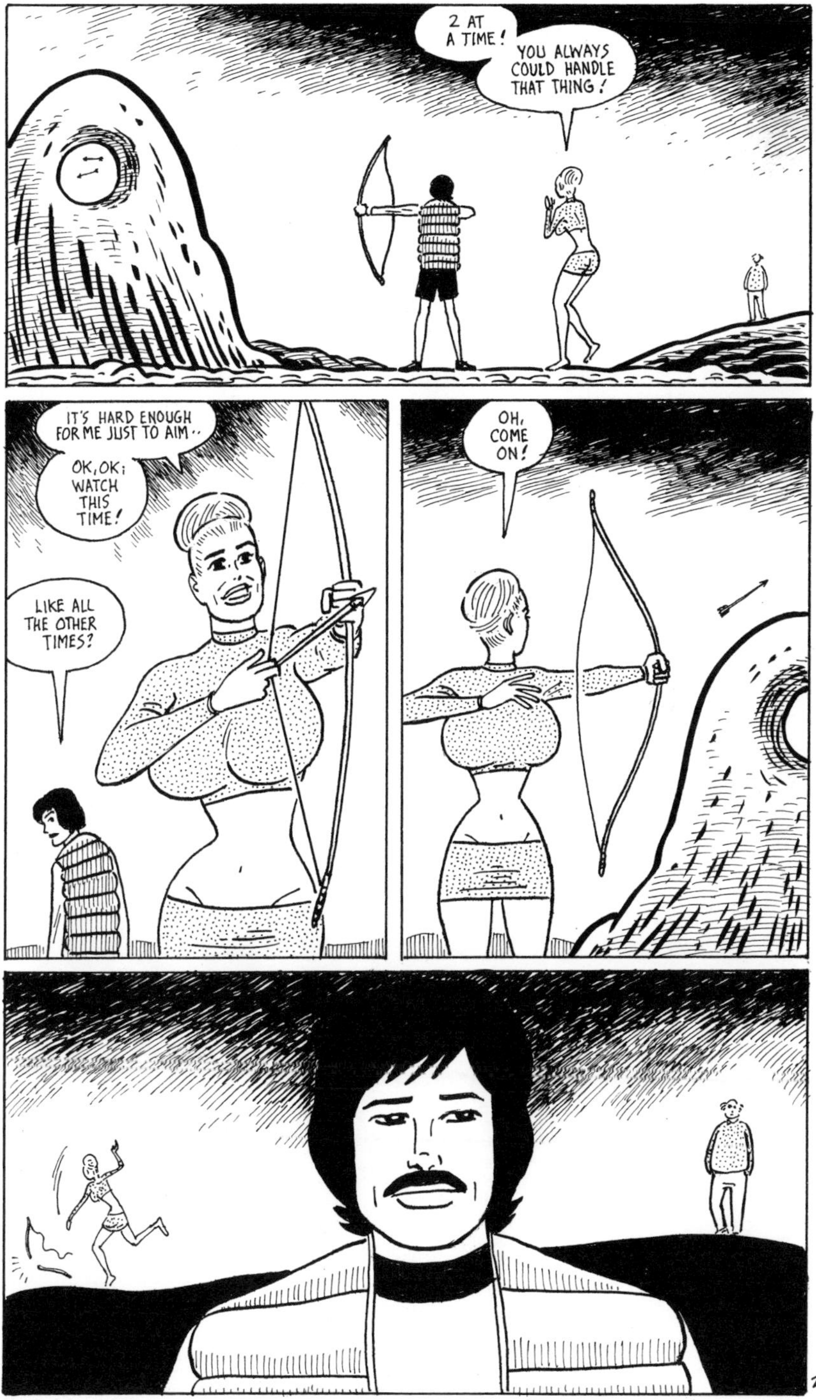
2 AT A TIME!
YOU ALWAYS COULD HANDLE THAT THING!
IT'S HARD ENOUGH FOR ME JUST TO AIM..
OK, OK; WATCH THIS TIME!
LIKE ALL THE OTHER TIMES?
OH, COME ON!

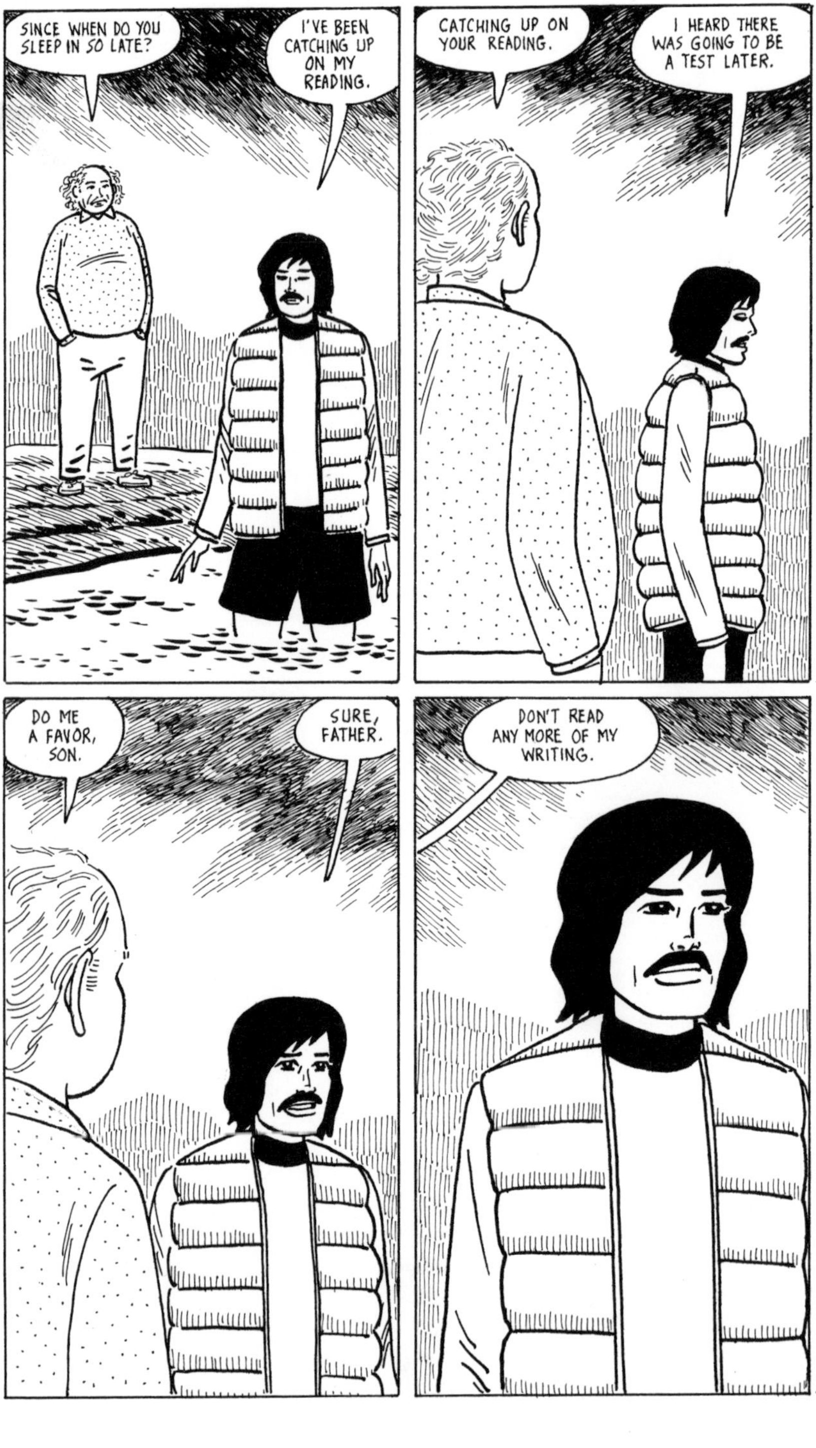
SINCE WHEN DO YOU SLEEP IN SO LATE?
I'VE BEEN CATCHING UP ON MY READING.
CATCHING UP ON YOUR READING.
I HEARD THERE WAS GOING TO BE A TEST LATER.
DO ME A FAVOR, SON.
SURE, FATHER.
DON'T READ ANY MORE OF MY WRITING.

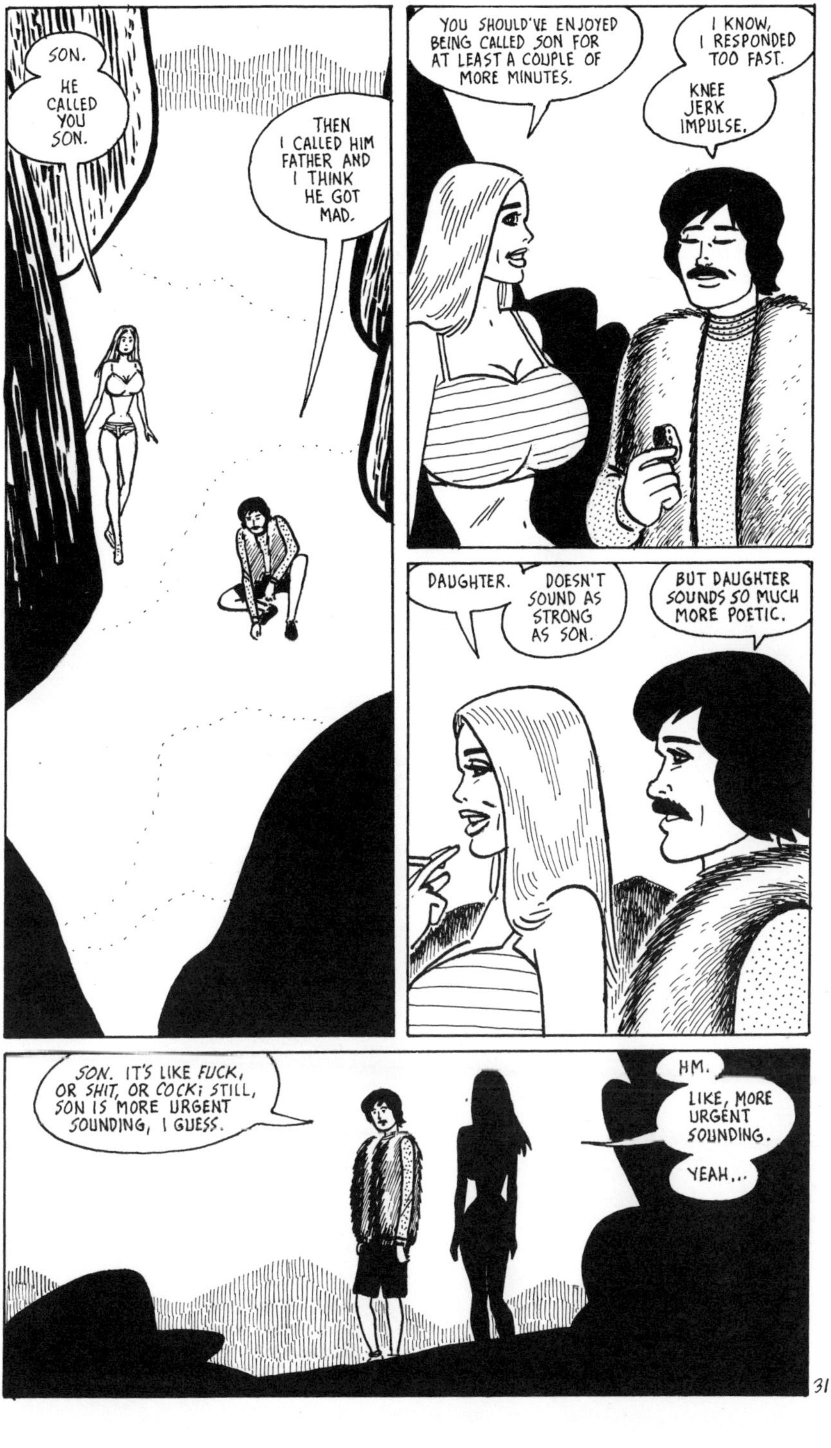
SON.
HE CALLED YOU SON.
THEN I CALLED HIM FATHER AND I THINK HE GOT MAD.
YOU SHOULD'VE ENJOYED BEING CALLED SON FOR AT LEAST A COUPLE OF MORE MINUTES.
I KNOW, I RESPONDED TOO FAST.
KNEE JERK IMPULSE.
DAUGHTER.
DOESN'T SOUND AS STRONG AS SON.
BUT DAUGHTER SOUNDS SO MUCH MORE POETIC.
SON. IT'S LIKE FUCK, OR SHIT, OR COCK; STILL, SON IS MORE URGENT SOUNDING, I GUESS.
HM.
LIKE, MORE URGENT SOUNDING.
YEAH...

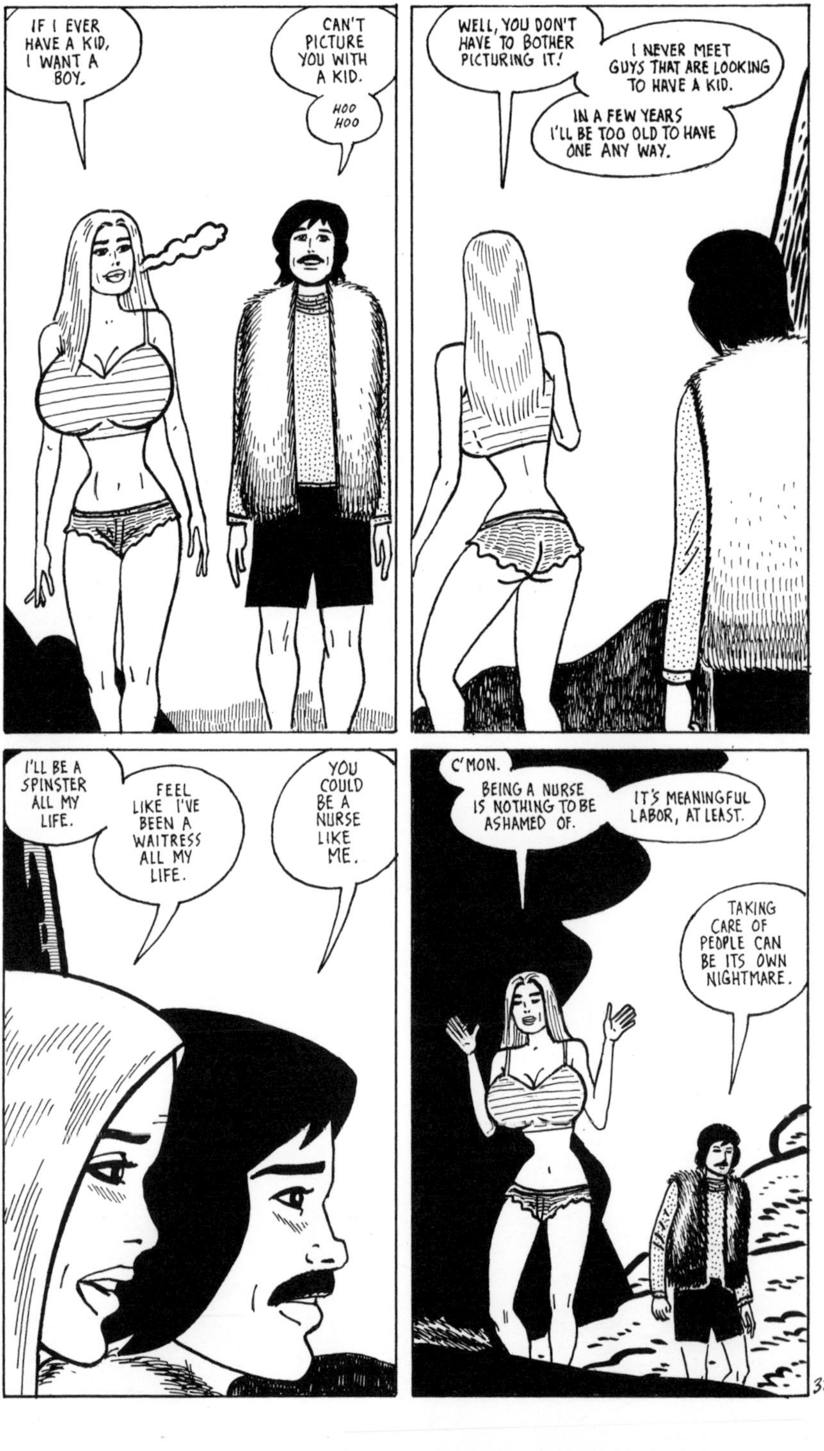
IF I EVER HAVE A KID, I WANT A BOY.
CAN'T PICTURE YOU WITH A KID.
HOO HOO
WELL, YOU DON'T HAVE TO BOTHER PICTURING IT!
I NEVER MEET GUYS THAT ARE LOOKING TO HAVE A KID.
IN A FEW YEARS I'LL BE TOO OLD TO HAVE ONE ANY WAY.
I'LL BE A SPINSTER ALL MY LIFE.
FEEL LIKE I'VE BEEN A WAITRESS ALL MY LIFE.
YOU COULD BE A NURSE LIKE ME.
C'MON.
BEING A NURSE IS NOTHING TO BE ASHAMED OF.
IT'S MEANINGFUL LABOR, AT LEAST.
TAKING CARE OF PEOPLE CAN BE ITS OWN NIGHTMARE.

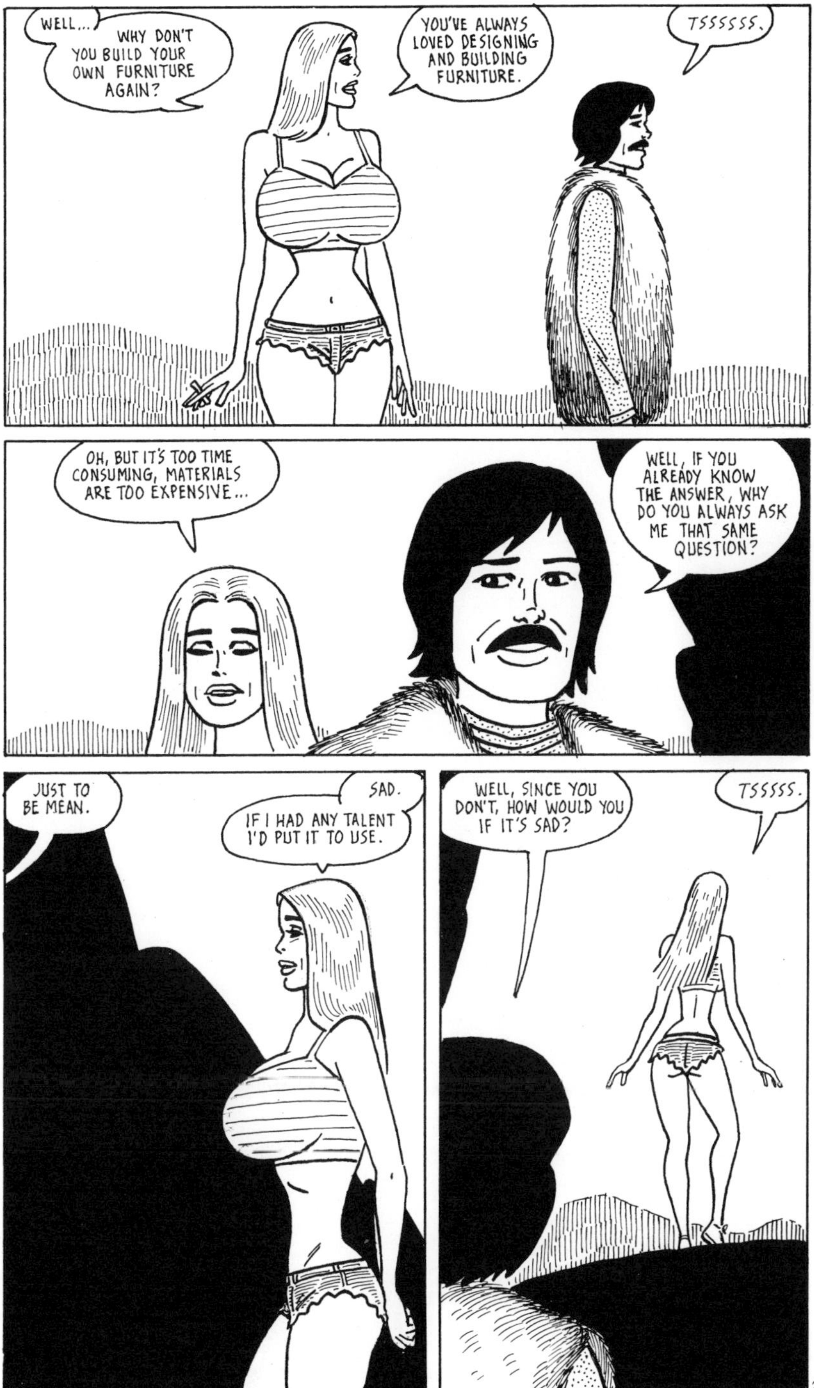
WELL... WHY DON'T YOU BUILD YOUR OWN FURNITURE AGAIN?
YOU'VE ALWAYS LOVED DESIGNING AND BUILDING FURNITURE.
TSSSSSS.
OH, BUT IT'S TOO TIME CONSUMING, MATERIALS ARE TOO EXPENSIVE...
WELL, IF YOU ALREADY KNOW THE ANSWER, WHY DO YOU ALWAYS ASK ME THAT SAME QUESTION?
JUST TO BE MEAN.
SAD.
IF I HAD ANY TALENT I'D PUT IT TO USE.
WELL, SINCE YOU DON'T, HOW WOULD YOU IF IT'S SAD?
TSSSSS.

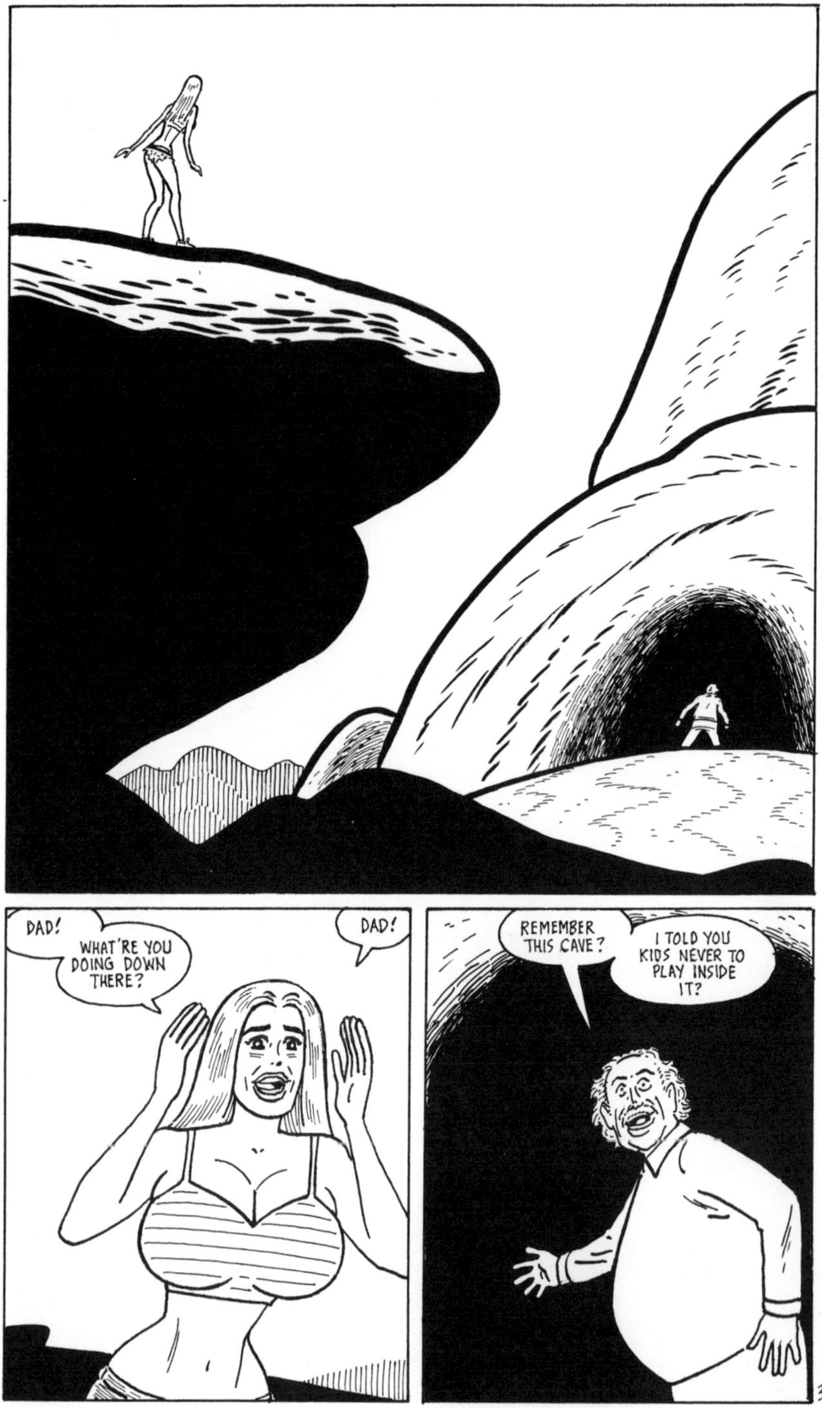
DAD!
WHAT'RE YOU DOING DOWN THERE?
DAD!
REMEMBER THIS CAVE?
I TOLD YOU KIDS NEVER TO PLAY INSIDE IT?

HOW'RE YOU GOING TO GET BACK UP?
HEE HEE!
DAD, DON'T..!

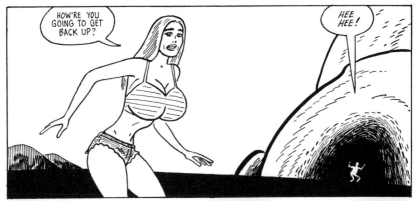

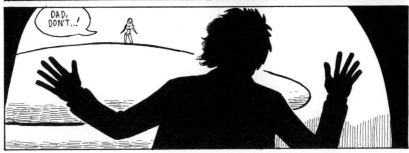

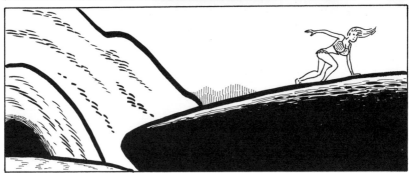

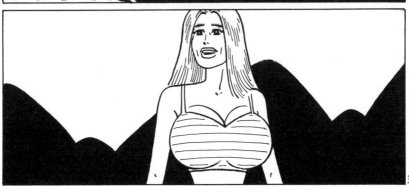

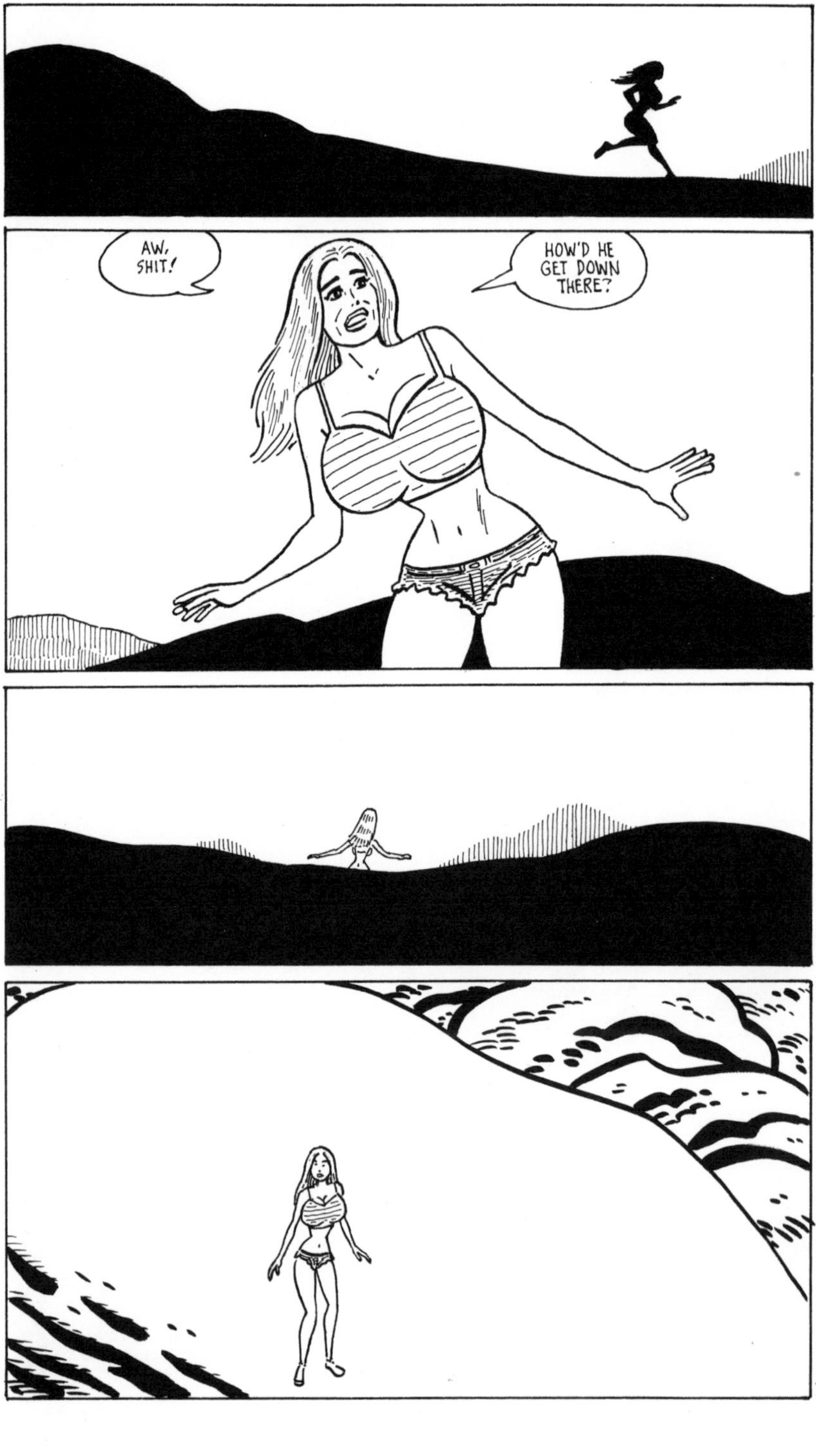
AW, SHIT!
HOW'D HE GET DOWN THERE?

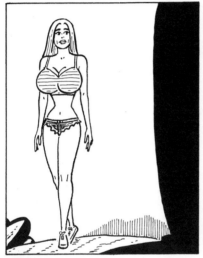

37

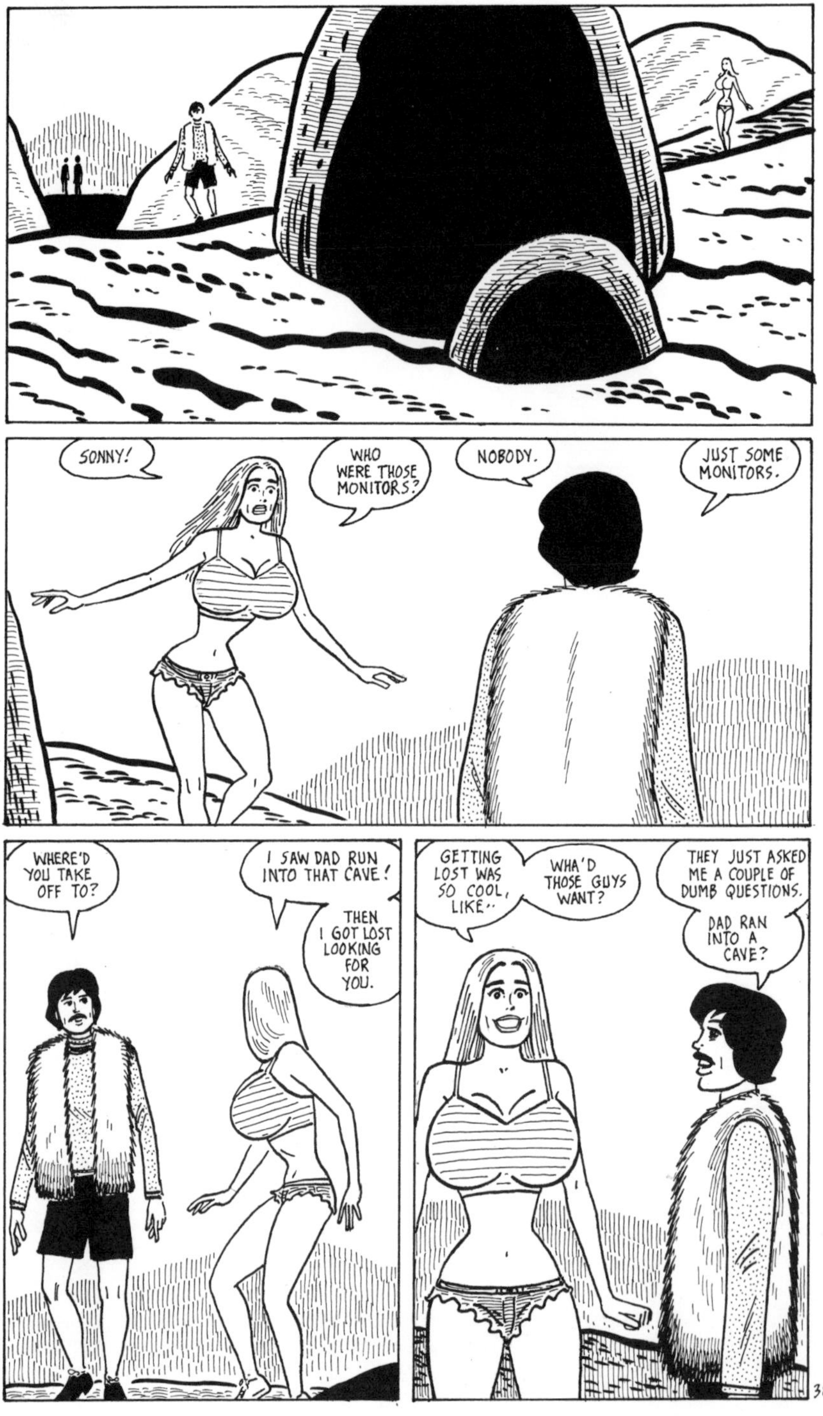
SONNY!
WHO WERE THOSE MONITORS?
NOBODY.
JUST SOME MONITORS.
WHERE'D YOU TAKE OFF TO?
I SAW DAD RUN INTO THAT CAVE!
THEN I GOT LOST LOOKING FOR YOU.
GETTING LOST WAS SO COOL, LIKE..
WHA'D THOSE GUYS WANT?
THEY JUST ASKED ME A COUPLE OF DUMB QUESTIONS.
DAD RAN INTO A CAVE?

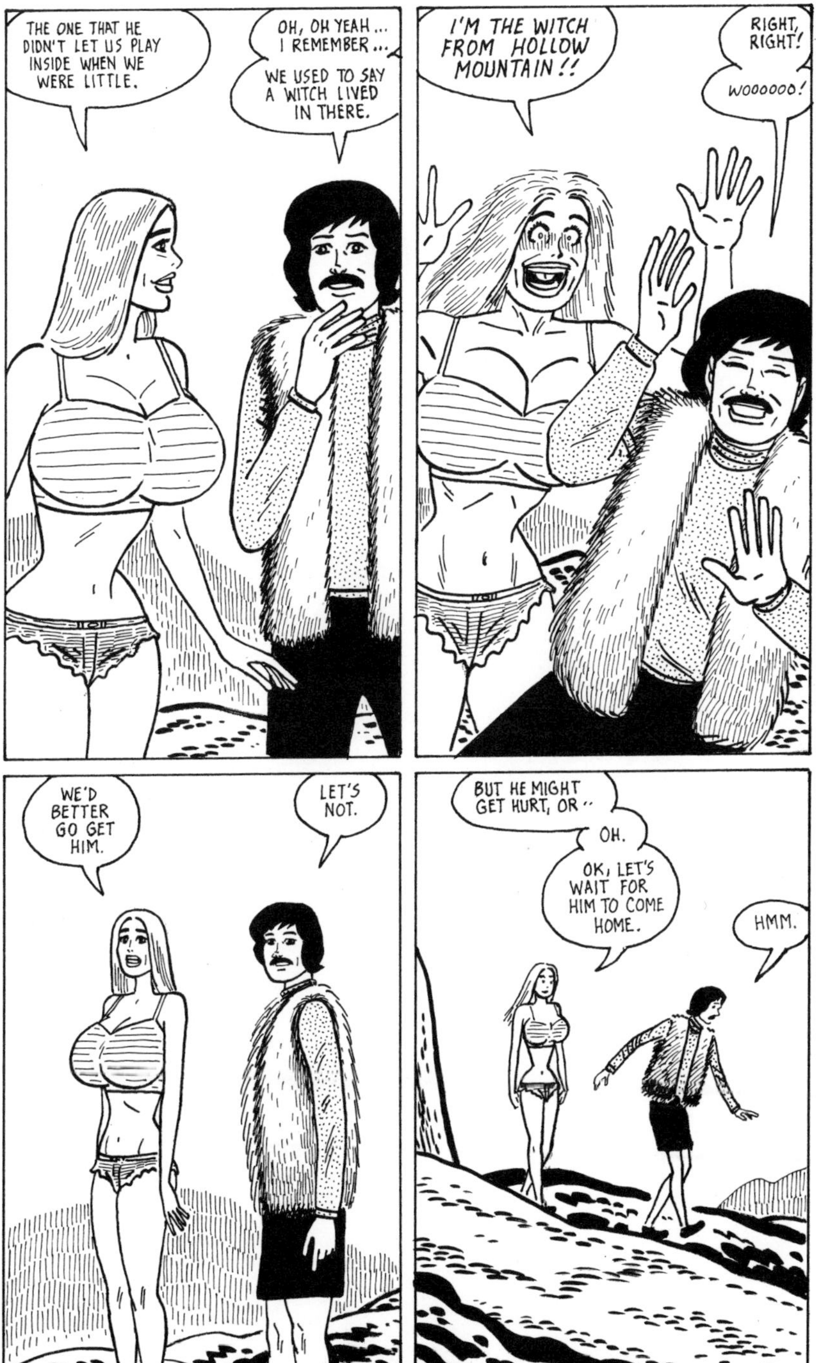
THE ONE THAT HE DIDN'T LET US PLAY INSIDE WHEN WE WERE LITTLE.
OH, OH YEAH ... I REMEMBER ...
WE USED TO SAY A WITCH LIVED IN THERE.
I'M THE WITCH FROM HOLLOW MOUNTAIN!!
RIGHT, RIGHT!
WOOOOOO!
WE'D BETTER GO GET HIM.
LET'S NOT.
BUT HE MIGHT GET HURT, OR ..
OH.
OK, LET'S WAIT FOR HIM TO COME HOME.
HMM.

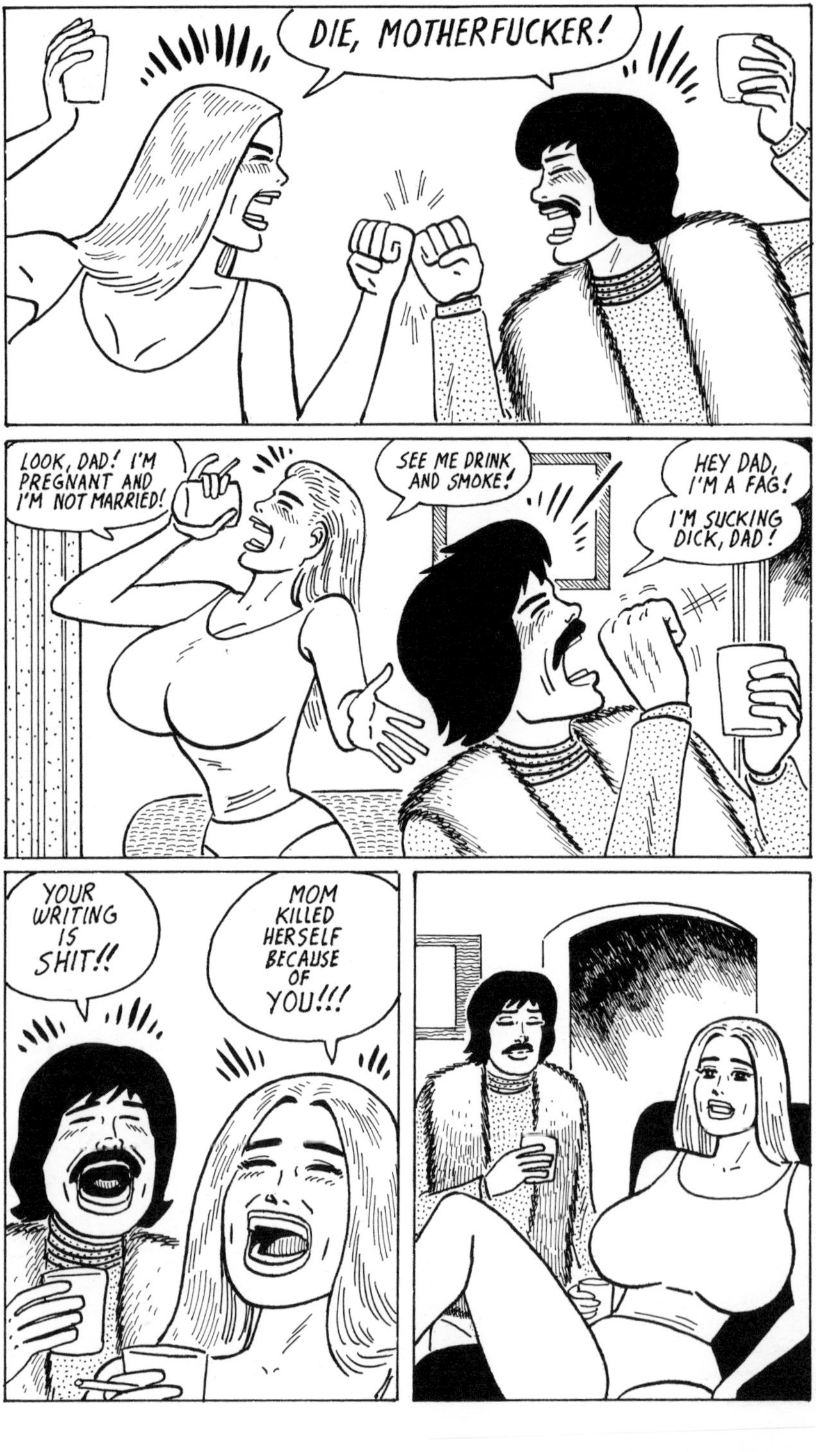
DIE, MOTHERFUCKER!
LOOK, DAD! I'M PREGNANT AND I'M NOT MARRIED!
SEE ME DRINK AND SMOKE!
HEY DAD, I'M A FAG!
I'M SUCKING DICK, DAD!
YOUR WRITING IS SHIT!!
MOM KILLED HERSELF BECAUSE OF YOU!!!

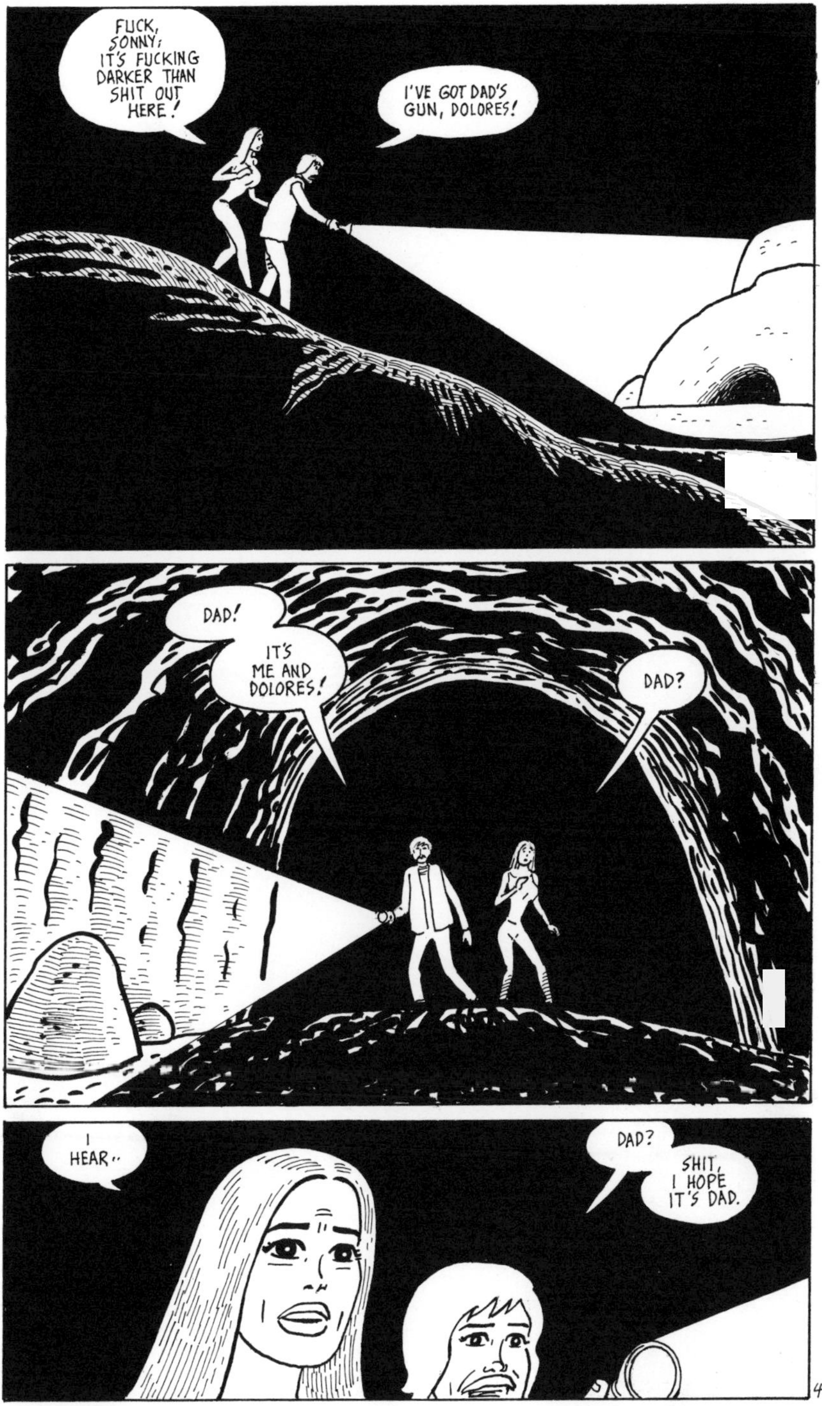
FUCK, SONNY; IT'S FUCKING DARKER THAN SHIT OUT HERE!
I'VE GOT DAD'S GUN, DOLORES!
DAD!
IT'S ME AND DOLORES!
DAD?
I HEAR..
DAD?
SHIT, I HOPE IT'S DAD.

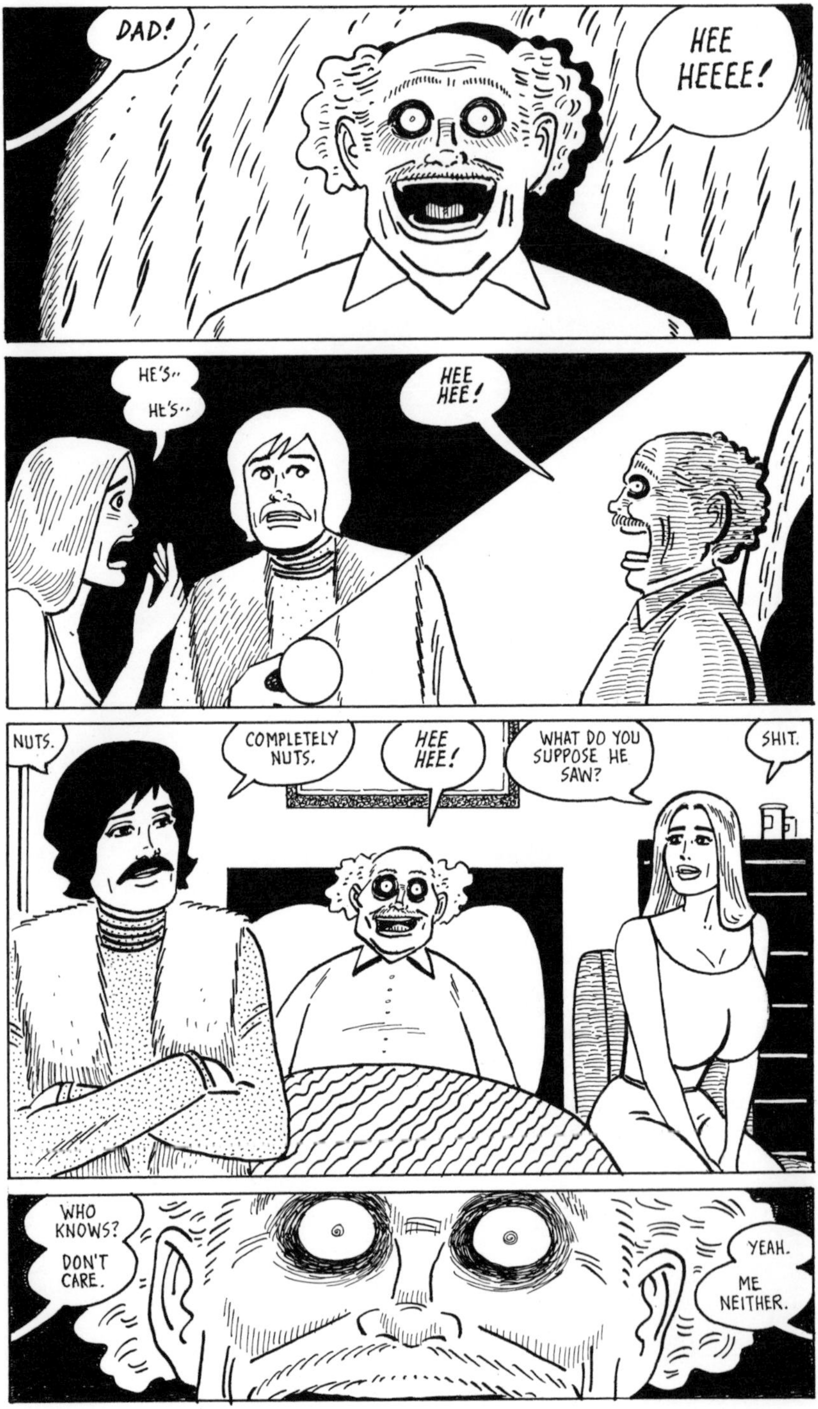
DAD!
HEE HEEEE!
HE'S..
HE'S..
HEE HEE!
NUTS.
COMPLETELY NUTS.
HEE HEE!
WHAT DO YOU SUPPOSE HE SAW?
SHIT.
WHO KNOWS?
DON'T CARE.
YEAH.
ME NEITHER.

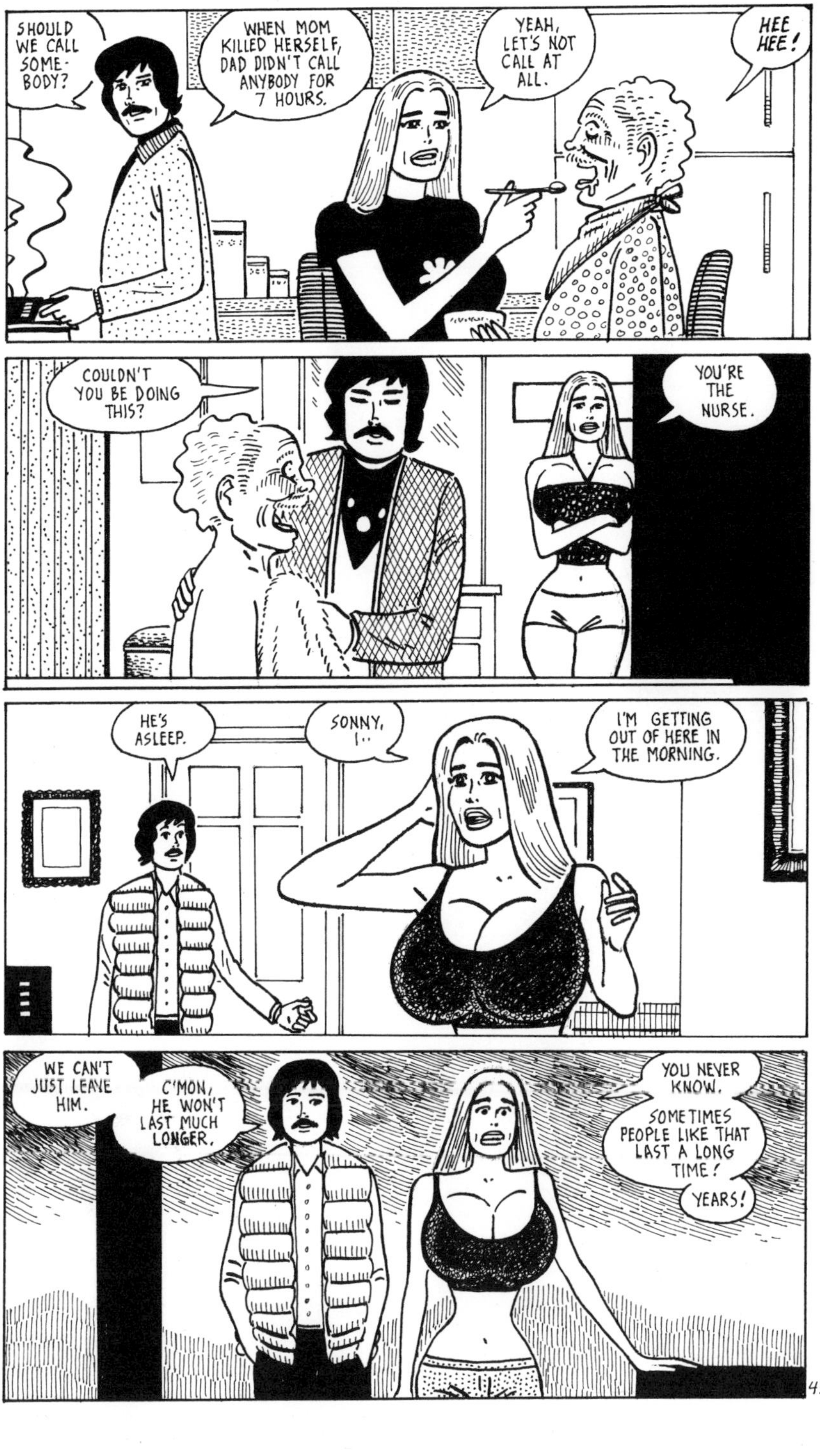
SHOULD WE CALL SOME-BODY?
WHEN MOM KILLED HERSELF, DAD DIDN'T CALL ANYBODY FOR 7 HOURS.
YEAH, LET'S NOT CALL AT ALL.
HEE HEE!
COULDN'T YOU BE DOING THIS?
YOU'RE THE NURSE.
HE'S ASLEEP.
SONNY, I..
I'M GETTING OUT OF HERE IN THE MORNING.
WE CAN'T JUST LEAVE HIM.
C'MON, HE WON'T LAST MUCH LONGER.
YOU NEVER KNOW.
SOMETIMES PEOPLE LIKE THAT LAST A LONG TIME!
YEARS!

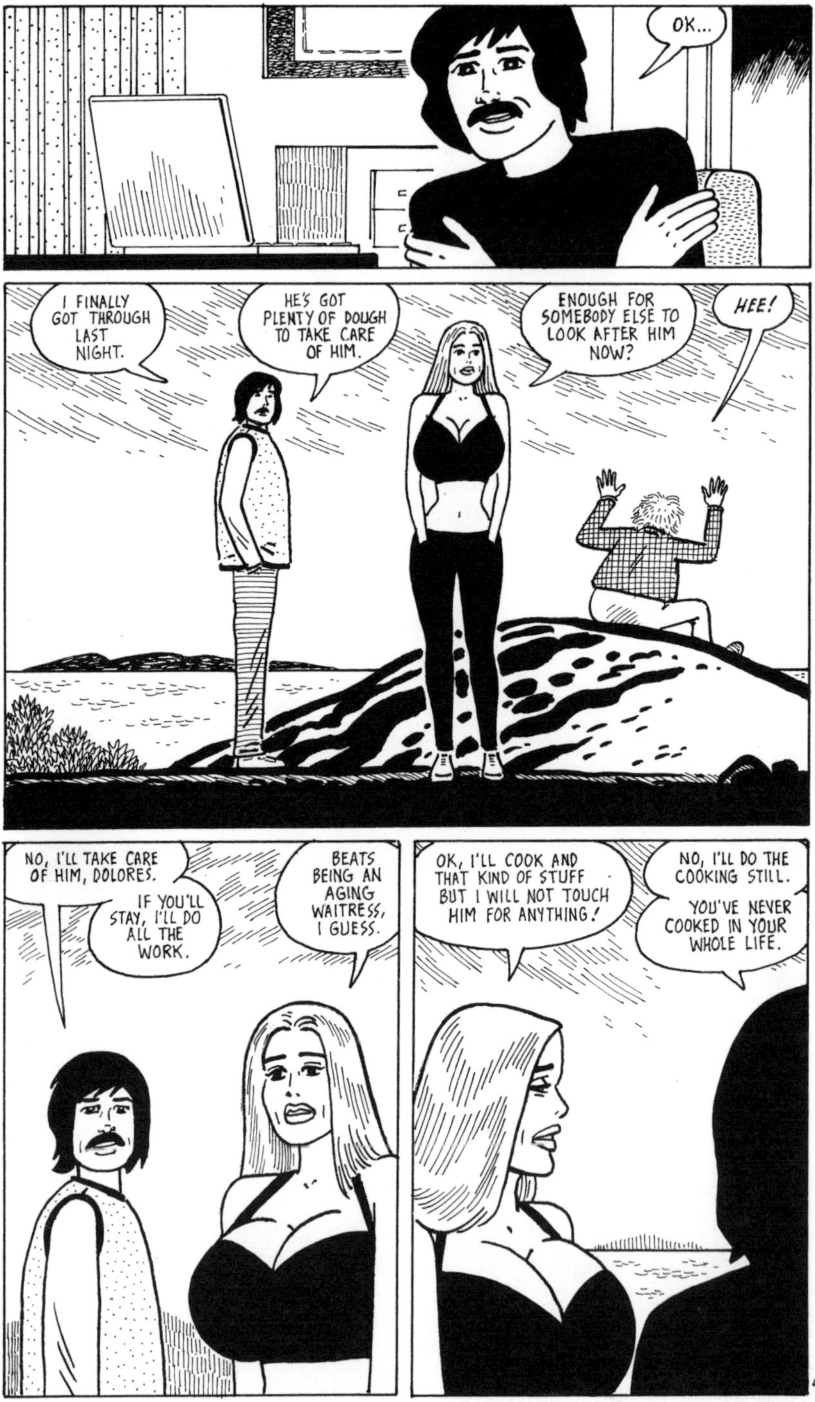

OK...
I FINALLY GOT THROUGH LAST NIGHT.
HE'S GOT PLENTY OF DOUGH TO TAKE CARE OF HIM.
ENOUGH FOR SOMEBODY ELSE TO LOOK AFTER HIM NOW?
HEE!
NO, I'LL TAKE CARE OF HIM, DOLORES.
IF YOU'LL STAY, I'LL DO ALL THE WORK.
BEATS BEING AN AGING WAITRESS, I GUESS.
OK, I'LL COOK AND THAT KIND OF STUFF BUT I WILL NOT TOUCH HIM FOR ANYTHING!
NO, I'LL DO THE COOKING STILL.
YOU'VE NEVER COOKED IN YOUR WHOLE LIFE.

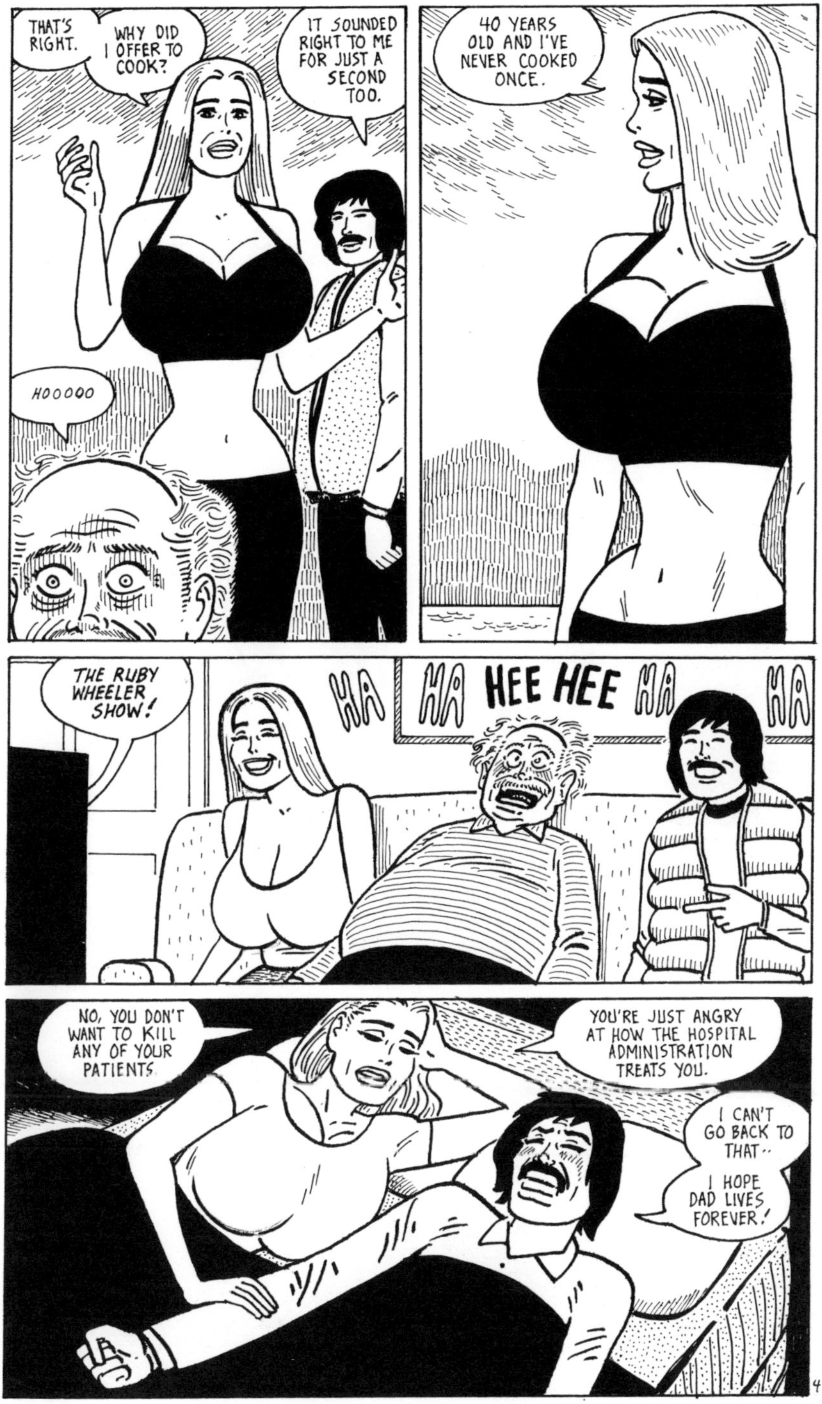
THAT'S RIGHT.
WHY DID I OFFER TO COOK?
IT SOUNDED RIGHT TO ME FOR JUST A SECOND TOO.
HOOOOO
40 YEARS OLD AND I'VE NEVER COOKED ONCE.
THE RUBY WHEELER SHOW!
HA HA HEE HEE HA HA
NO, YOU DON'T WANT TO KILL ANY OF YOUR PATIENTS.
YOU'RE JUST ANGRY AT HOW THE HOSPITAL ADMINISTRATION TREATS YOU.
I CAN'T GO BACK TO THAT..
I HOPE DAD LIVES FOREVER!

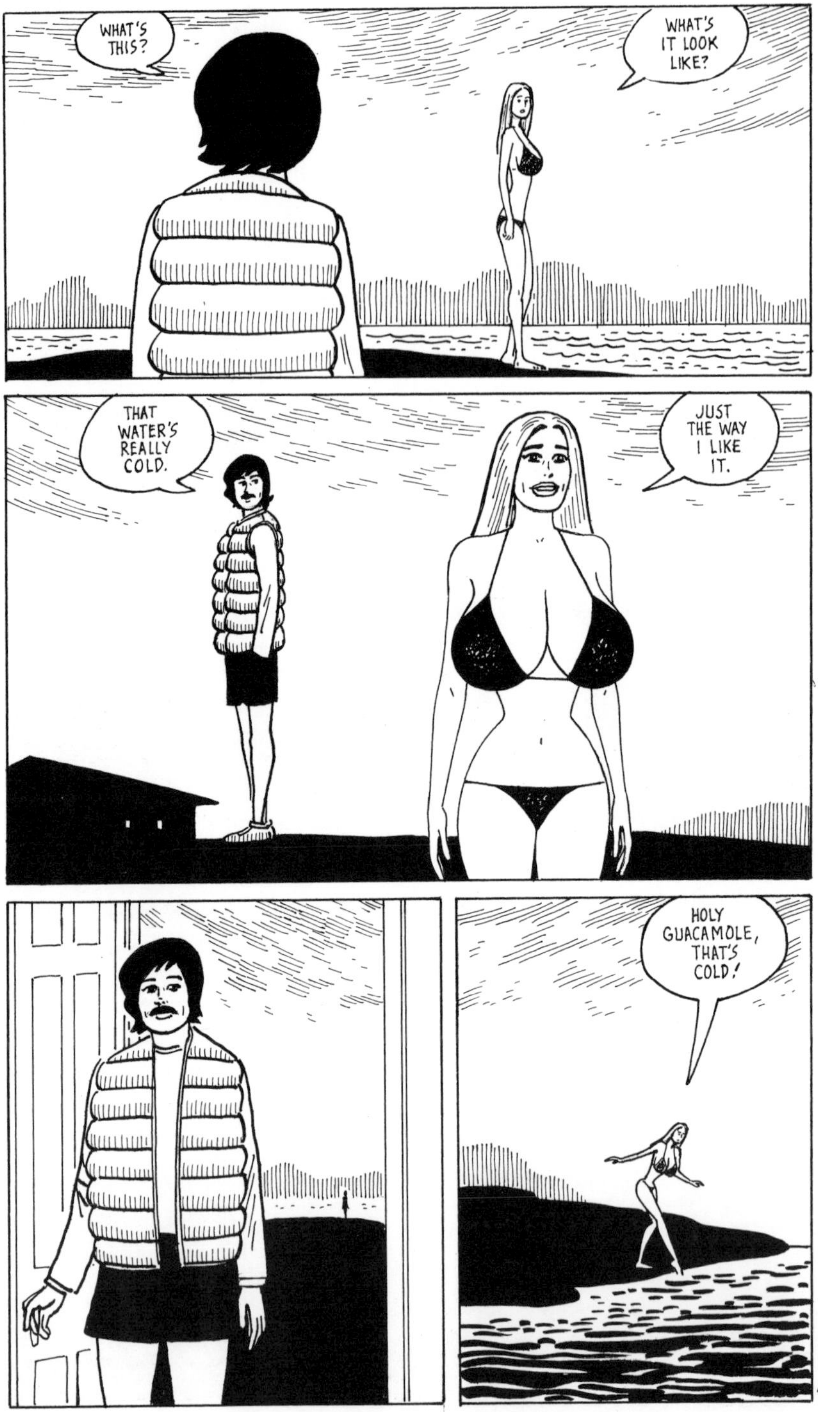
WHAT'S THIS?
WHAT'S IT LOOK LIKE?
THAT WATER'S REALLY COLD.
JUST THE WAY I LIKE IT.
HOLY GUACAMOLE, THAT'S COLD!

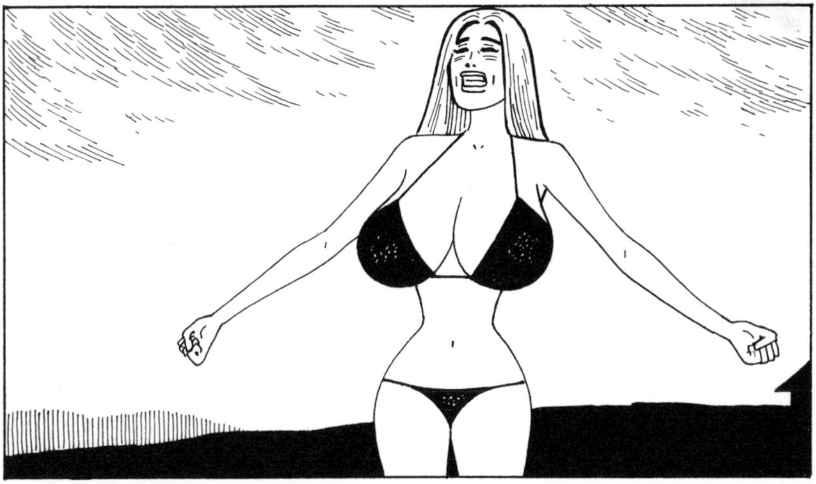

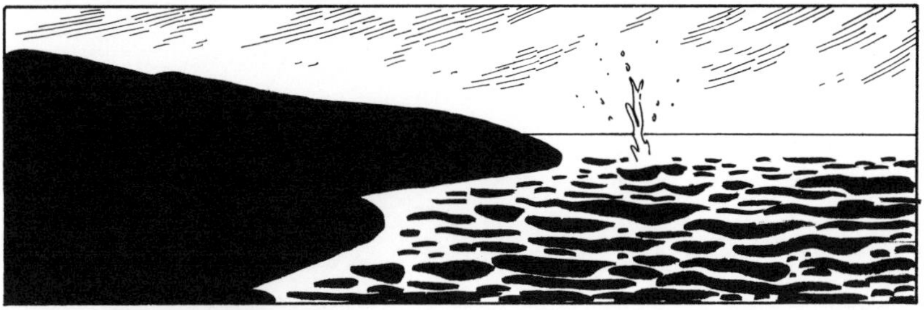

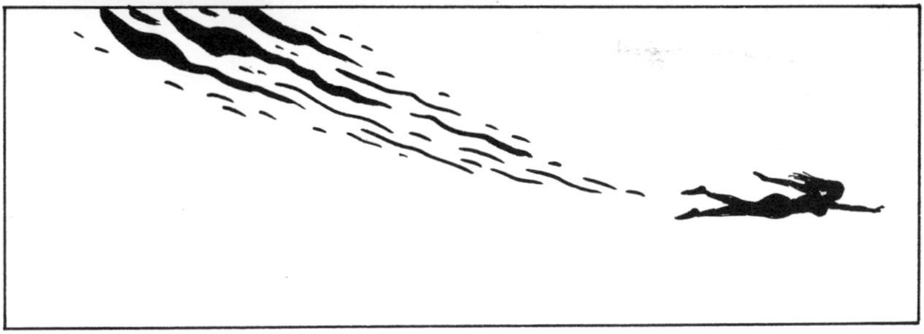

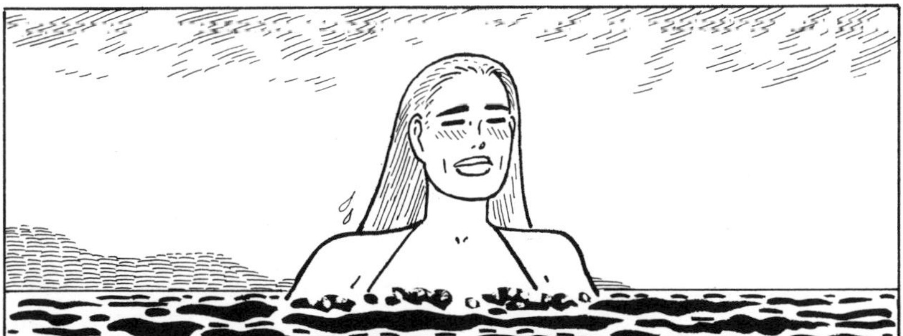

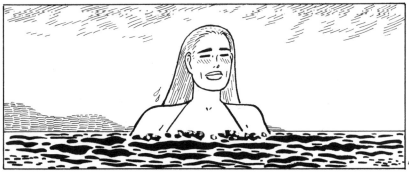

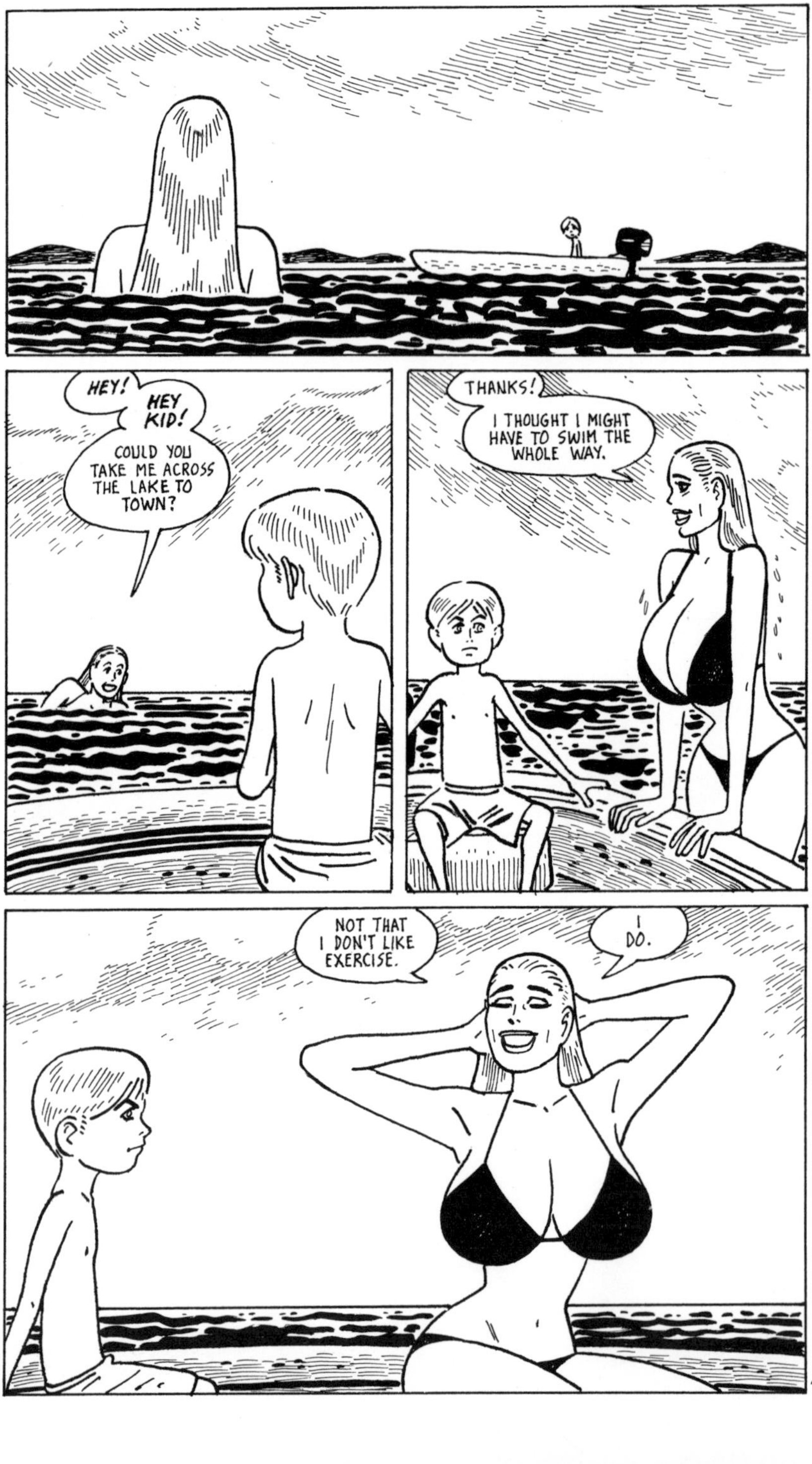
HEY!
HEY KID!
COULD YOU TAKE ME ACROSS THE LAKE TO TOWN?
THANKS!
I THOUGHT I MIGHT HAVE TO SWIM THE WHOLE WAY.
NOT THAT I DON'T LIKE EXERCISE.
I DO.

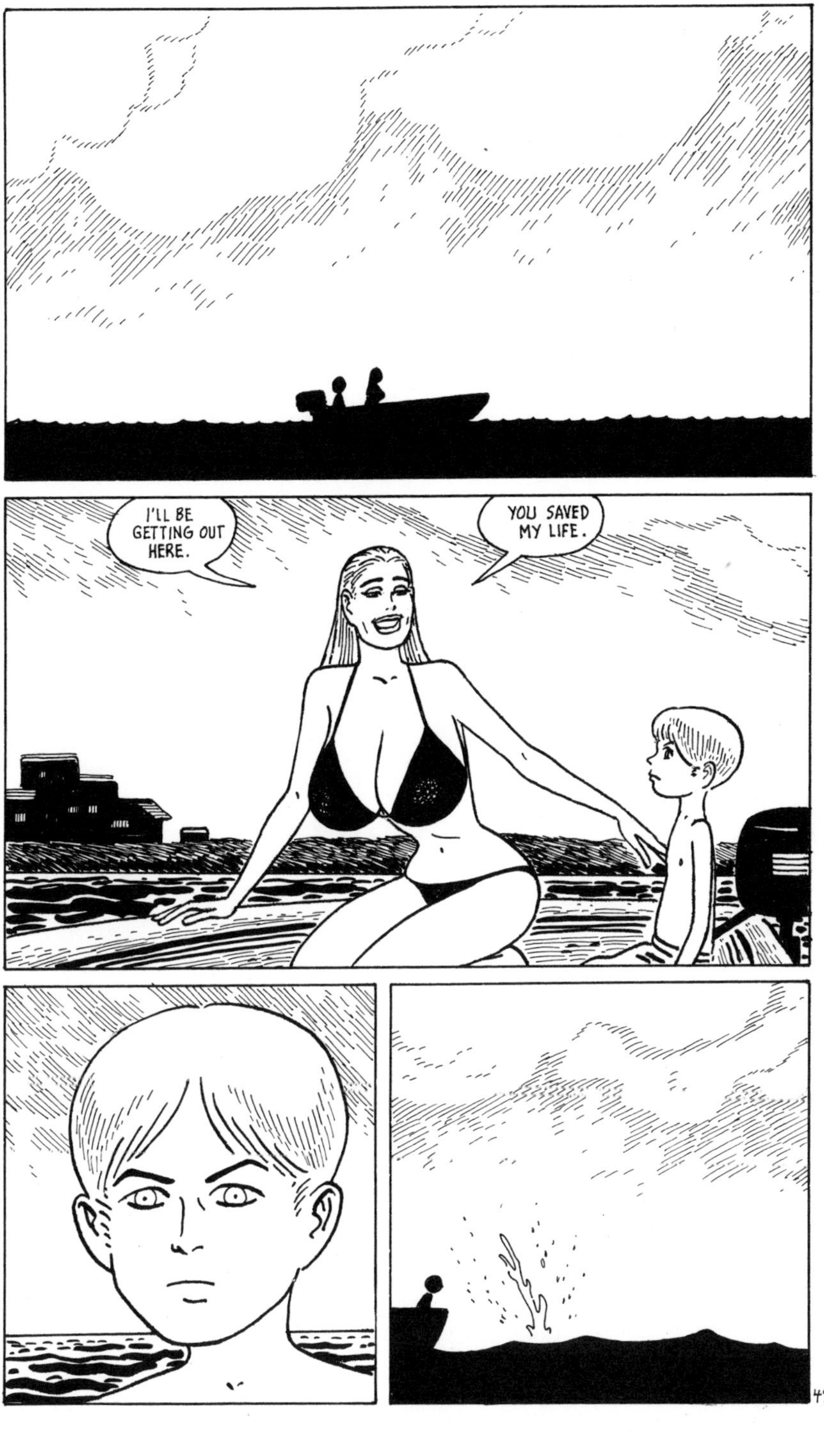
I'LL BE GETTING OUT HERE.
YOU SAVED MY LIFE.

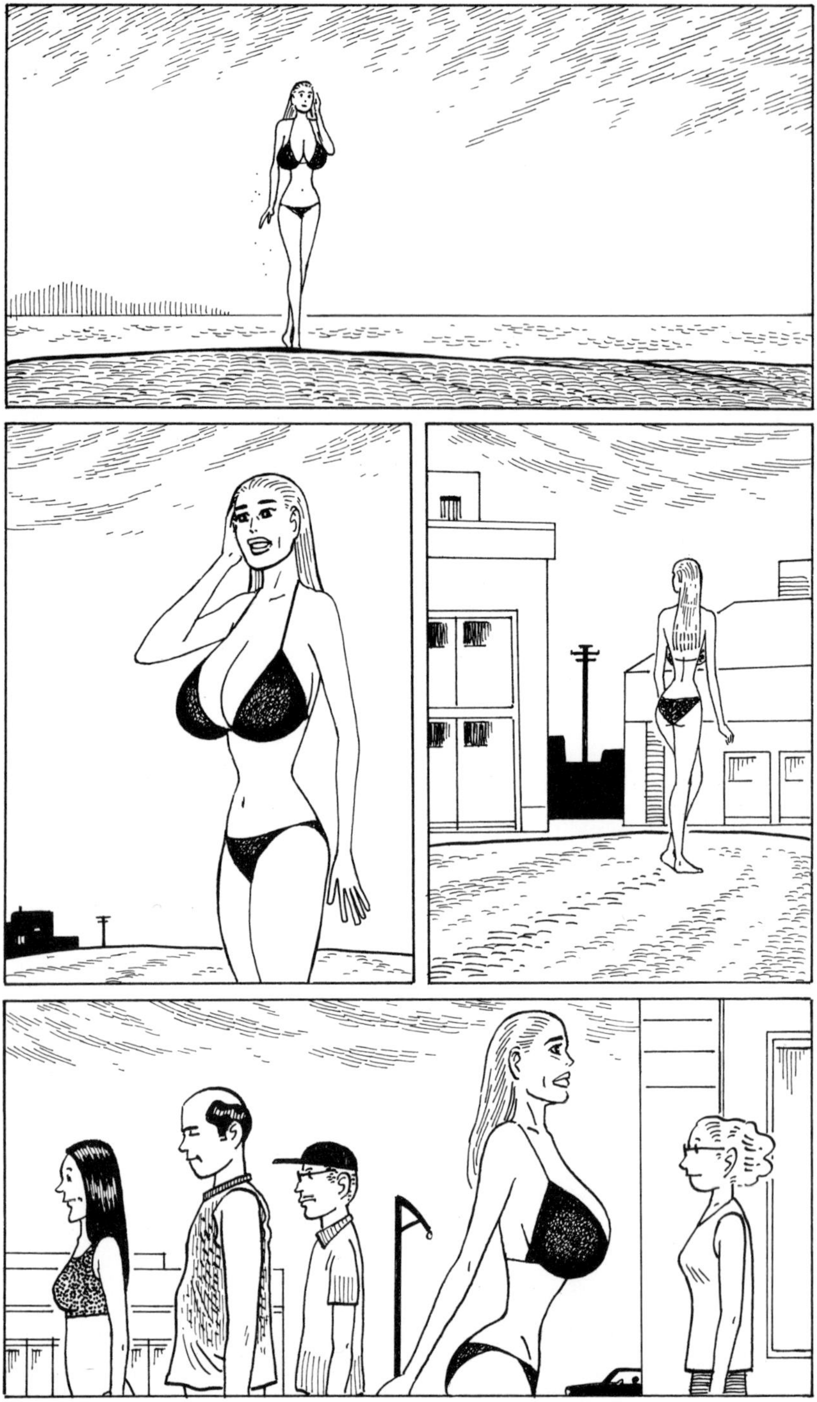

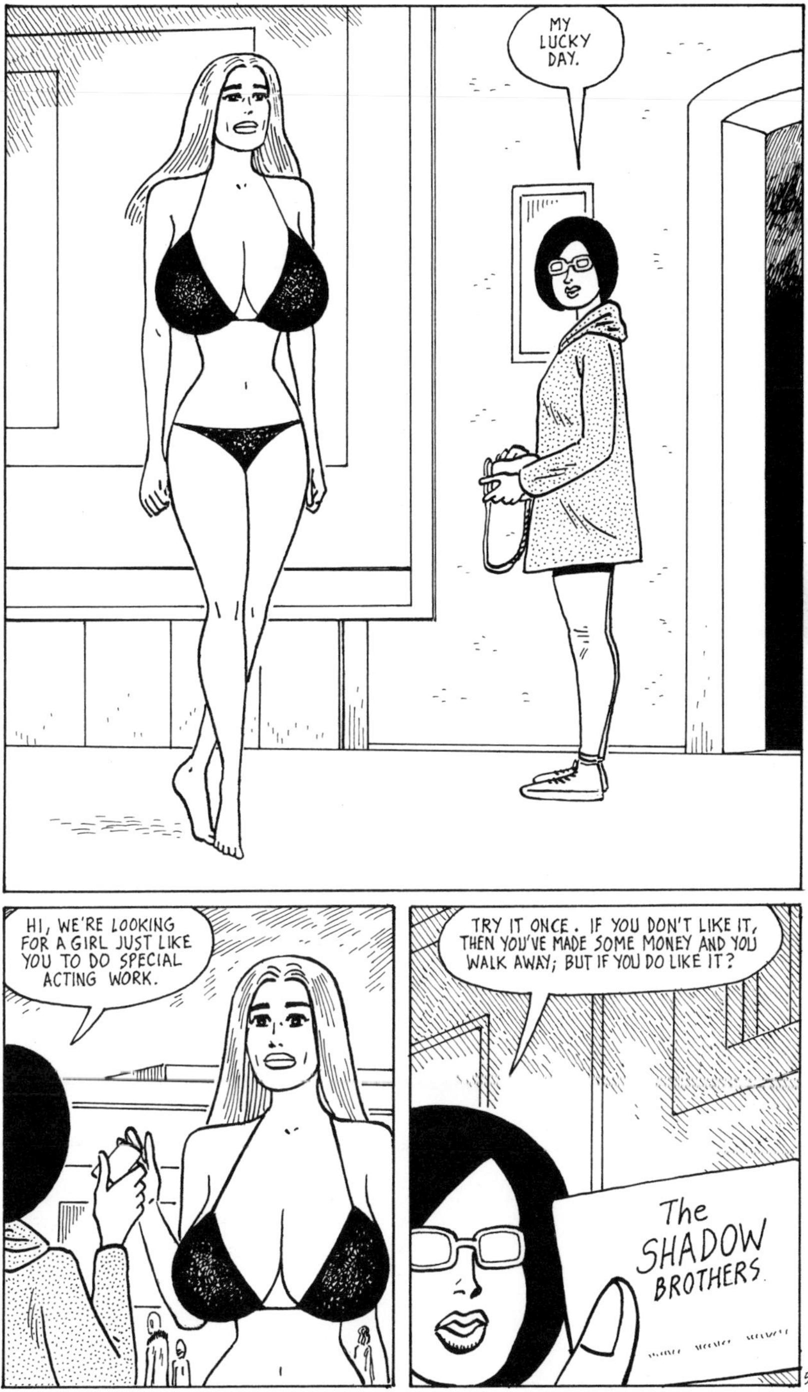
MY LUCKY DAY.
HI, WE'RE LOOKING FOR A GIRL JUST LIKE YOU TO DO SPECIAL ACTING WORK.
TRY IT ONCE. IF YOU DON'T LIKE IT, THEN YOU'VE MADE SOME MONEY AND YOU WALK AWAY; BUT IF YOU DO LIKE IT?
The SHADOW BROTHERS

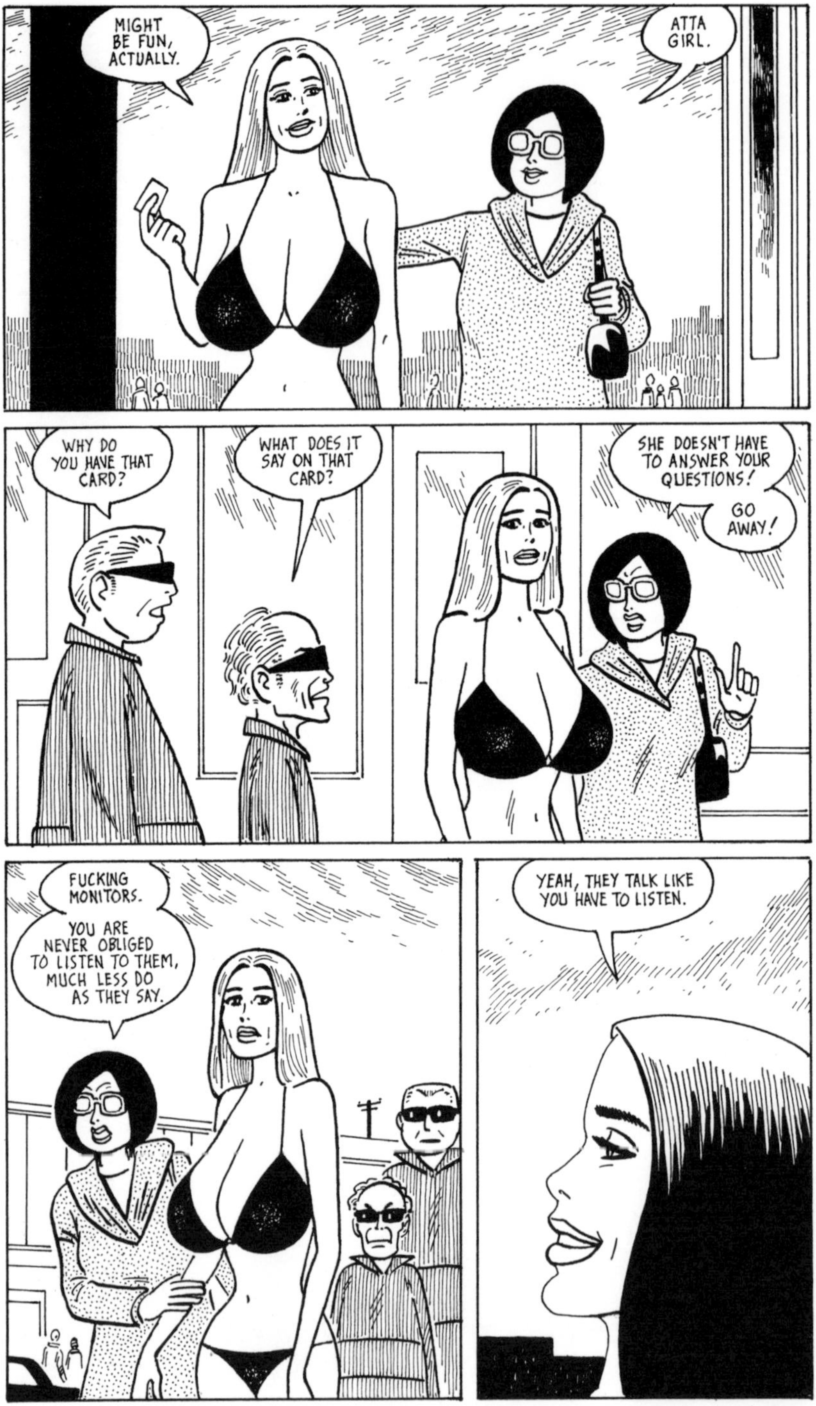
MIGHT BE FUN, ACTUALLY.
ATTA GIRL.
WHY DO YOU HAVE THAT CARD?
WHAT DOES IT SAY ON THAT CARD?
SHE DOESN'T HAVE TO ANSWER YOUR QUESTIONS!
GO AWAY!
FUCKING MONITORS.
YOU ARE NEVER OBLIGED TO LISTEN TO THEM, MUCH LESS DO AS THEY SAY.
YEAH, THEY TALK LIKE YOU HAVE TO LISTEN.

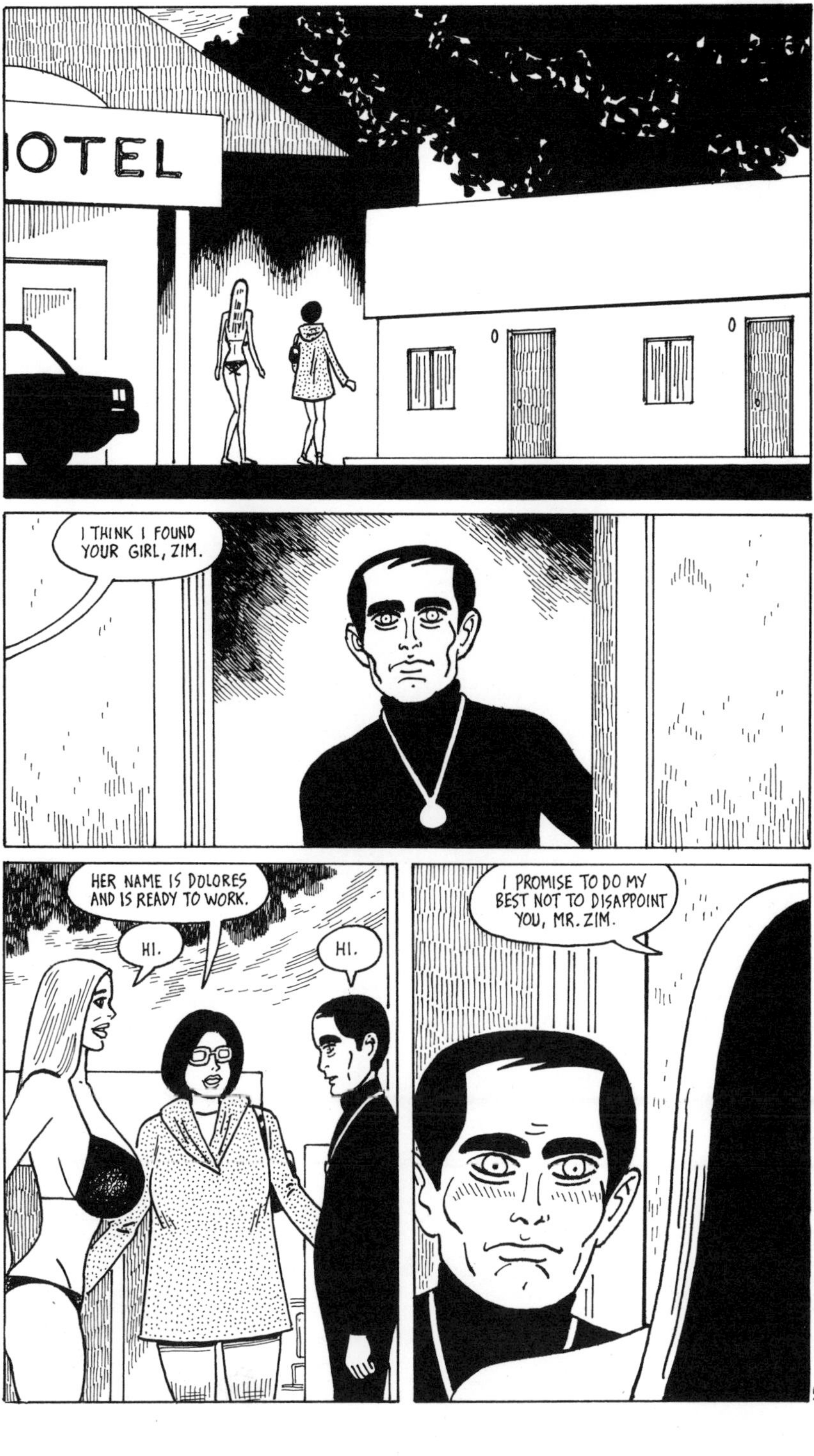
OTEL
I THINK I FOUND YOUR GIRL, ZIM.
HER NAME IS DOLORES AND IS READY TO WORK.
HI.
HI.
I PROMISE TO DO MY BEST NOT TO DISAPPOINT YOU, MR. ZIM.

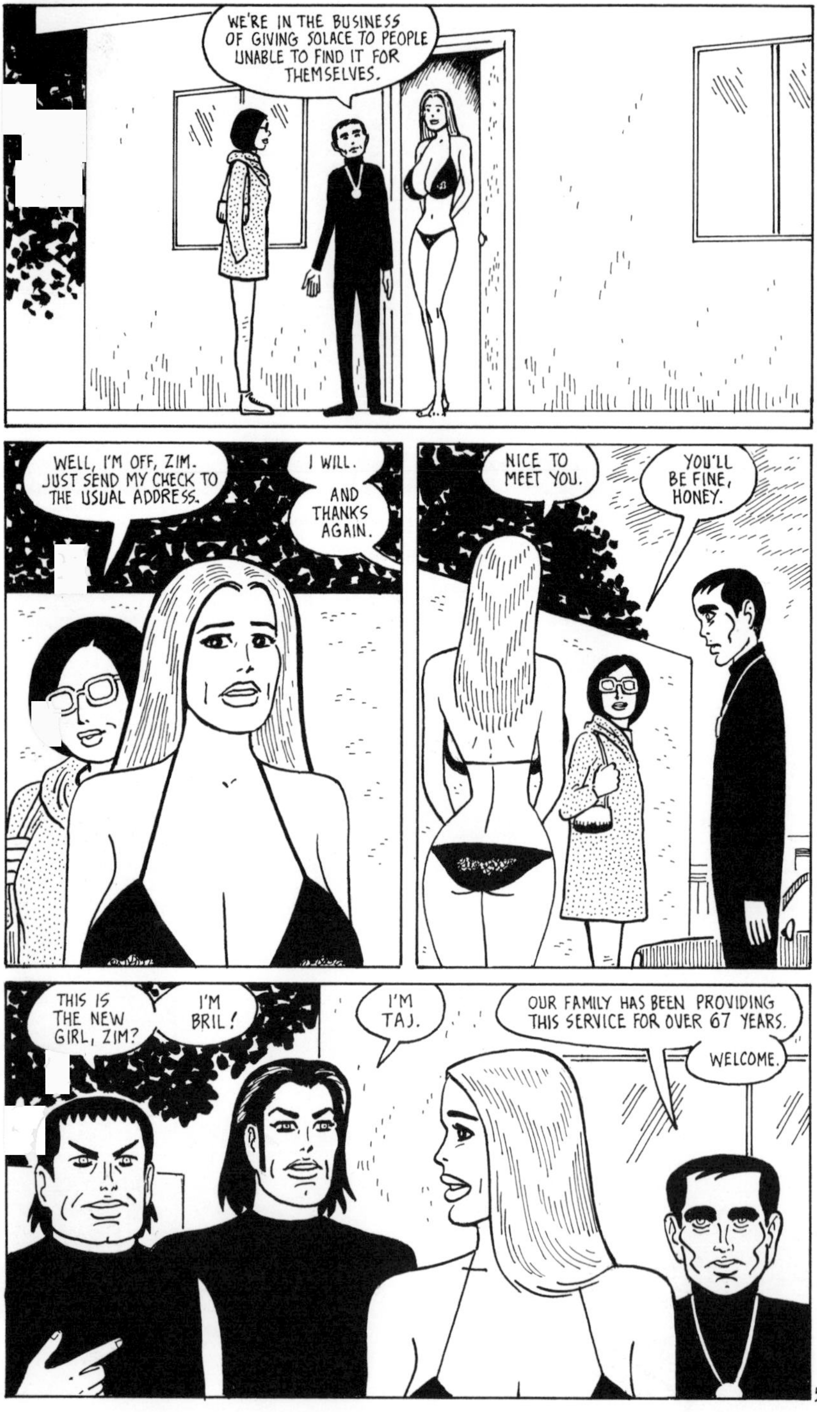
WE'RE IN THE BUSINESS OF GIVING SOLACE TO PEOPLE UNABLE TO FIND IT FOR THEMSELVES.
WELL, I'M OFF, ZIM. JUST SEND MY CHECK TO THE USUAL ADDRESS.
I WILL.
AND THANKS AGAIN.
NICE TO MEET YOU.
YOU'LL BE FINE, HONEY.
THIS IS THE NEW GIRL, ZIM?
I'M BRIL!
I'M TAJ.
OUR FAMILY HAS BEEN PROVIDING THIS SERVICE FOR OVER 67 YEARS.
WELCOME.

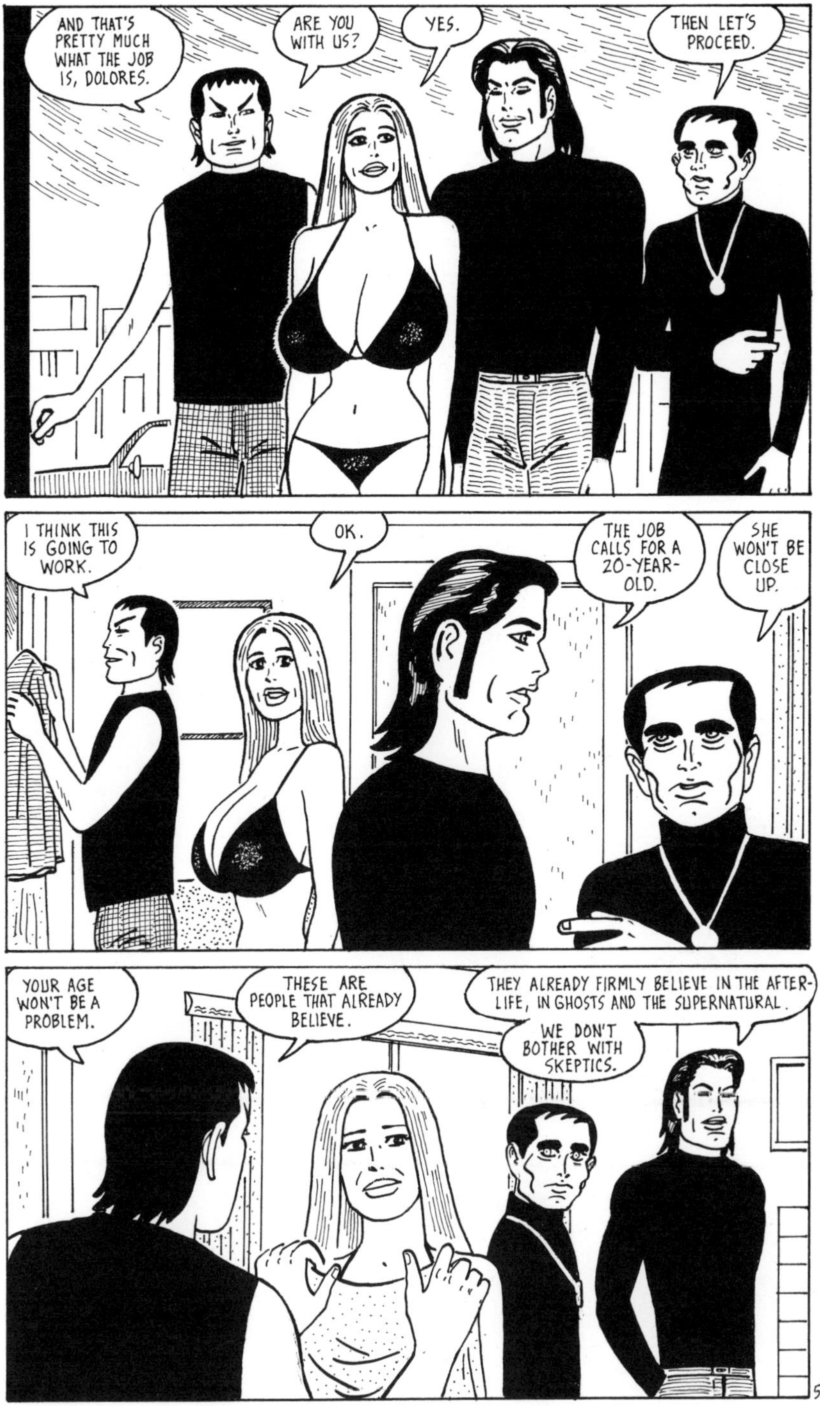
AND THAT'S PRETTY MUCH WHAT THE JOB IS, DOLORES.
ARE YOU WITH US?
YES.
THEN LET'S PROCEED.
I THINK THIS IS GOING TO WORK.
OK.
THE JOB CALLS FOR A 20-YEAR-OLD.
SHE WON'T BE CLOSE UP.
YOUR AGE WON'T BE A PROBLEM.
THESE ARE PEOPLE THAT ALREADY BELIEVE.
THEY ALREADY FIRMLY BELIEVE IN THE AFTER-LIFE, IN GHOSTS AND THE SUPERNATURAL.
WE DON'T BOTHER WITH SKEPTICS.

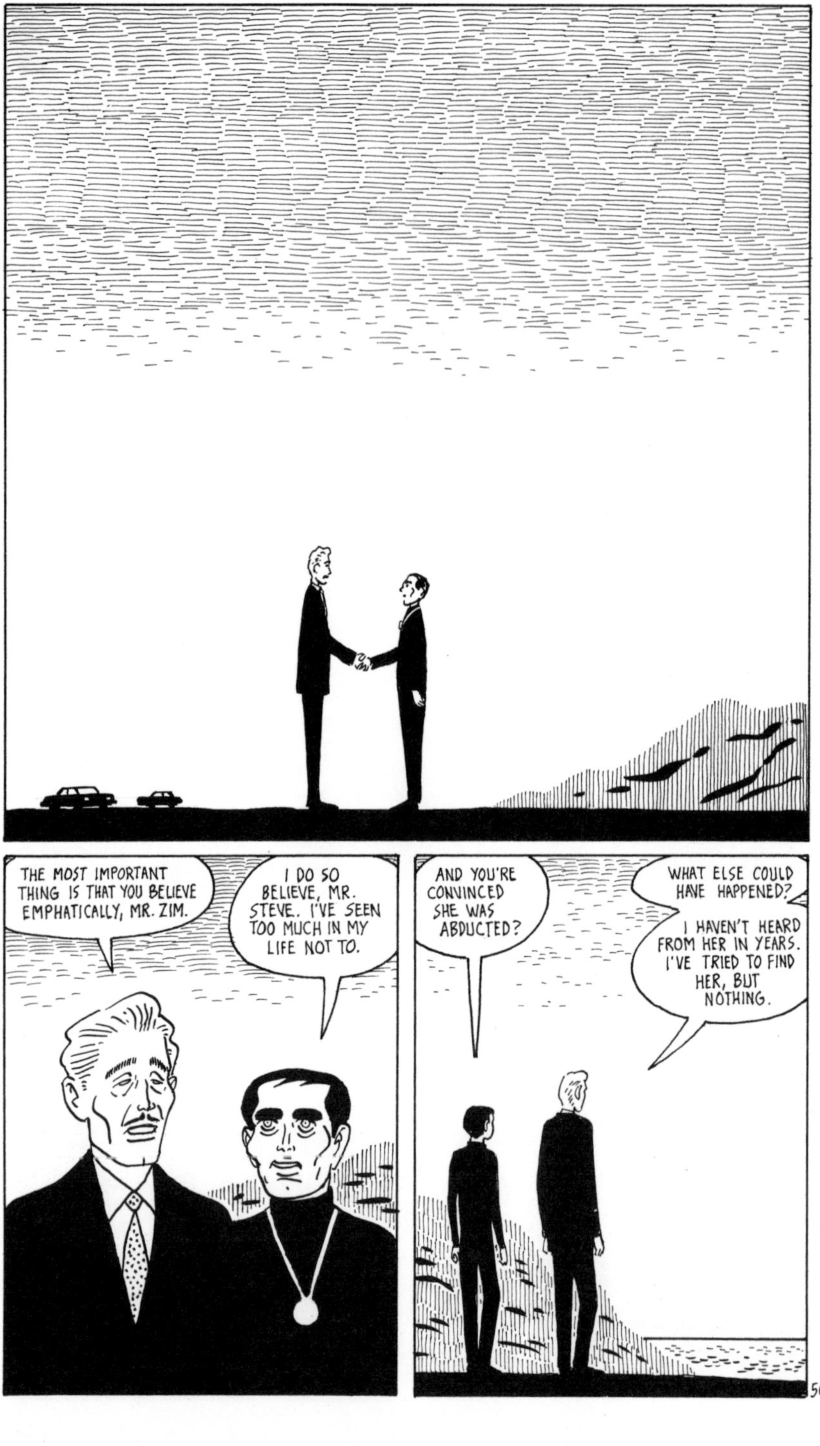
THE MOST IMPORTANT THING IS THAT YOU BELIEVE EMPHATICALLY, MR. ZIM.
I DO SO BELIEVE, MR. STEVE. I'VE SEEN TOO MUCH IN MY LIFE NOT TO.
AND YOU'RE CONVINCED SHE WAS ABDUCTED?
WHAT ELSE COULD HAVE HAPPENED?
I HAVEN'T HEARD FROM HER IN YEARS. I'VE TRIED TO FIND HER, BUT NOTHING.

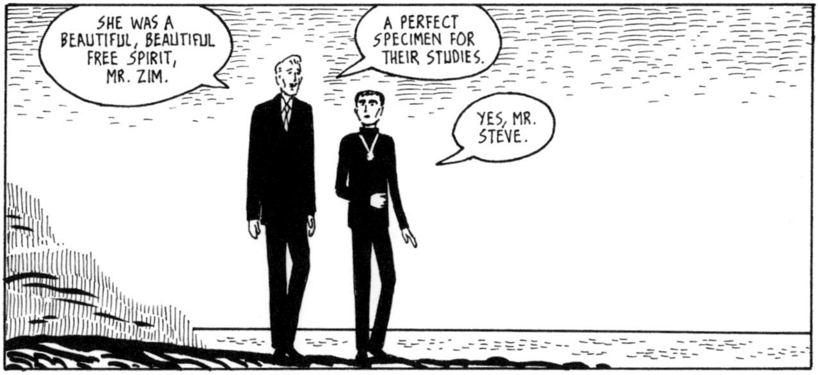
SHE WAS A BEAUTIFUL, BEAUTIFUL FREE SPIRIT, MR. ZIM.
A PERFECT SPECIMEN FOR THEIR STUDIES.
YES, MR. STEVE.

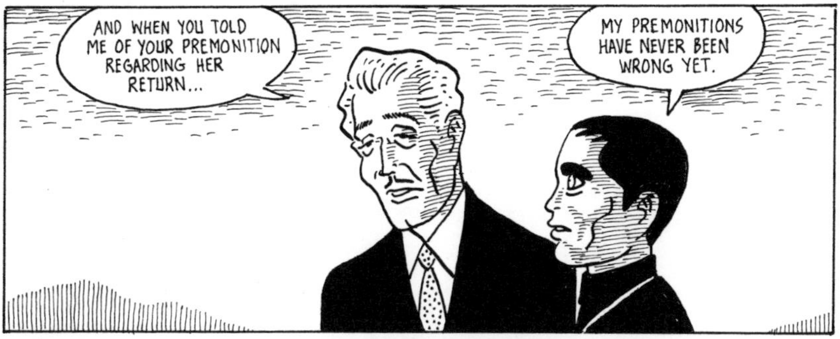
AND WHEN YOU TOLD ME OF YOUR PREMONITION REGARDING HER RETURN...
MY PREMONITIONS HAVE NEVER BEEN WRONG YET.

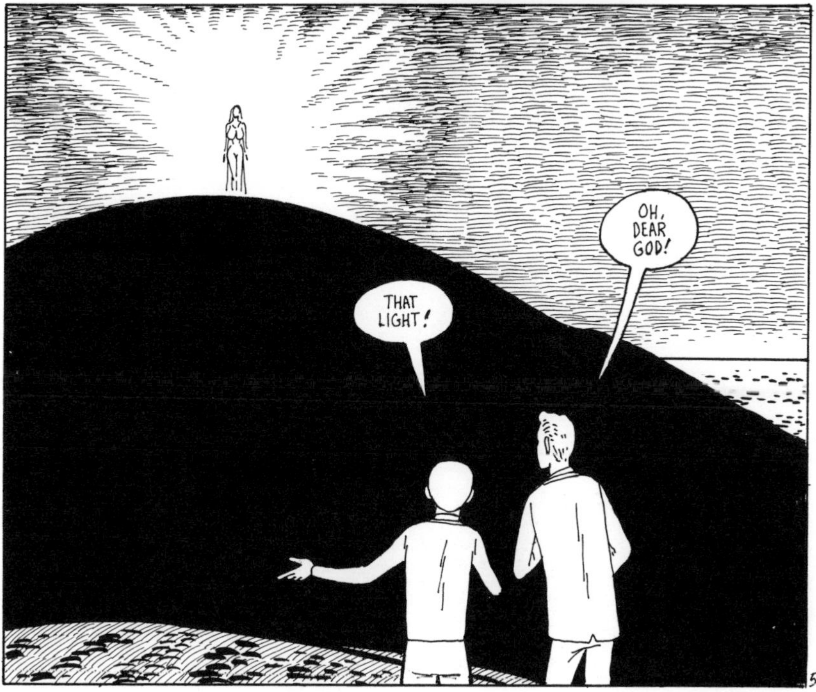
OH, DEAR GOD!
THAT LIGHT!

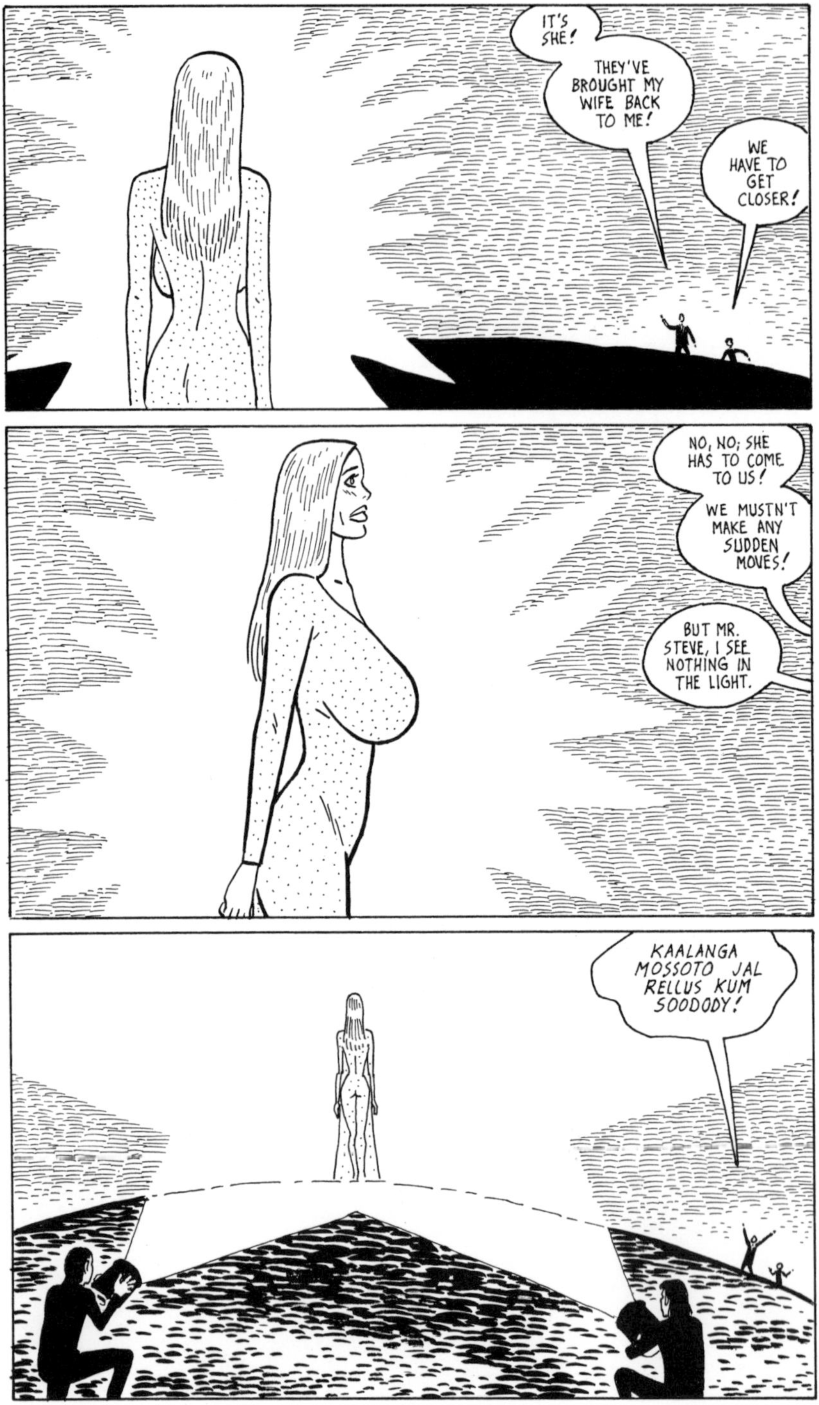
IT'S SHE!
THEY'VE BROUGHT MY WIFE BACK TO ME!
WE HAVE TO GET CLOSER!
NO, NO; SHE HAS TO COME TO US!
WE MUSTN'T MAKE ANY SUDDEN MOVES!
BUT MR. STEVE, I SEE NOTHING IN THE LIGHT.
KAALANGA MOSSOTO JAL RELLUS KUM SOODODY!

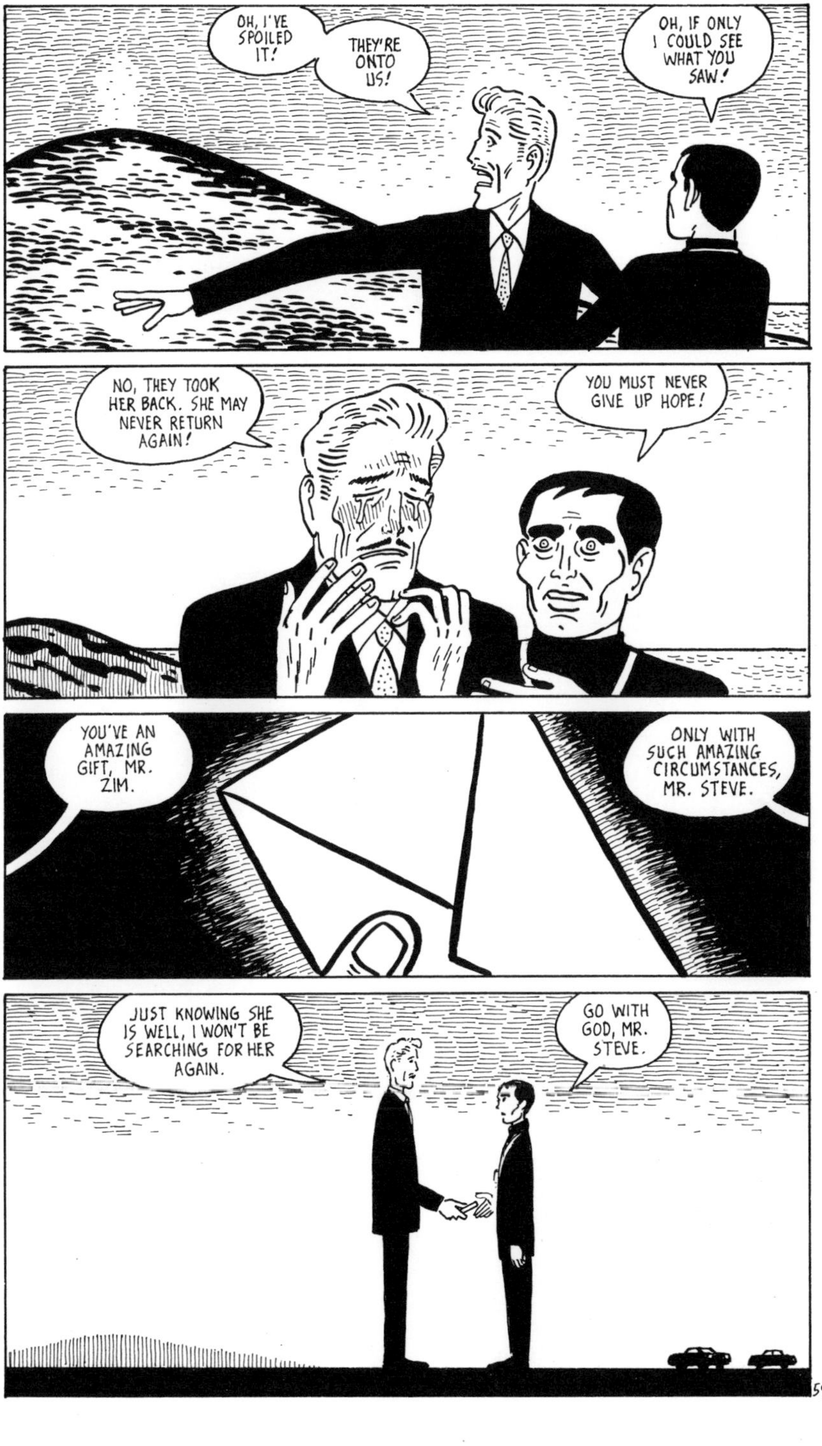
OH, I'VE SPOILED IT!
THEY'RE ONTO US!
OH, IF ONLY I COULD SEE WHAT YOU SAW!
NO, THEY TOOK HER BACK. SHE MAY NEVER RETURN AGAIN!
YOU MUST NEVER GIVE UP HOPE!
YOU'VE AN AMAZING GIFT, MR. ZIM.
ONLY WITH SUCH AMAZING CIRCUMSTANCES, MR. STEVE.
JUST KNOWING SHE IS WELL, I WON'T BE SEARCHING FOR HER AGAIN.
GO WITH GOD, MR. STEVE.

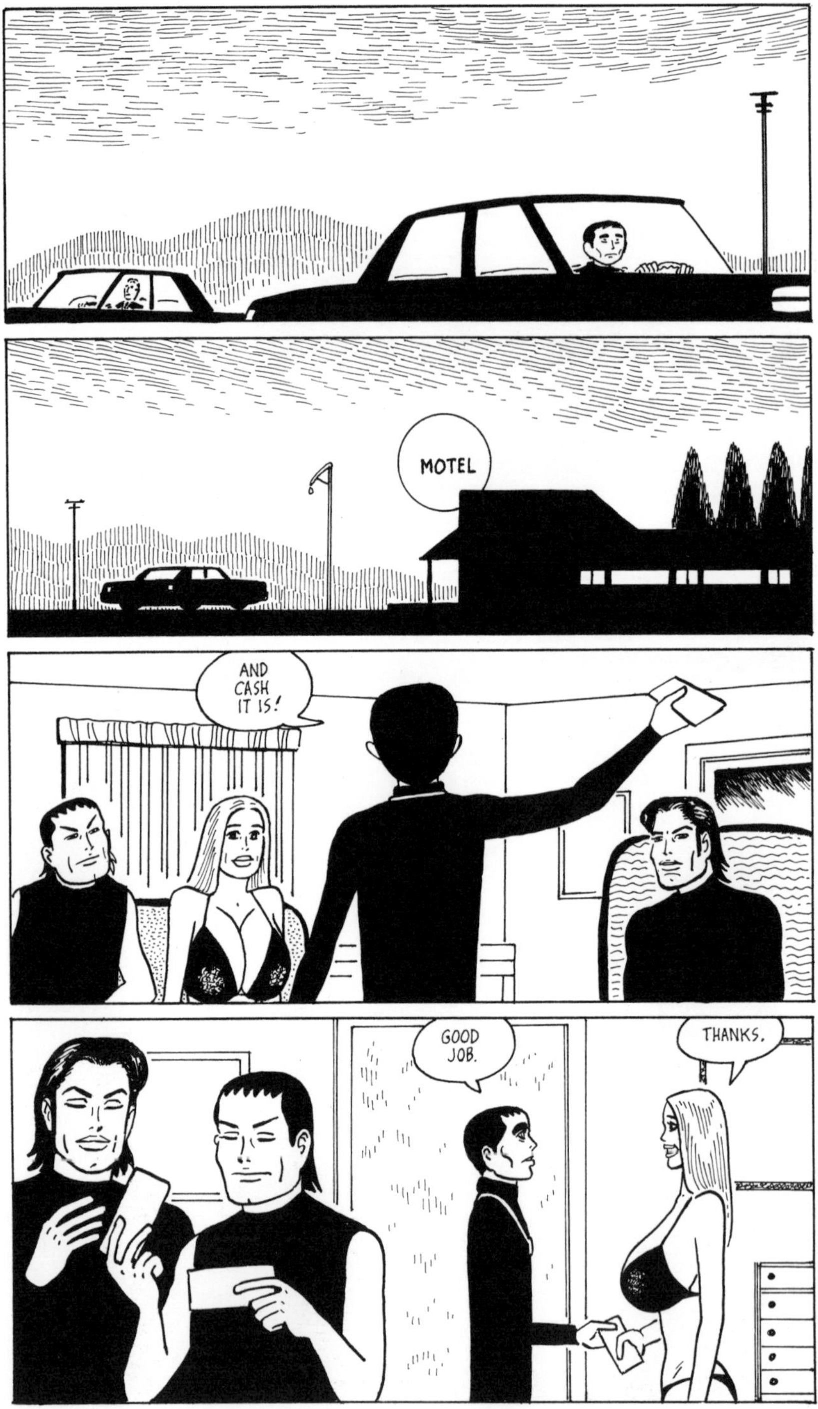
MOTEL
AND CASH IT IS!
GOOD JOB.
THANKS.

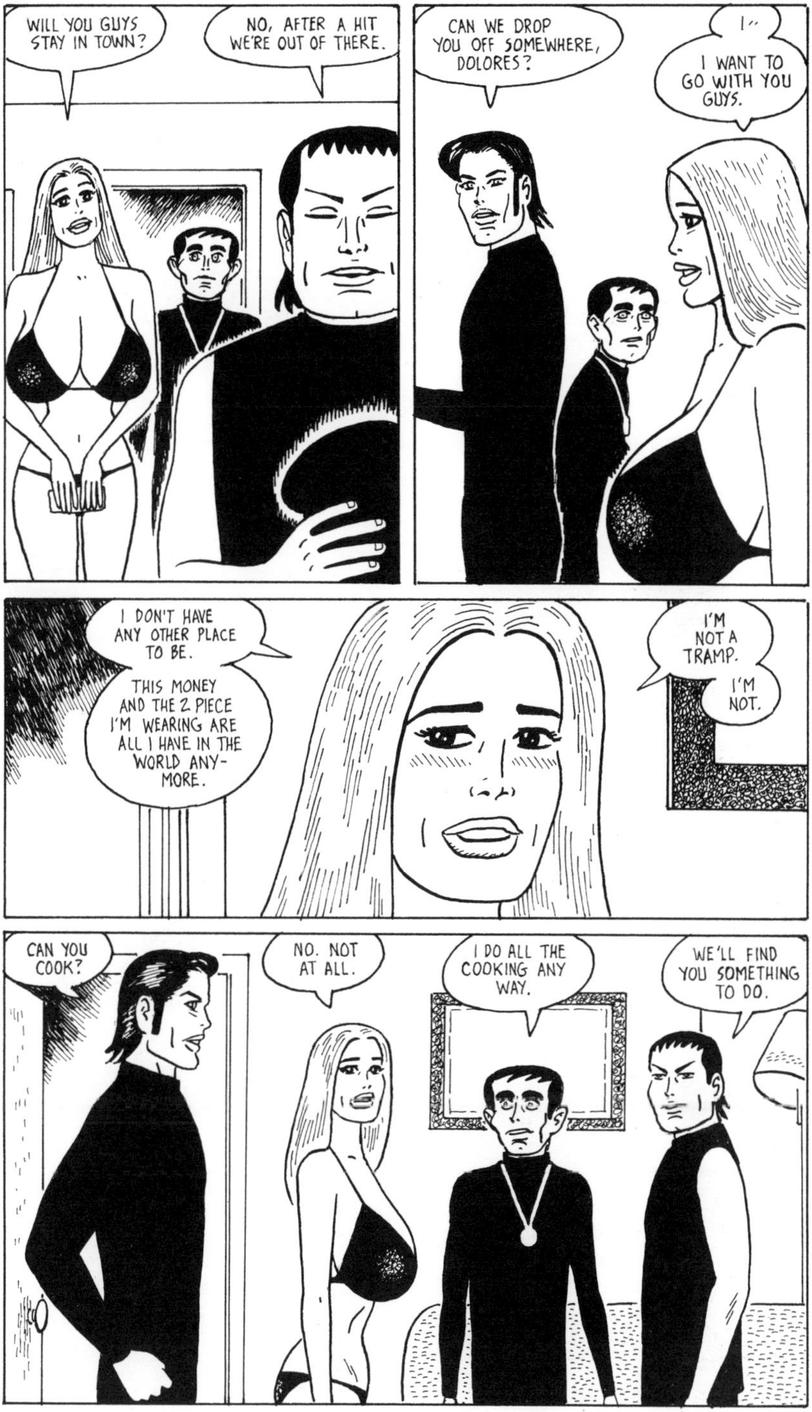
WILL YOU GUYS STAY IN TOWN?
NO, AFTER A HIT WE'RE OUT OF THERE.
CAN WE DROP YOU OFF SOMEWHERE, DOLORES?
I--
I WANT TO GO WITH YOU GUYS.
I DON'T HAVE ANY OTHER PLACE TO BE.
THIS MONEY AND THE 2 PIECE I'M WEARING ARE ALL I HAVE IN THE WORLD ANY-MORE.
I'M NOT A TRAMP.
I'M NOT.
CAN YOU COOK?
NO. NOT AT ALL.
I DO ALL THE COOKING ANY WAY.
WE'LL FIND YOU SOMETHING TO DO.

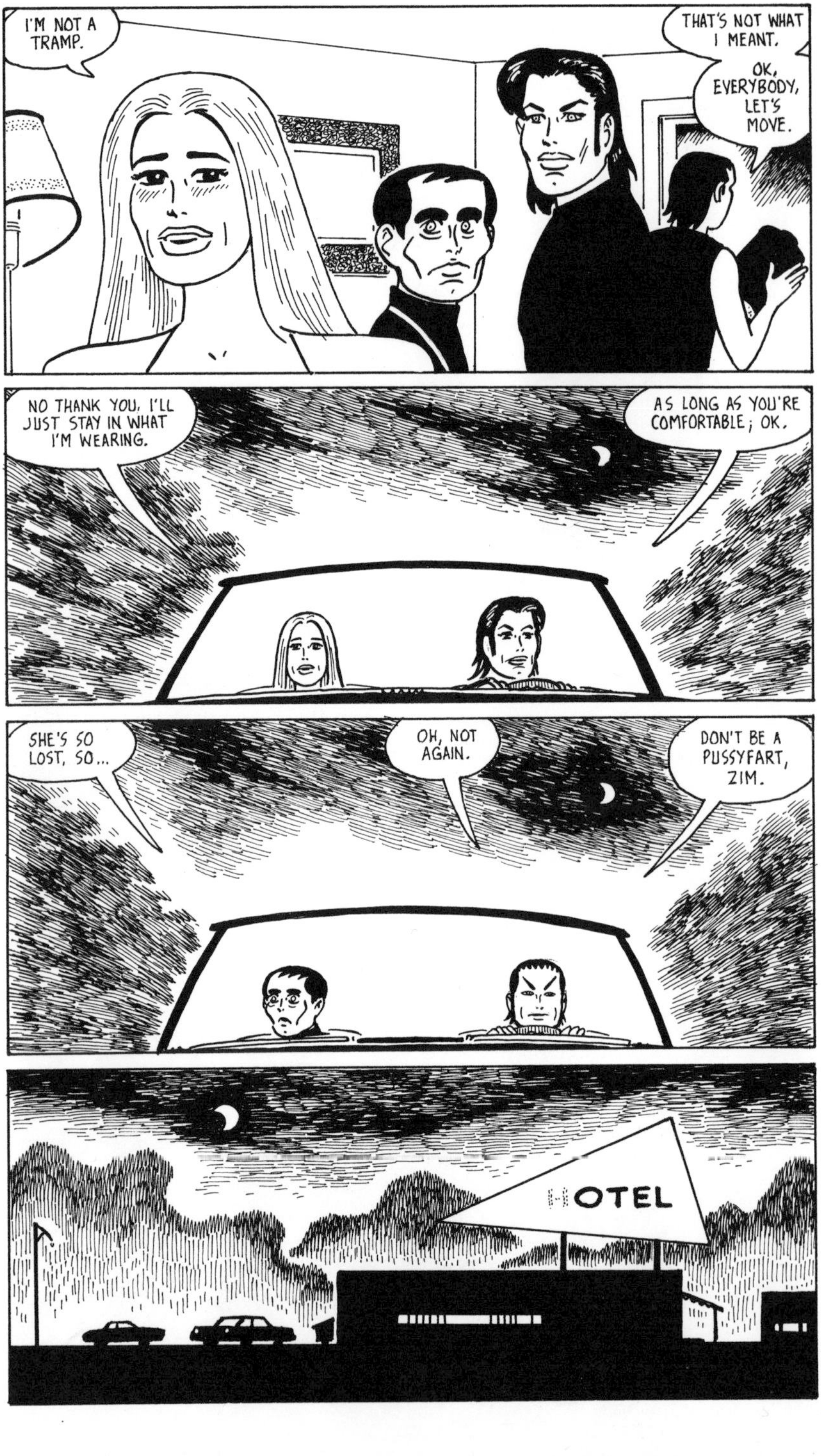
I'M NOT A TRAMP.
THAT'S NOT WHAT I MEANT.
OK, EVERYBODY, LET'S MOVE.
NO THANK YOU, I'LL JUST STAY IN WHAT I'M WEARING.
AS LONG AS YOU'RE COMFORTABLE; OK.
SHE'S SO LOST, SO...
OH, NOT AGAIN.
DON'T BE A PUSSYFART, ZIM.
HOTEL

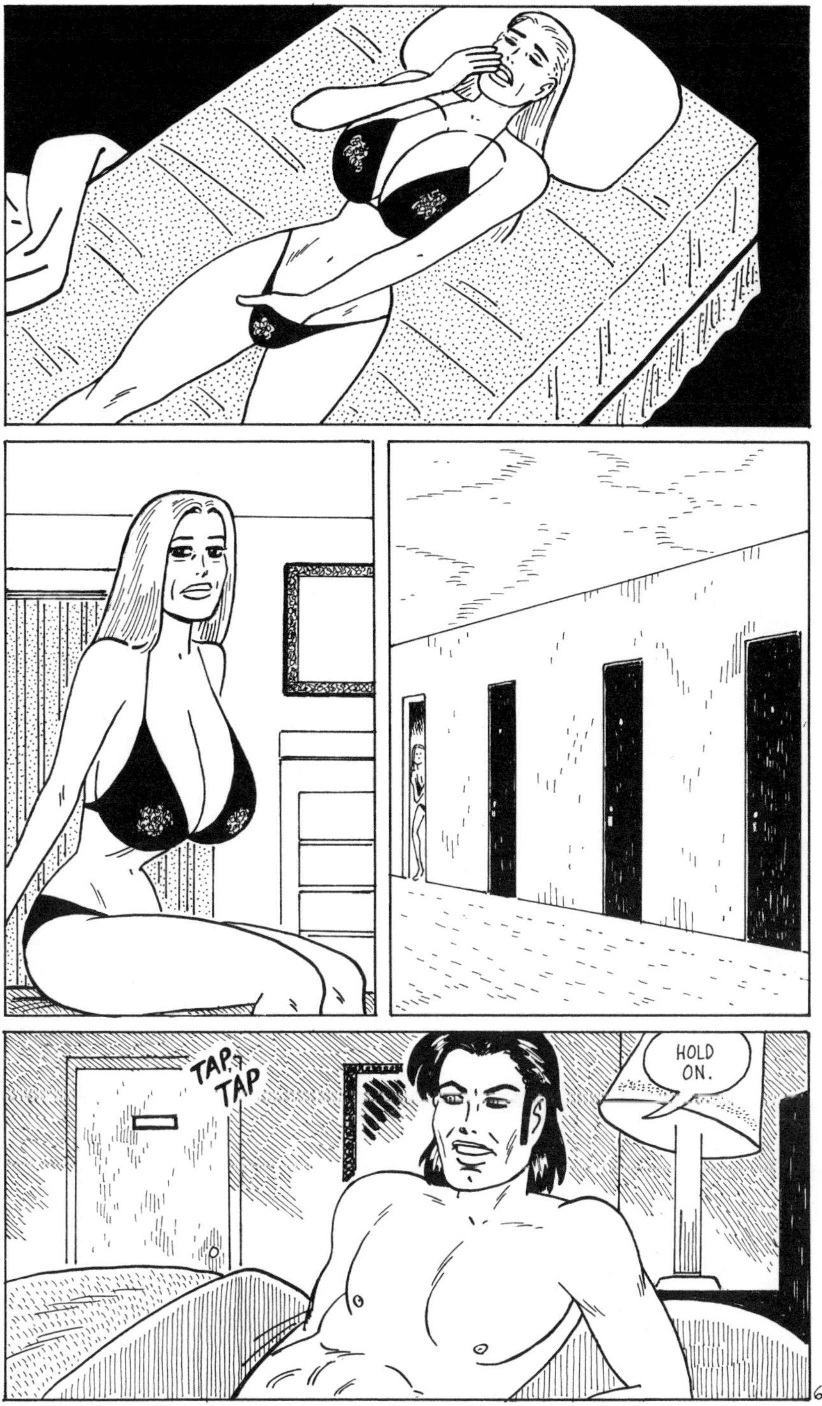
TAP, TAP
HOLD ON.

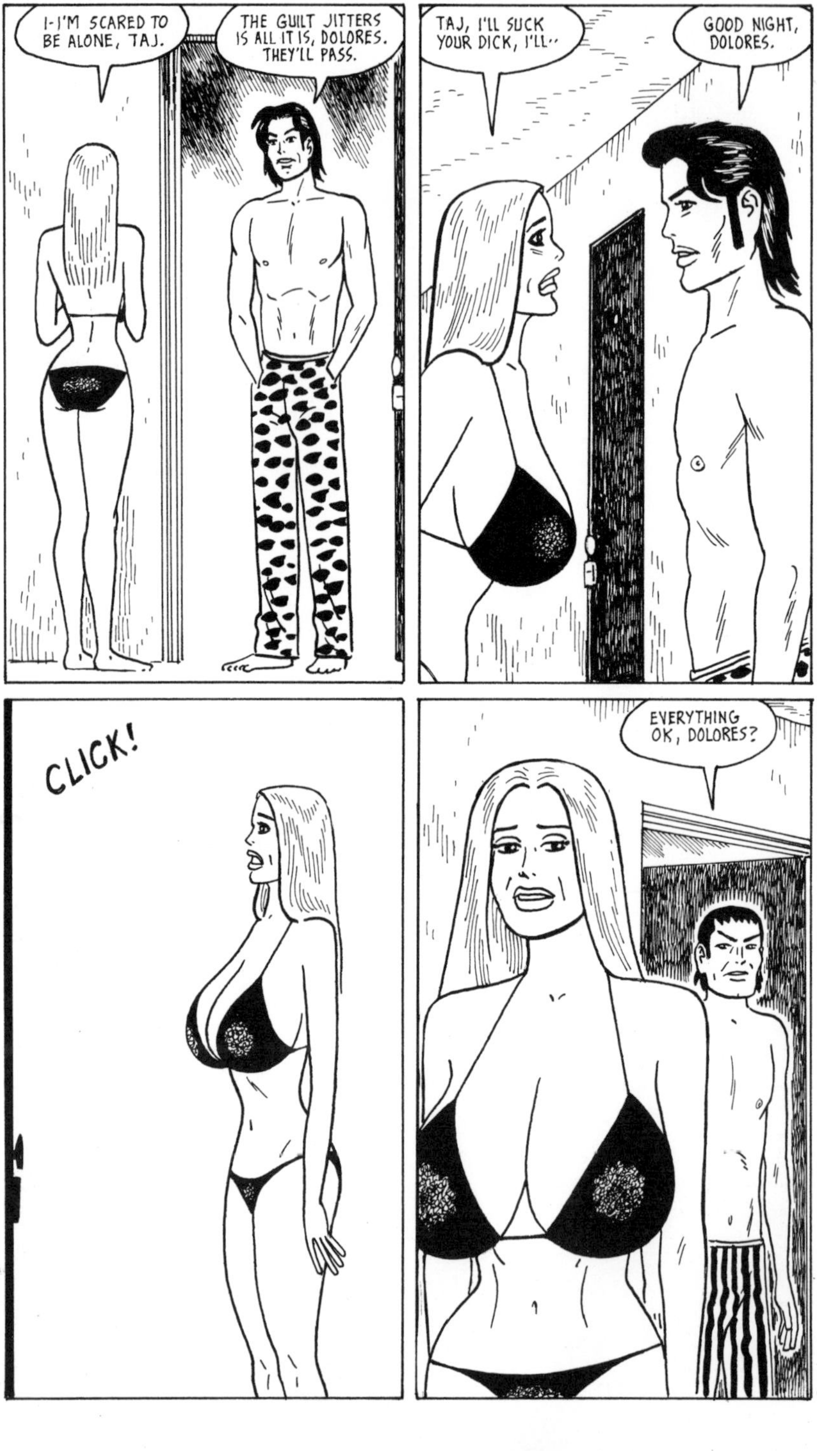
I-I'M SCARED TO BE ALONE, TAJ.
THE GUILT JITTERS IS ALL IT IS, DOLORES. THEY'LL PASS.
TAJ, I'LL SUCK YOUR DICK, I'LL..
GOOD NIGHT, DOLORES.
CLICK!
EVERYTHING OK, DOLORES?

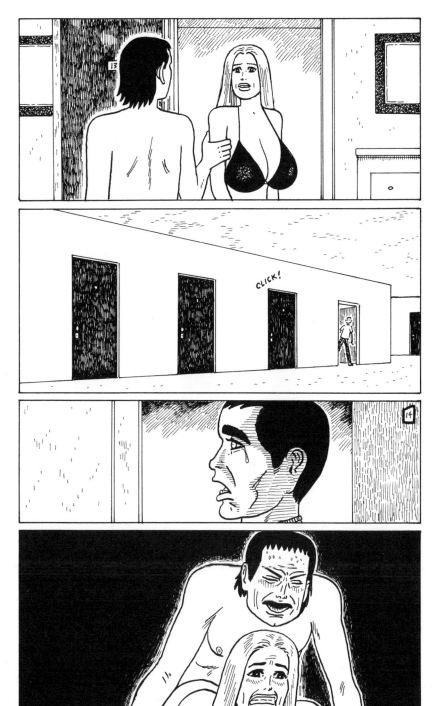

CLICK!

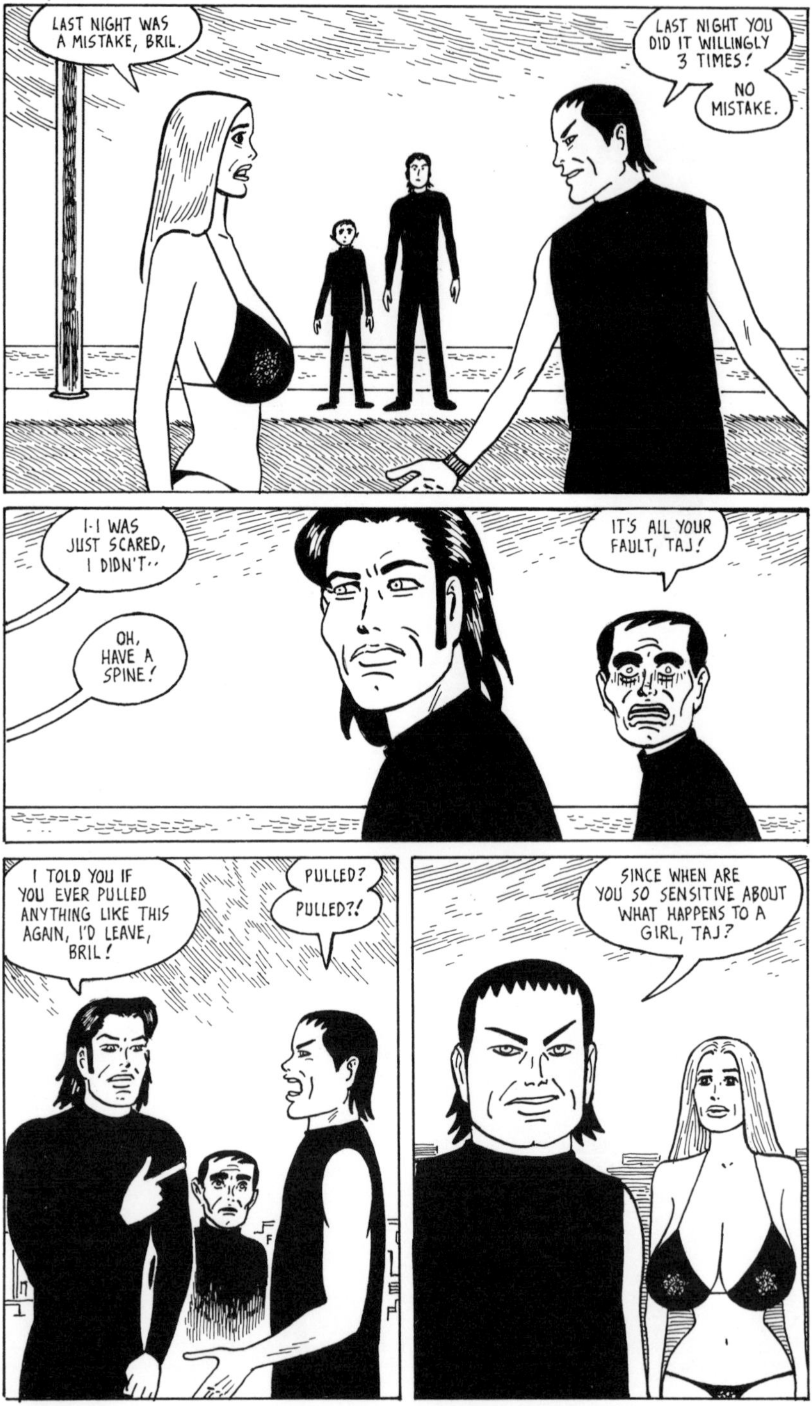
LAST NIGHT WAS A MISTAKE, BRIL.
LAST NIGHT YOU DID IT WILLINGLY 3 TIMES!
NO MISTAKE.
I-I WAS JUST SCARED, I DIDN'T..
OH, HAVE A SPINE!
IT'S ALL YOUR FAULT, TAJ!
I TOLD YOU IF YOU EVER PULLED ANYTHING LIKE THIS AGAIN, I'D LEAVE, BRIL!
PULLED?
PULLED?!
SINCE WHEN ARE YOU SO SENSITIVE ABOUT WHAT HAPPENS TO A GIRL, TAJ?

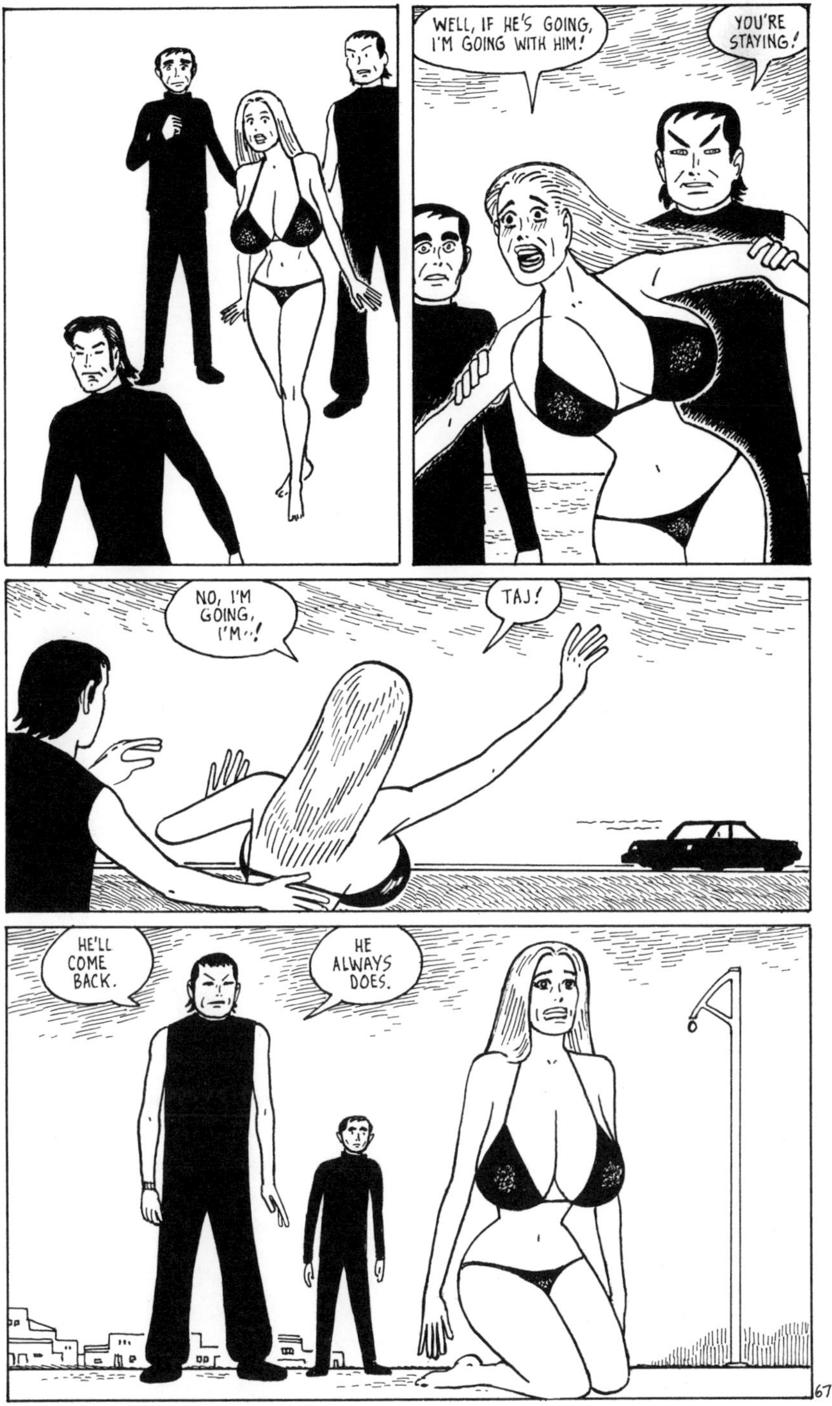
WELL, IF HE'S GOING, I'M GOING WITH HIM!
YOU'RE STAYING!
NO, I'M GOING, I'M--!
TAJ!
HE'LL COME BACK.
HE ALWAYS DOES.

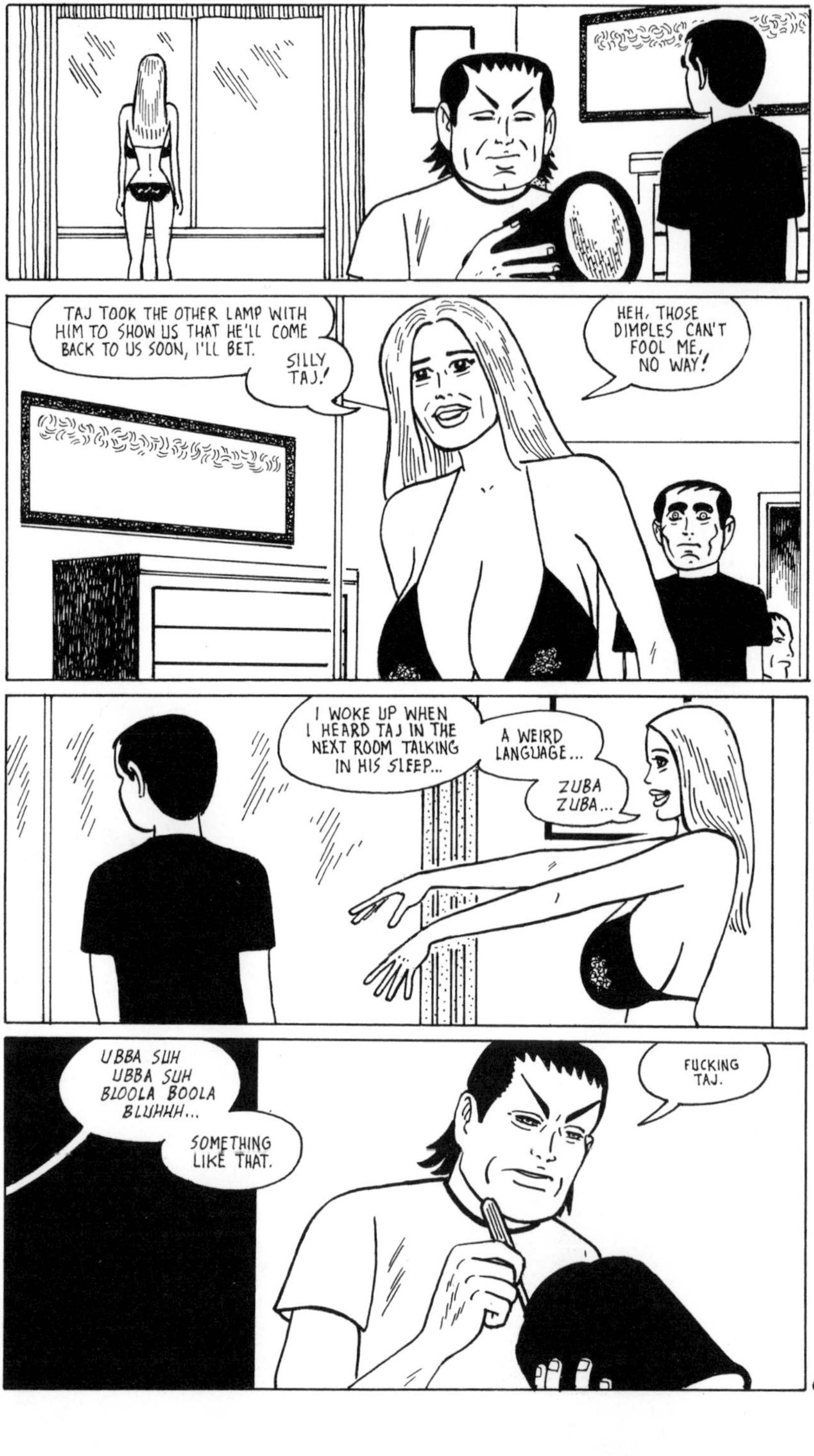
TAJ TOOK THE OTHER LAMP WITH HIM TO SHOW US THAT HE'LL COME BACK TO US SOON, I'LL BET.
SILLY TAJ!
HEH, THOSE DIMPLES CAN'T FOOL ME, NO WAY!
I WOKE UP WHEN I HEARD TAJ IN THE NEXT ROOM TALKING IN HIS SLEEP...
A WEIRD LANGUAGE...
ZUBA ZUBA...
UBBA SUH UBBA SUH BLOOLA BOOLA BLUHHH...
SOMETHING LIKE THAT.
FUCKING TAJ.

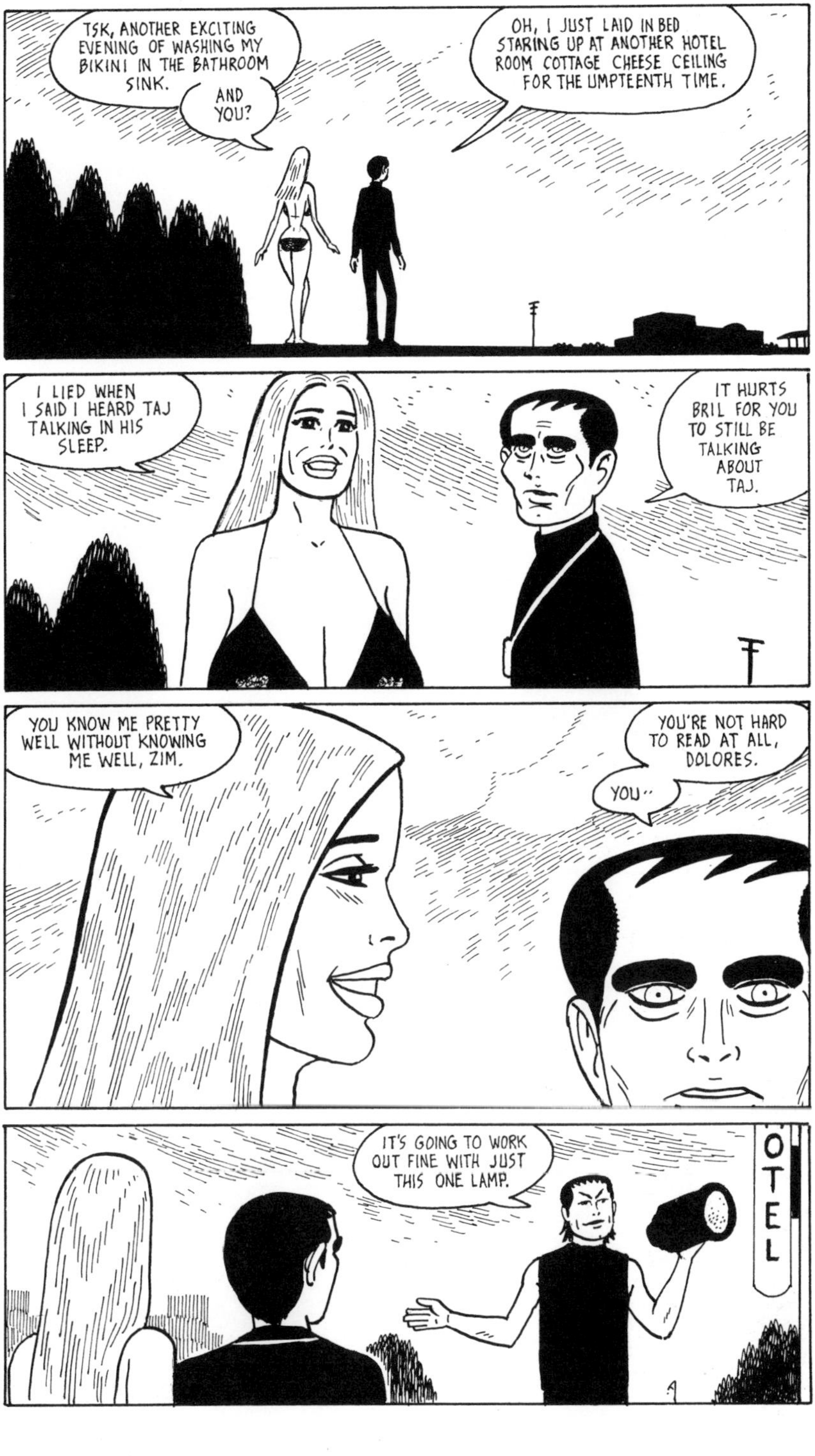
TSK, ANOTHER EXCITING EVENING OF WASHING MY BIKINI IN THE BATHROOM SINK.
AND YOU?
OH, I JUST LAID IN BED STARING UP AT ANOTHER HOTEL ROOM COTTAGE CHEESE CEILING FOR THE UMPTEENTH TIME.
I LIED WHEN I SAID I HEARD TAJ TALKING IN HIS SLEEP.
IT HURTS BRIL FOR YOU TO STILL BE TALKING ABOUT TAJ.
YOU KNOW ME PRETTY WELL WITHOUT KNOWING ME WELL, ZIM.
YOU'RE NOT HARD TO READ AT ALL, DOLORES.
YOU..
IT'S GOING TO WORK OUT FINE WITH JUST THIS ONE LAMP.
OTEL

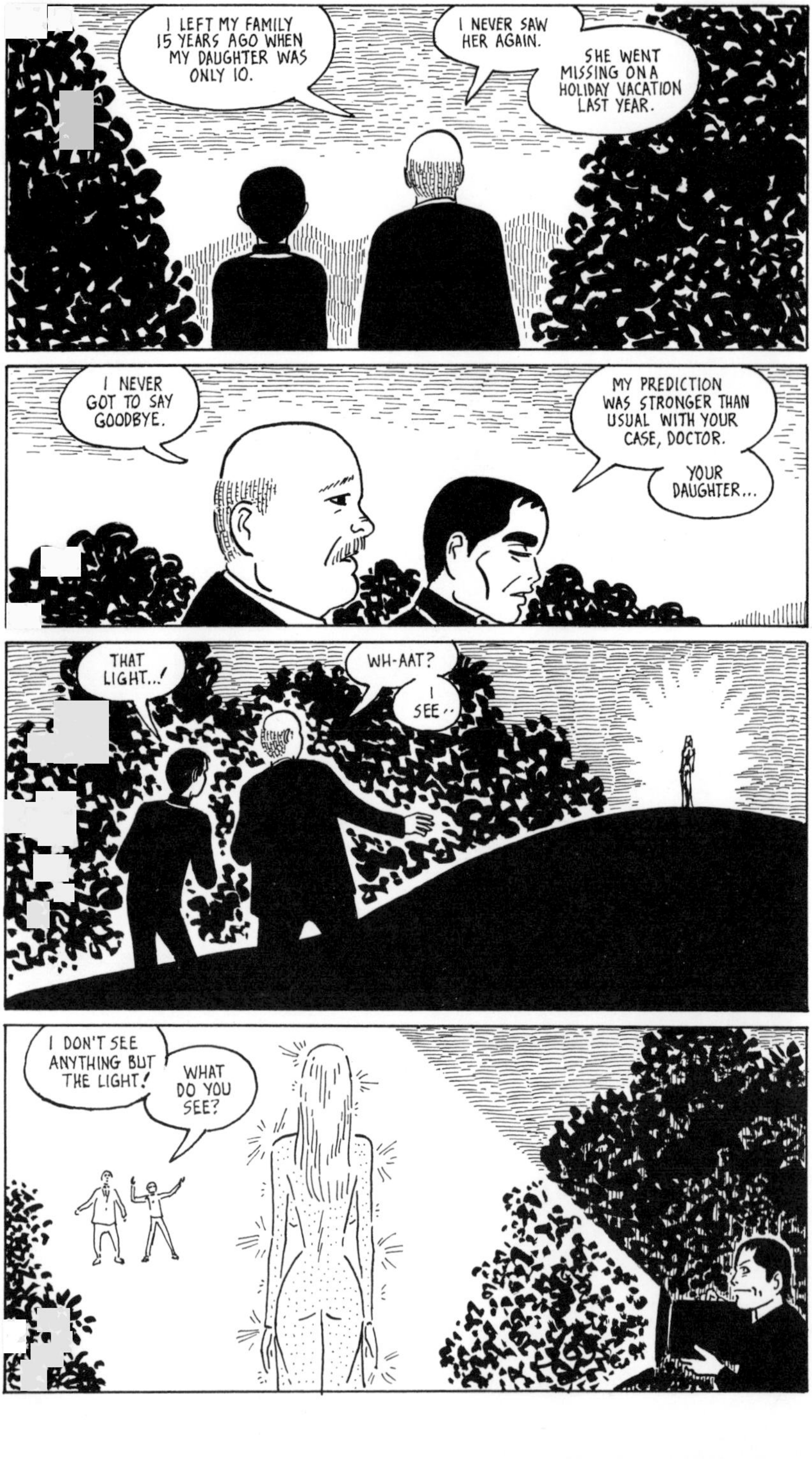
I LEFT MY FAMILY 15 YEARS AGO WHEN MY DAUGHTER WAS ONLY 10.
I NEVER SAW HER AGAIN.
SHE WENT MISSING ON A HOLIDAY VACATION LAST YEAR.
I NEVER GOT TO SAY GOODBYE.
MY PREDICTION WAS STRONGER THAN USUAL WITH YOUR CASE, DOCTOR.
YOUR DAUGHTER...
THAT LIGHT...!
WH-AAT?
I SEE..
I DON'T SEE ANYTHING BUT THE LIGHT!
WHAT DO YOU SEE?

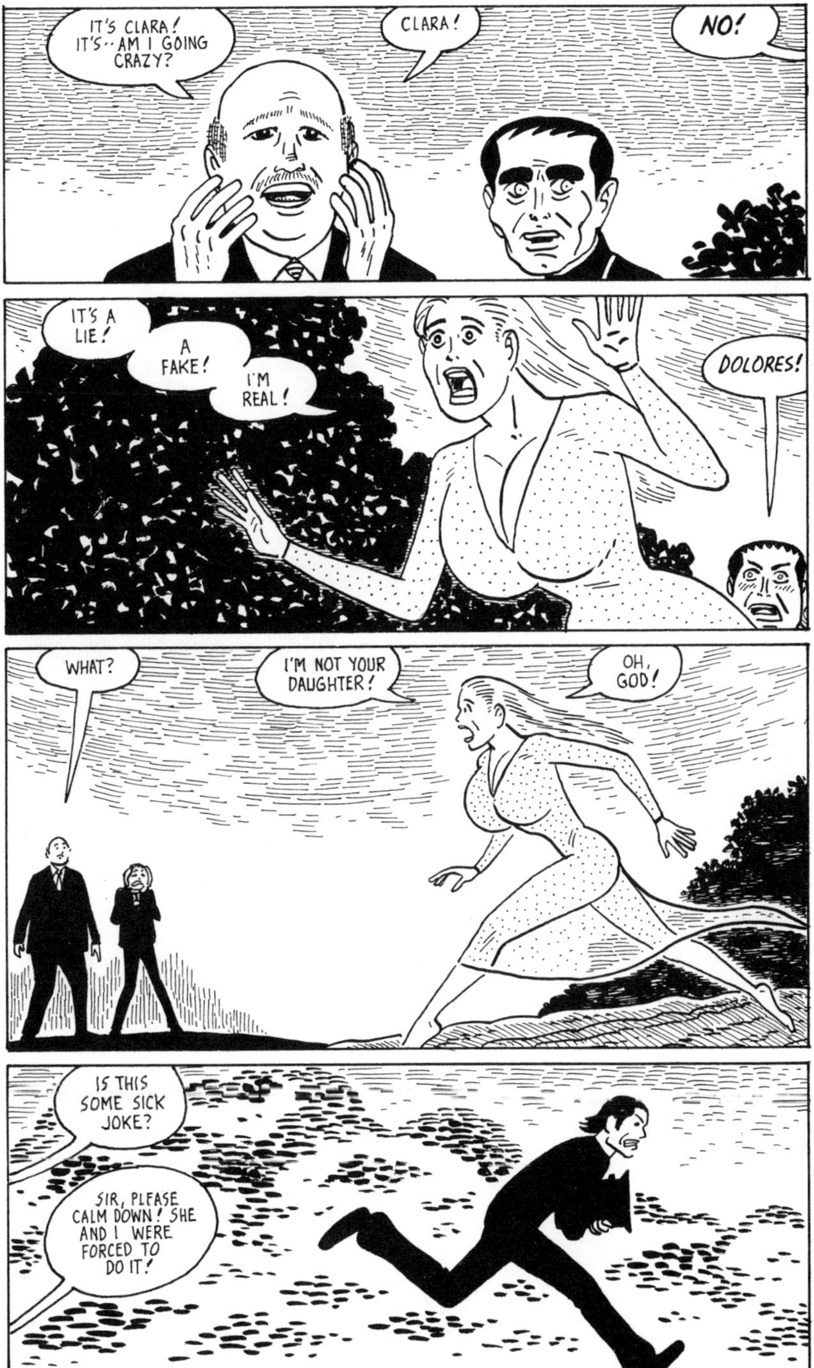
IT'S CLARA! IT'S.. AM I GOING CRAZY?
CLARA!
NO!
IT'S A LIE!
A FAKE!
I'M REAL!
DOLORES!
WHAT?
I'M NOT YOUR DAUGHTER!
OH, GOD!
IS THIS SOME SICK JOKE?
SIR, PLEASE CALM DOWN! SHE AND I WERE FORCED TO DO IT!

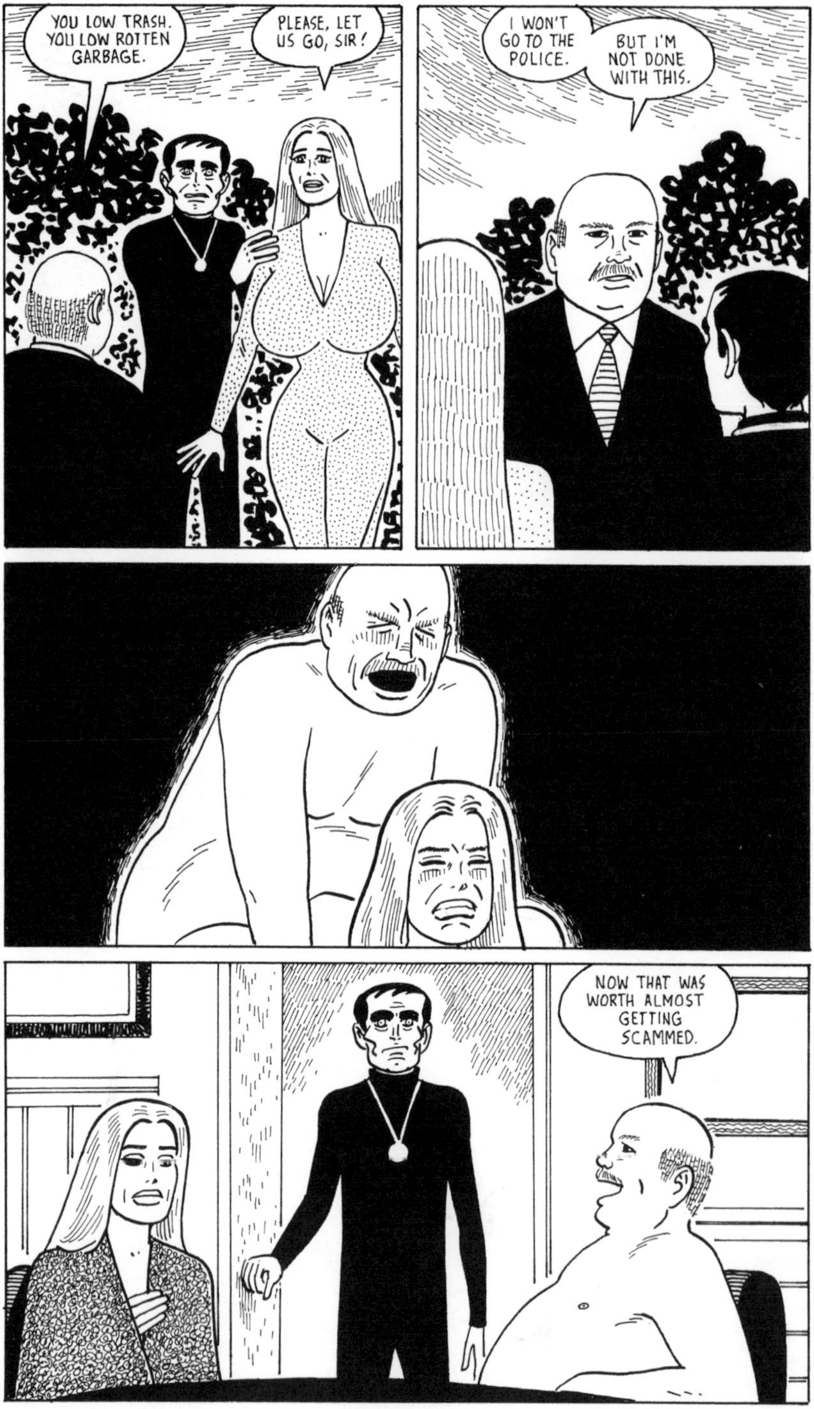
YOU LOW TRASH. YOU LOW ROTTEN GARBAGE.
PLEASE, LET US GO, SIR!
I WON'T GO TO THE POLICE.
BUT I'M NOT DONE WITH THIS.
NOW THAT WAS WORTH ALMOST GETTING SCAMMED.

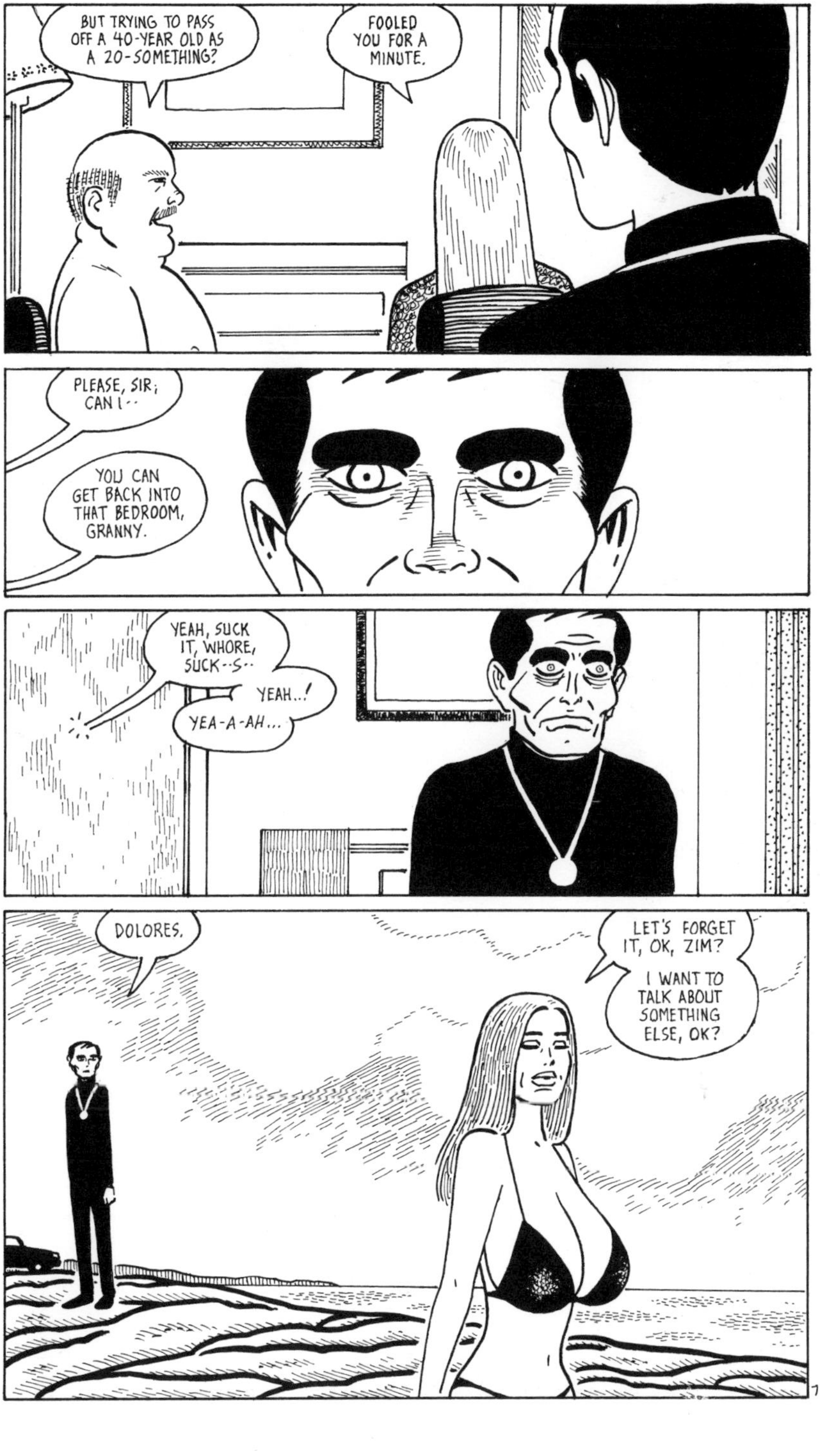
BUT TRYING TO PASS OFF A 40-YEAR OLD AS A 20-SOMETHING?
FOOLED YOU FOR A MINUTE.
PLEASE, SIR; CAN I··
YOU CAN GET BACK INTO THAT BEDROOM, GRANNY.
YEAH, SUCK IT, WHORE, SUCK··S··
YEAH..!
YEA-A-AH...
DOLORES.
LET'S FORGET IT, OK, ZIM?
I WANT TO TALK ABOUT SOMETHING ELSE, OK?

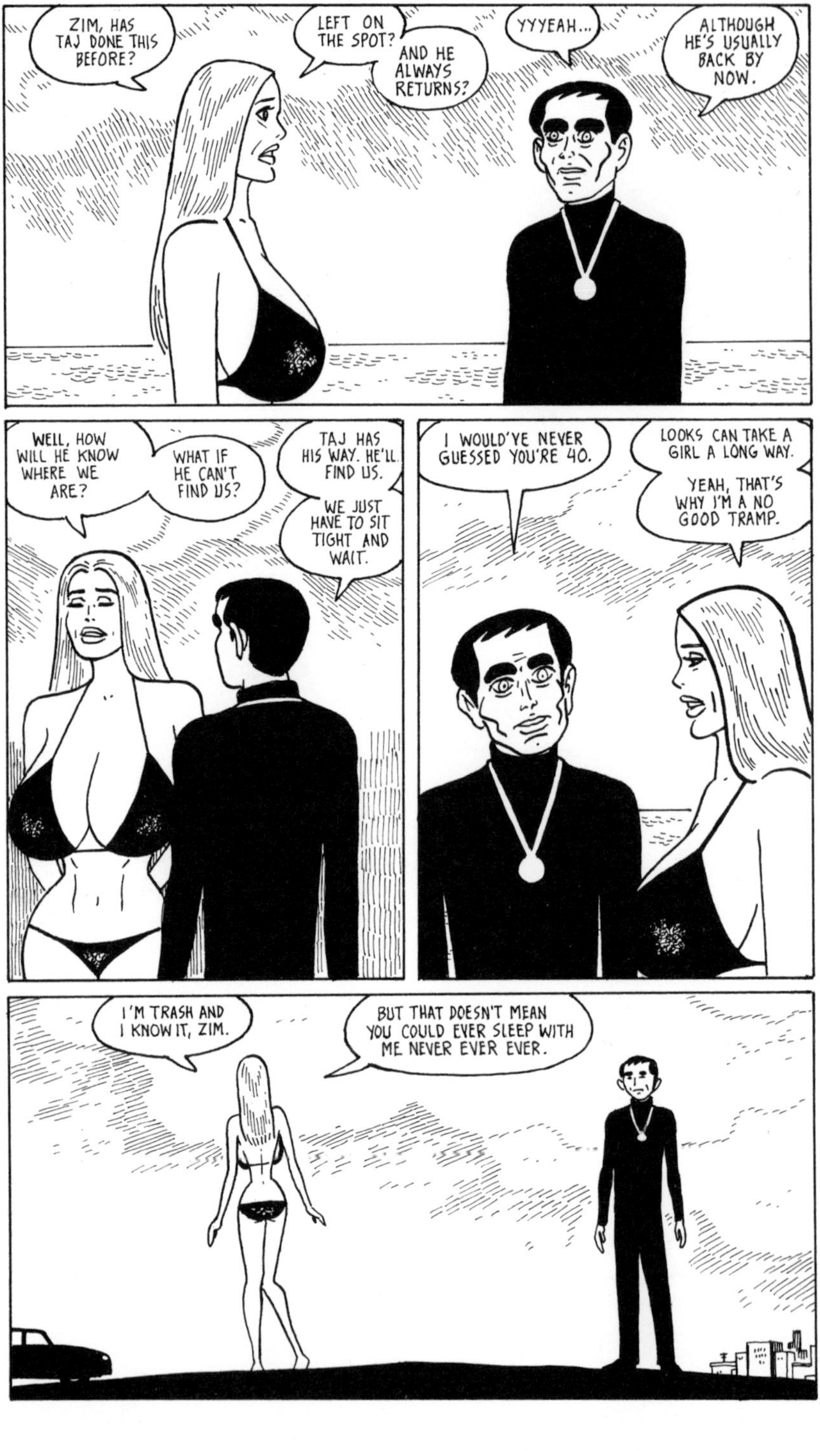
ZIM, HAS TAJ DONE THIS BEFORE?
LEFT ON THE SPOT?
AND HE ALWAYS RETURNS?
YYYEAH...
ALTHOUGH HE'S USUALLY BACK BY NOW.
WELL, HOW WILL HE KNOW WHERE WE ARE?
WHAT IF HE CAN'T FIND US?
TAJ HAS HIS WAY. HE'LL FIND US.
WE JUST HAVE TO SIT TIGHT AND WAIT.
I WOULD'VE NEVER GUESSED YOU'RE 40.
LOOKS CAN TAKE A GIRL A LONG WAY.
YEAH, THAT'S WHY I'M A NO GOOD TRAMP.
I'M TRASH AND I KNOW IT, ZIM.
BUT THAT DOESN'T MEAN YOU COULD EVER SLEEP WITH ME NEVER EVER EVER.

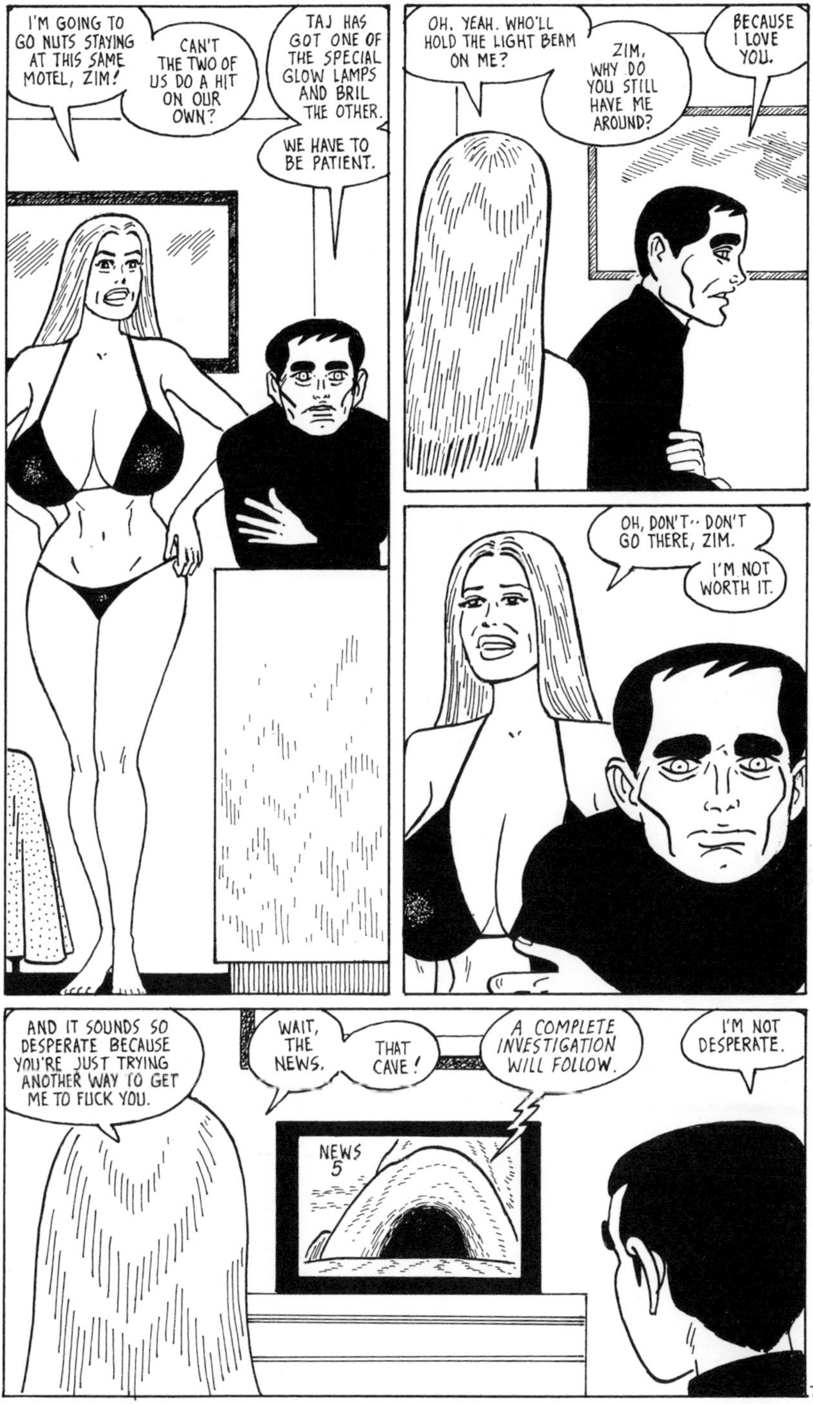
I'M GOING TO GO NUTS STAYING AT THIS SAME MOTEL, ZIM!
CAN'T THE TWO OF US DO A HIT ON OUR OWN?
TAJ HAS GOT ONE OF THE SPECIAL GLOW LAMPS AND BRIL THE OTHER.
WE HAVE TO BE PATIENT.
OH, YEAH. WHO'LL HOLD THE LIGHT BEAM ON ME?
ZIM, WHY DO YOU STILL HAVE ME AROUND?
BECAUSE I LOVE YOU.
OH, DON'T.. DON'T GO THERE, ZIM.
I'M NOT WORTH IT.
AND IT SOUNDS SO DESPERATE BECAUSE YOU'RE JUST TRYING ANOTHER WAY TO GET ME TO FUCK YOU.
WAIT, THE NEWS.
THAT CAVE!
A COMPLETE INVESTIGATION WILL FOLLOW.
NEWS 5
I'M NOT DESPERATE.

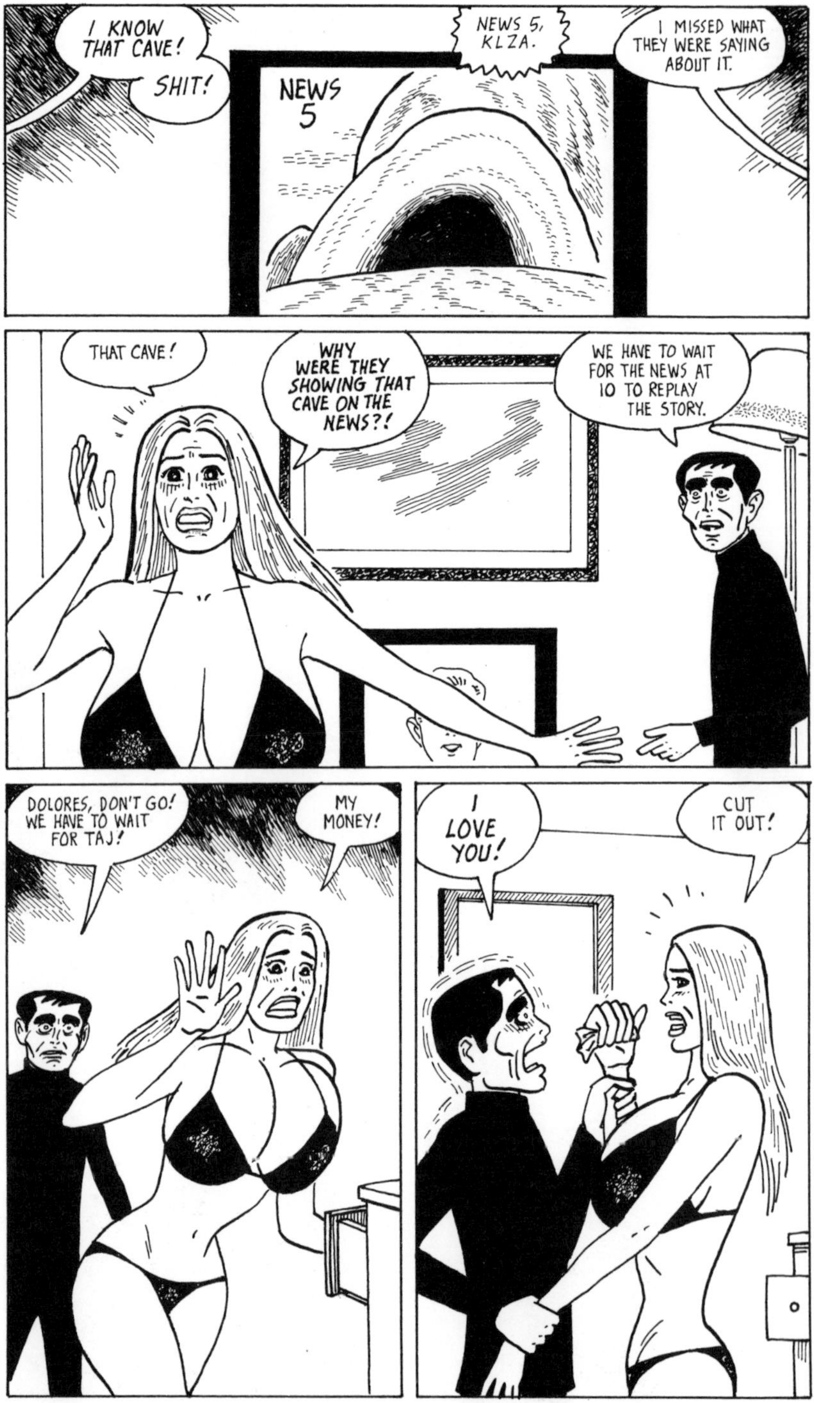
I KNOW THAT CAVE!
SHIT!
NEWS 5, KLZA.
NEWS 5
I MISSED WHAT THEY WERE SAYING ABOUT IT.
THAT CAVE!
WHY WERE THEY SHOWING THAT CAVE ON THE NEWS?!
WE HAVE TO WAIT FOR THE NEWS AT 10 TO REPLAY THE STORY.
DOLORES, DON'T GO! WE HAVE TO WAIT FOR TAJ!
MY MONEY!
I LOVE YOU!
CUT IT OUT!

FUCKING SHIT!
SLAM..
CALL ME, BRIL!
HEY, BRIL!
MORON.
HEY, YOU KIDS!
THERE BETTER HAVE NOT BEEN ANY HANKY PANKY BETWEEN YOU TWO.
SHE'S GONE, BRIL.

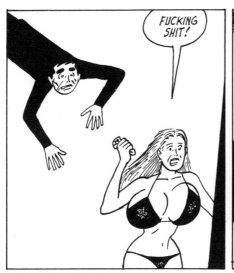

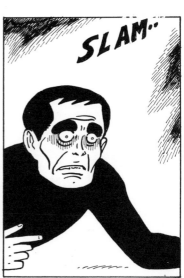

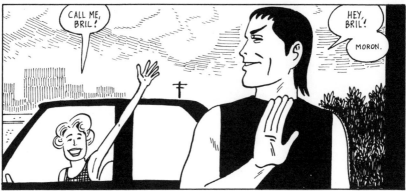

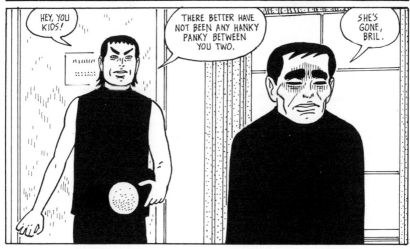

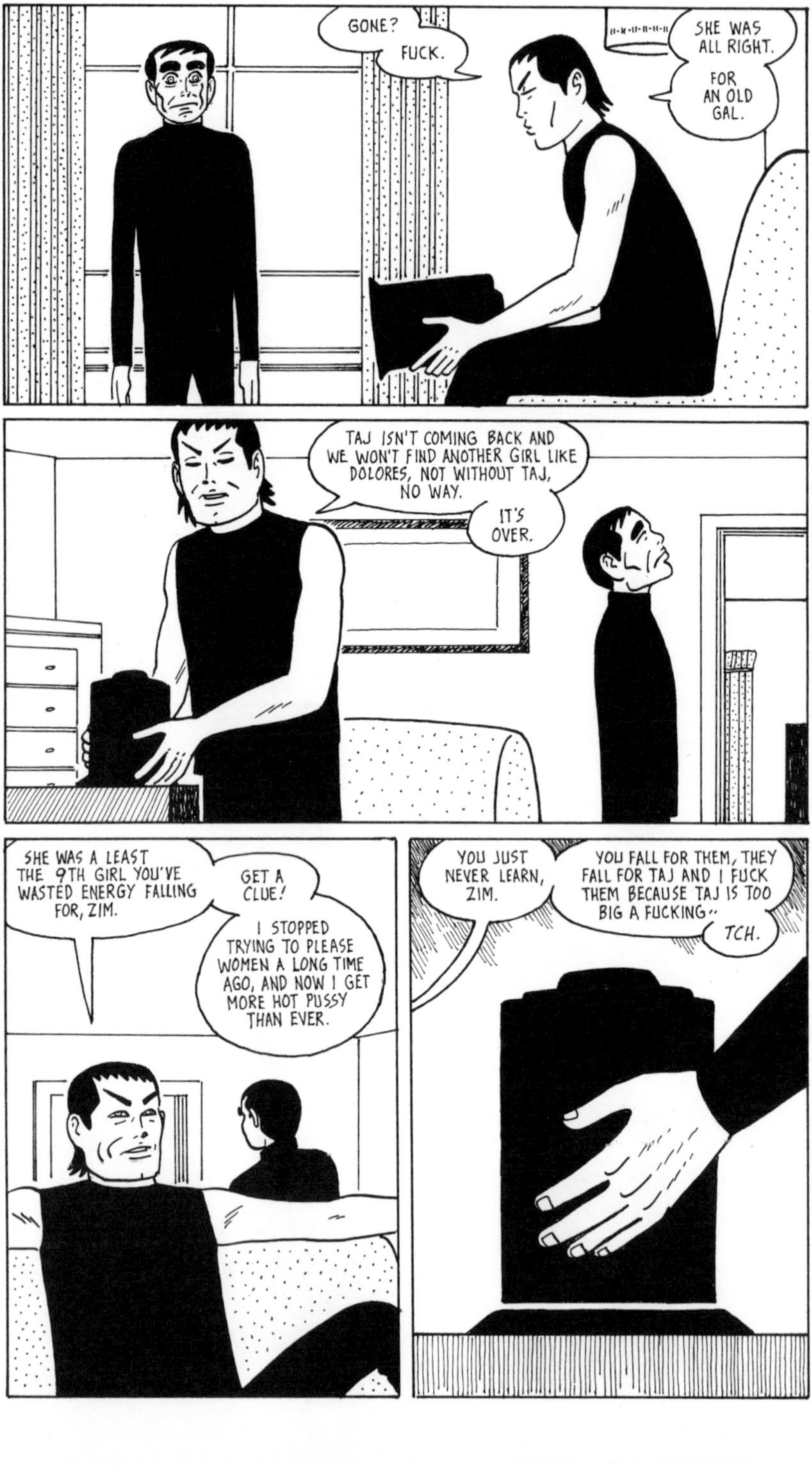
GONE?
FUCK.
SHE WAS ALL RIGHT.
FOR AN OLD GAL.
TAJ ISN'T COMING BACK AND WE WON'T FIND ANOTHER GIRL LIKE DOLORES, NOT WITHOUT TAJ, NO WAY.
IT'S OVER.
SHE WAS A LEAST THE 9TH GIRL YOU'VE WASTED ENERGY FALLING FOR, ZIM.
GET A CLUE!
I STOPPED TRYING TO PLEASE WOMEN A LONG TIME AGO, AND NOW I GET MORE HOT PUSSY THAN EVER.
YOU JUST NEVER LEARN, ZIM.
YOU FALL FOR THEM, THEY FALL FOR TAJ AND I FUCK THEM BECAUSE TAJ IS TOO BIG A FUCKING..
TCH.

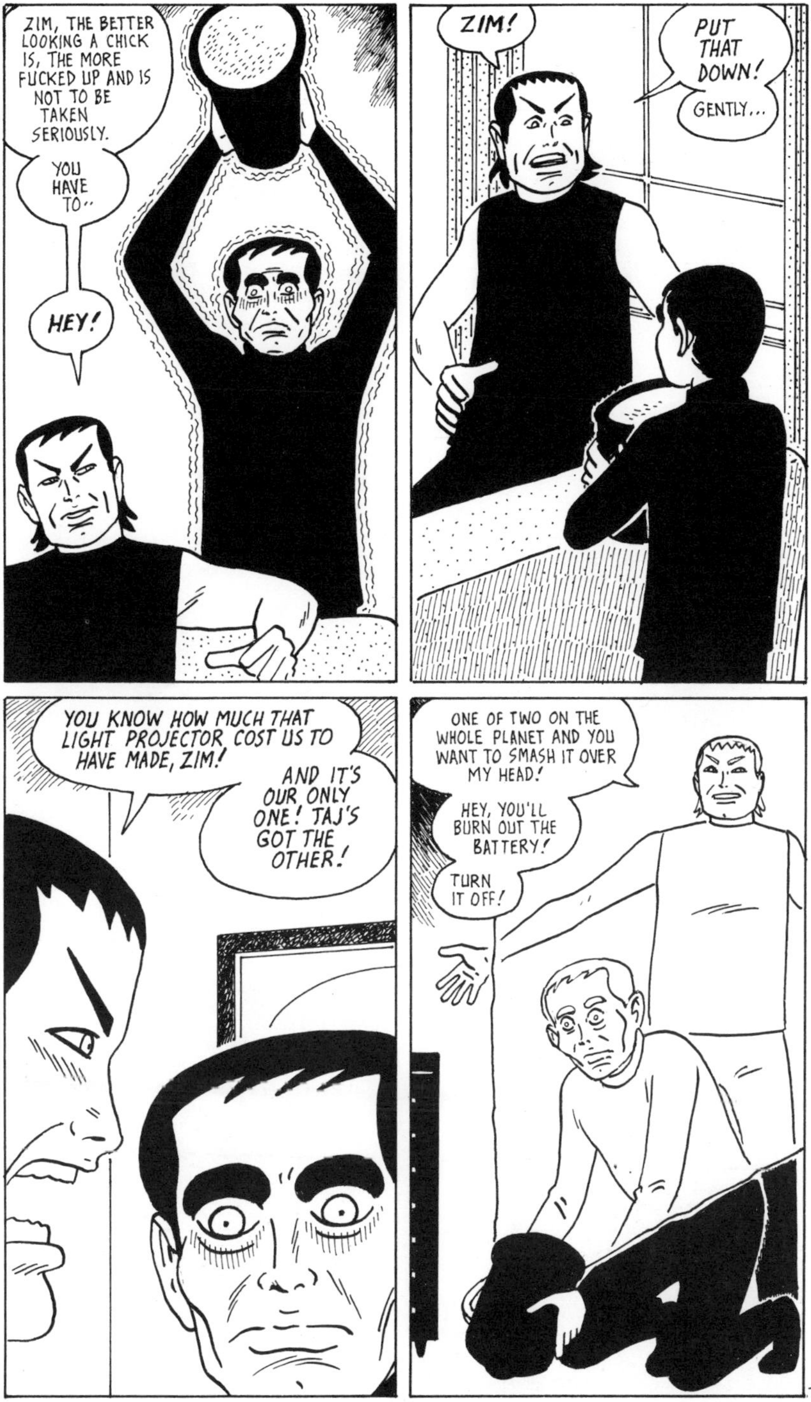
ZIM, THE BETTER LOOKING A CHICK IS, THE MORE FUCKED UP AND IS NOT TO BE TAKEN SERIOUSLY.
YOU HAVE TO..
HEY!
ZIM!
PUT THAT DOWN!
GENTLY...
YOU KNOW HOW MUCH THAT LIGHT PROJECTOR COST US TO HAVE MADE, ZIM!
AND IT'S OUR ONLY ONE! TAJ'S GOT THE OTHER!
ONE OF TWO ON THE WHOLE PLANET AND YOU WANT TO SMASH IT OVER MY HEAD!
HEY, YOU'LL BURN OUT THE BATTERY!
TURN IT OFF!

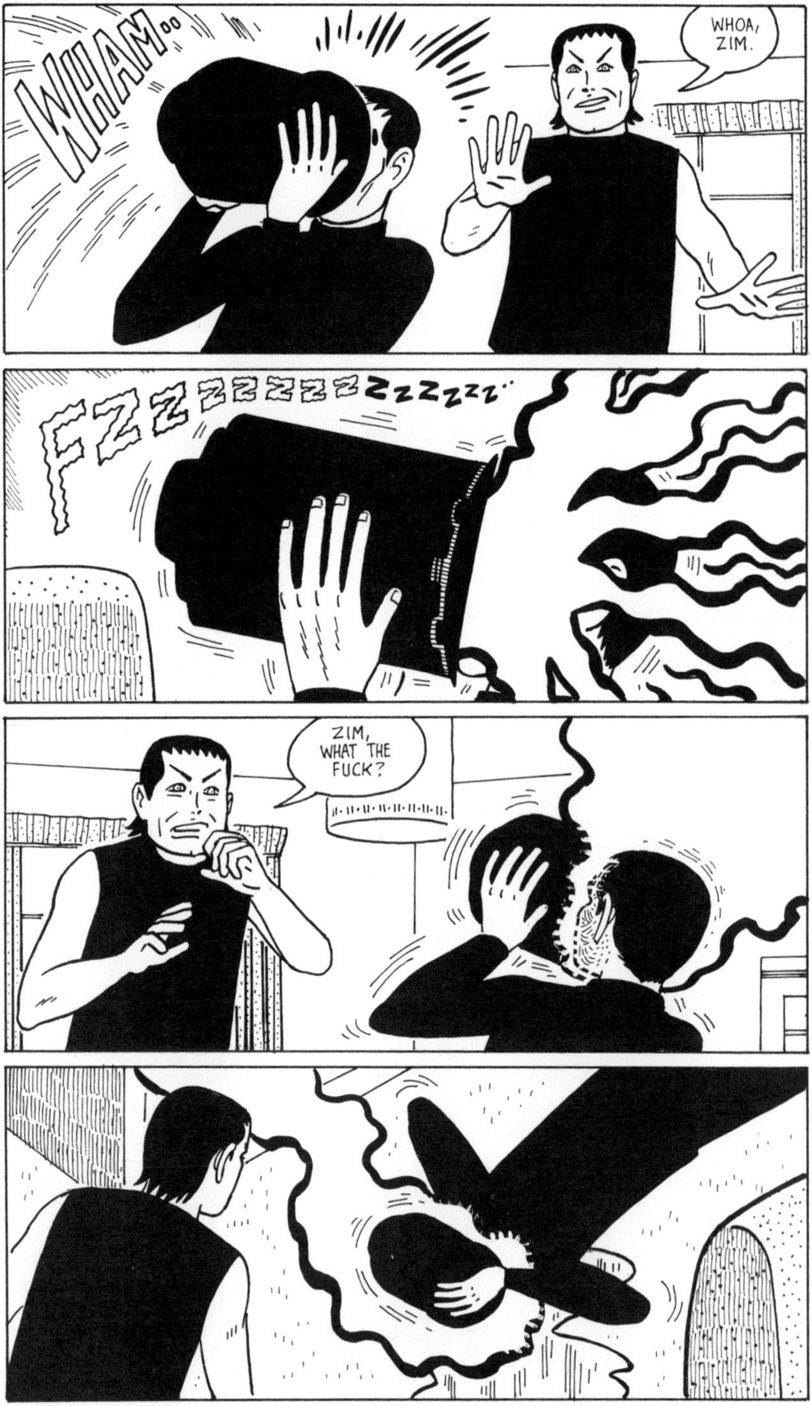
WHAM
WHOA, ZIM.
FZZZZZZZZZZZZ
ZIM, WHAT THE FUCK?

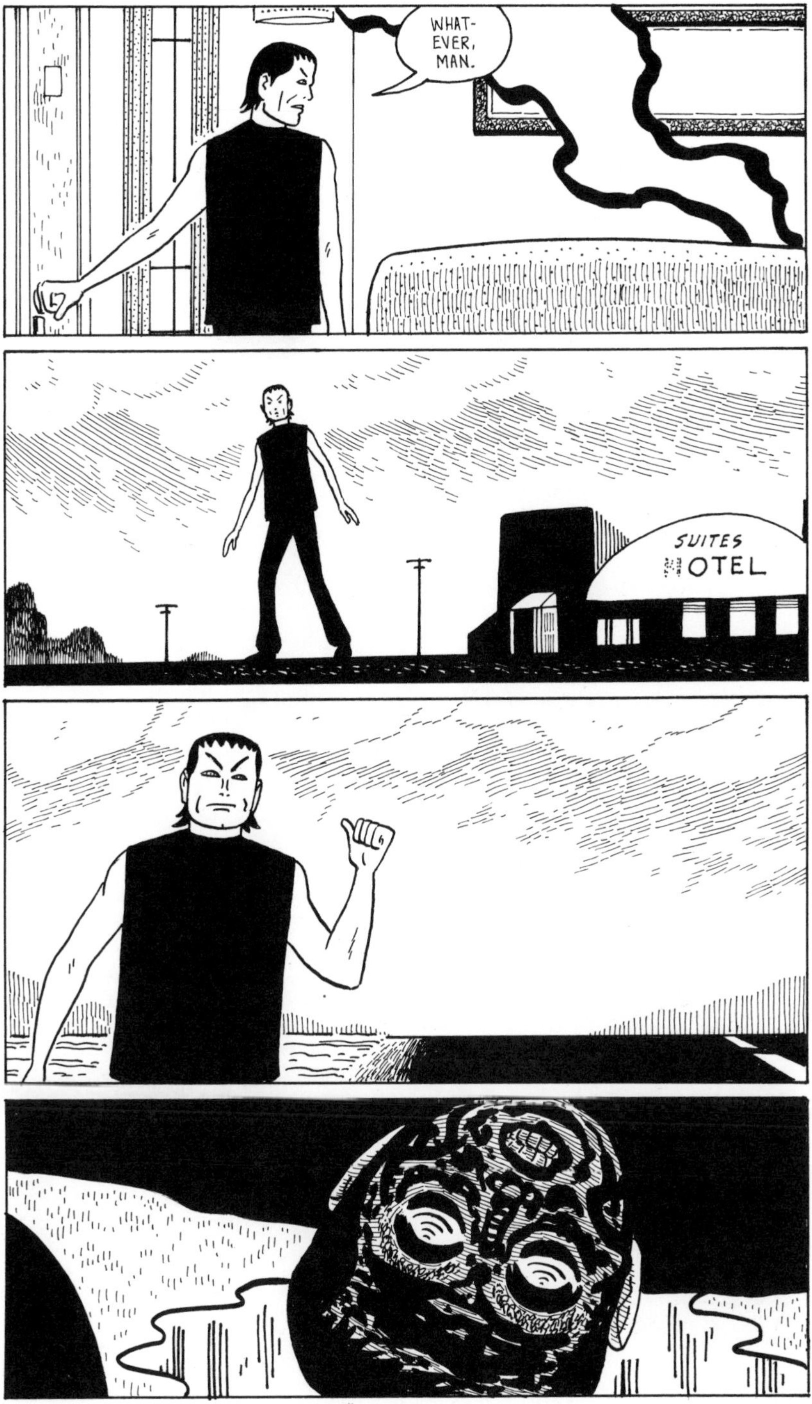
WHAT-EVER, MAN.
SUITES
OTEL

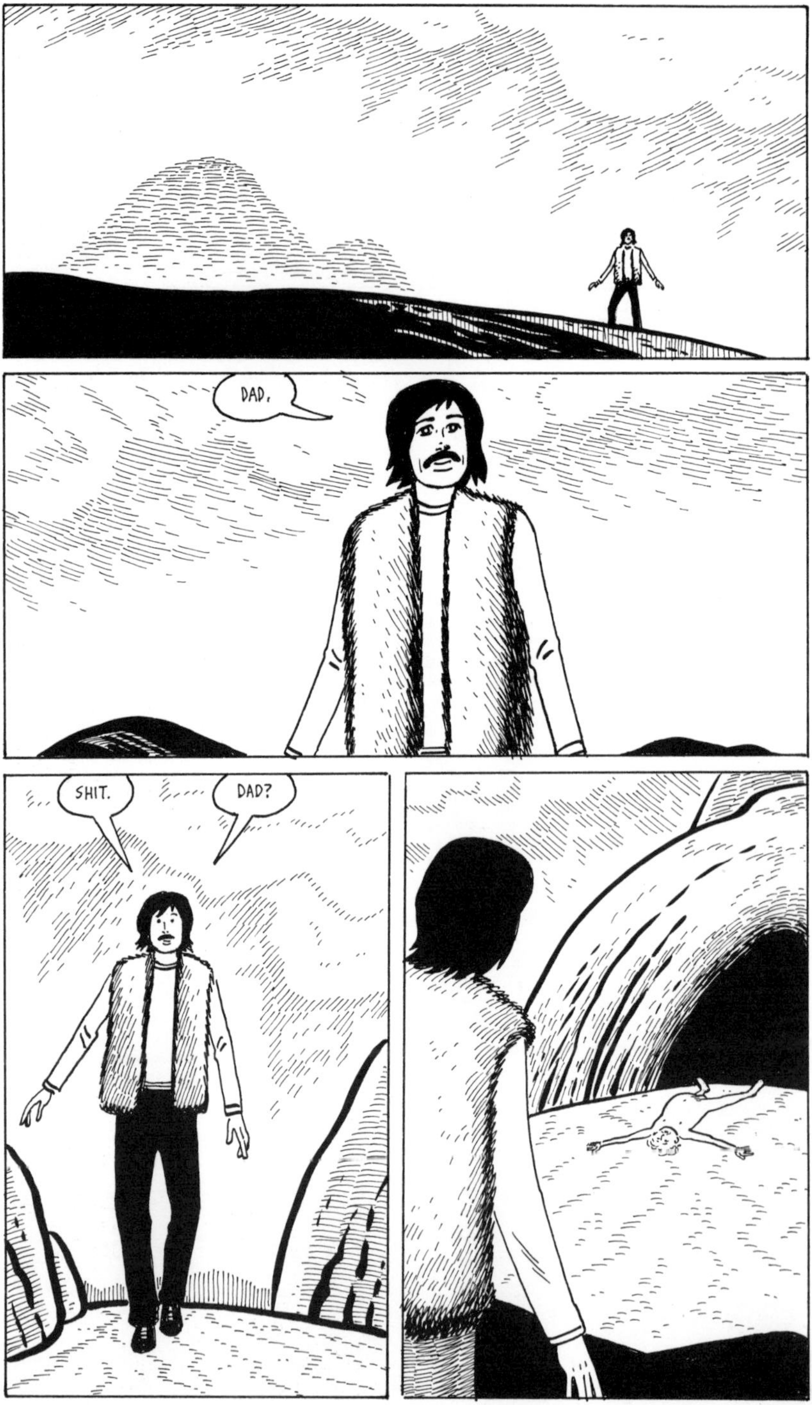
DAD,
SHIT.
DAD?

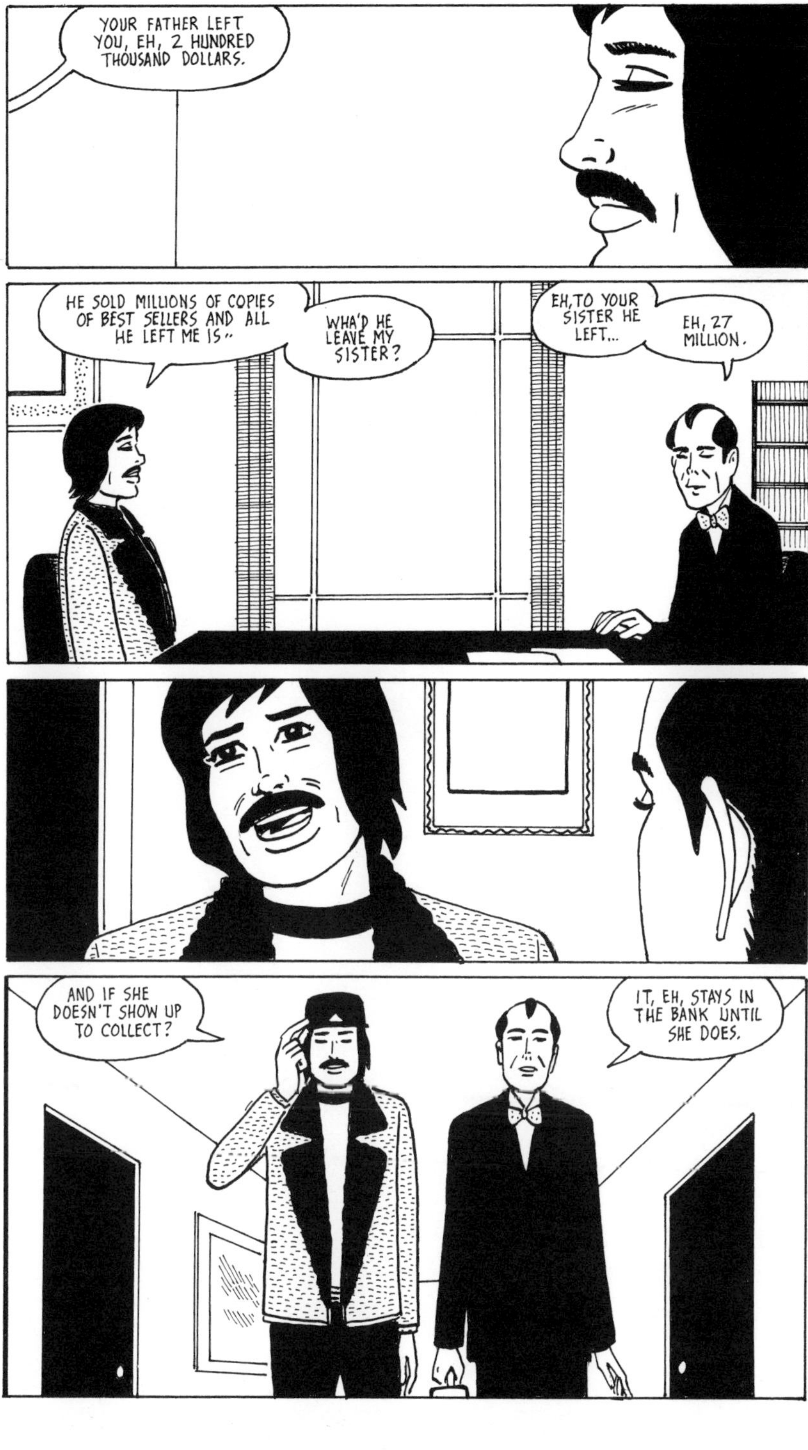
YOUR FATHER LEFT YOU, EH, 2 HUNDRED THOUSAND DOLLARS.
HE SOLD MILLIONS OF COPIES OF BEST SELLERS AND ALL HE LEFT ME IS..
WHA'D HE LEAVE MY SISTER?
EH,TO YOUR SISTER HE LEFT...
EH, 27 MILLION.
AND IF SHE DOESN'T SHOW UP TO COLLECT?
IT, EH, STAYS IN THE BANK UNTIL SHE DOES.

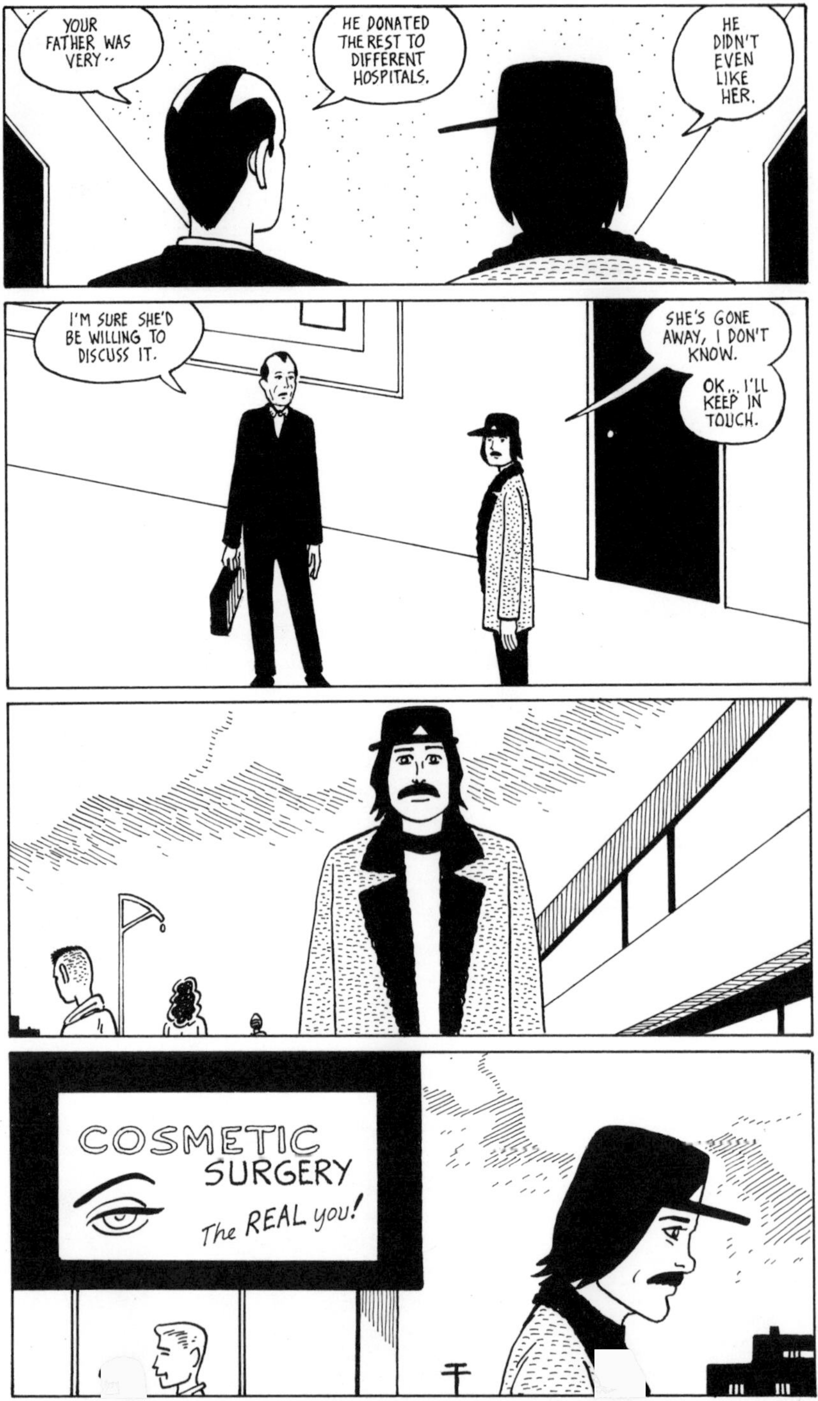
YOUR FATHER WAS VERY ..
HE DONATED THE REST TO DIFFERENT HOSPITALS.
HE DIDN'T EVEN LIKE HER.
I'M SURE SHE'D BE WILLING TO DISCUSS IT.
SHE'S GONE AWAY, I DON'T KNOW.
OK... I'LL KEEP IN TOUCH.
COSMETIC SURGERY
The REAL you!

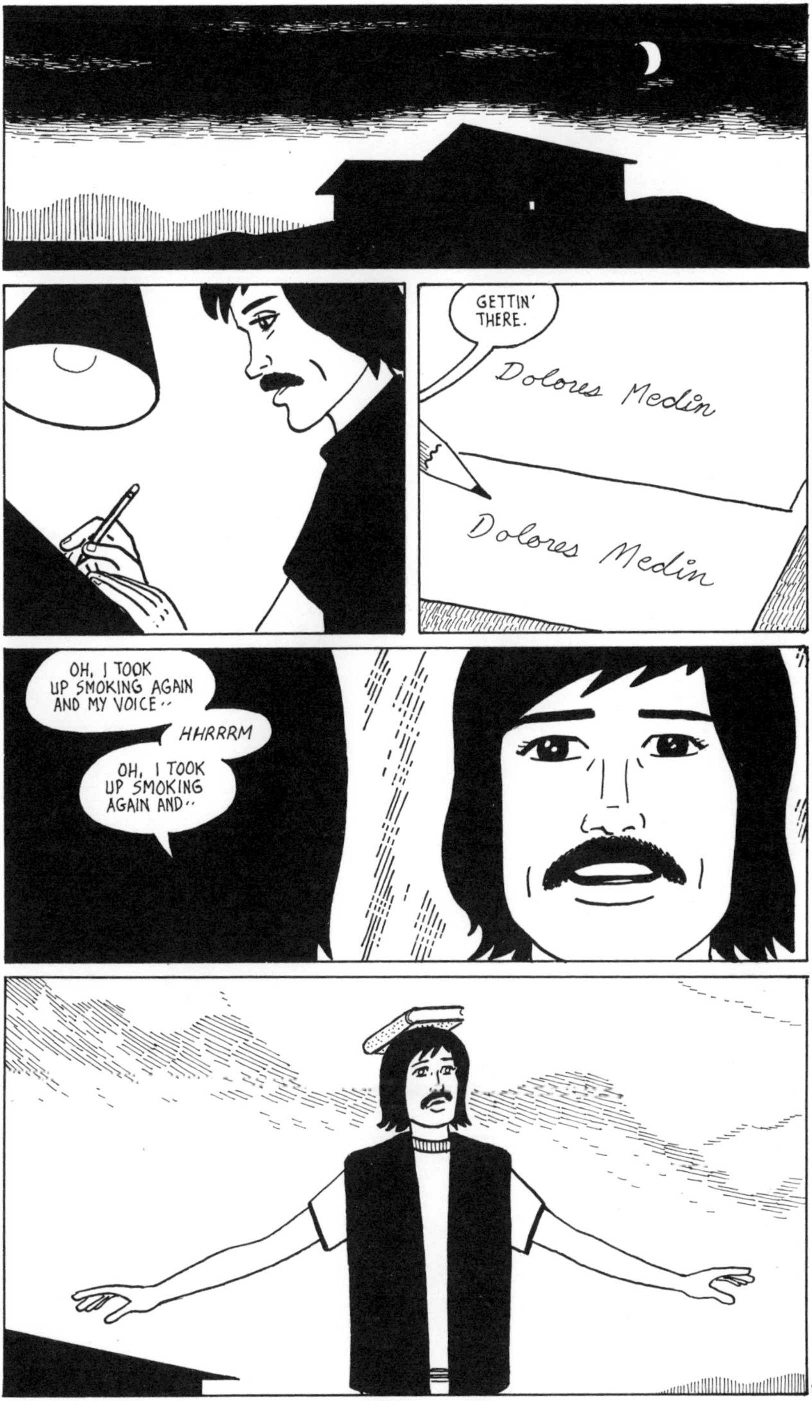
GETTIN' THERE.
Dolores Medin
Dolores Medin
OH, I TOOK UP SMOKING AGAIN AND MY VOICE..
HHRRRM
OH, I TOOK UP SMOKING AGAIN AND..

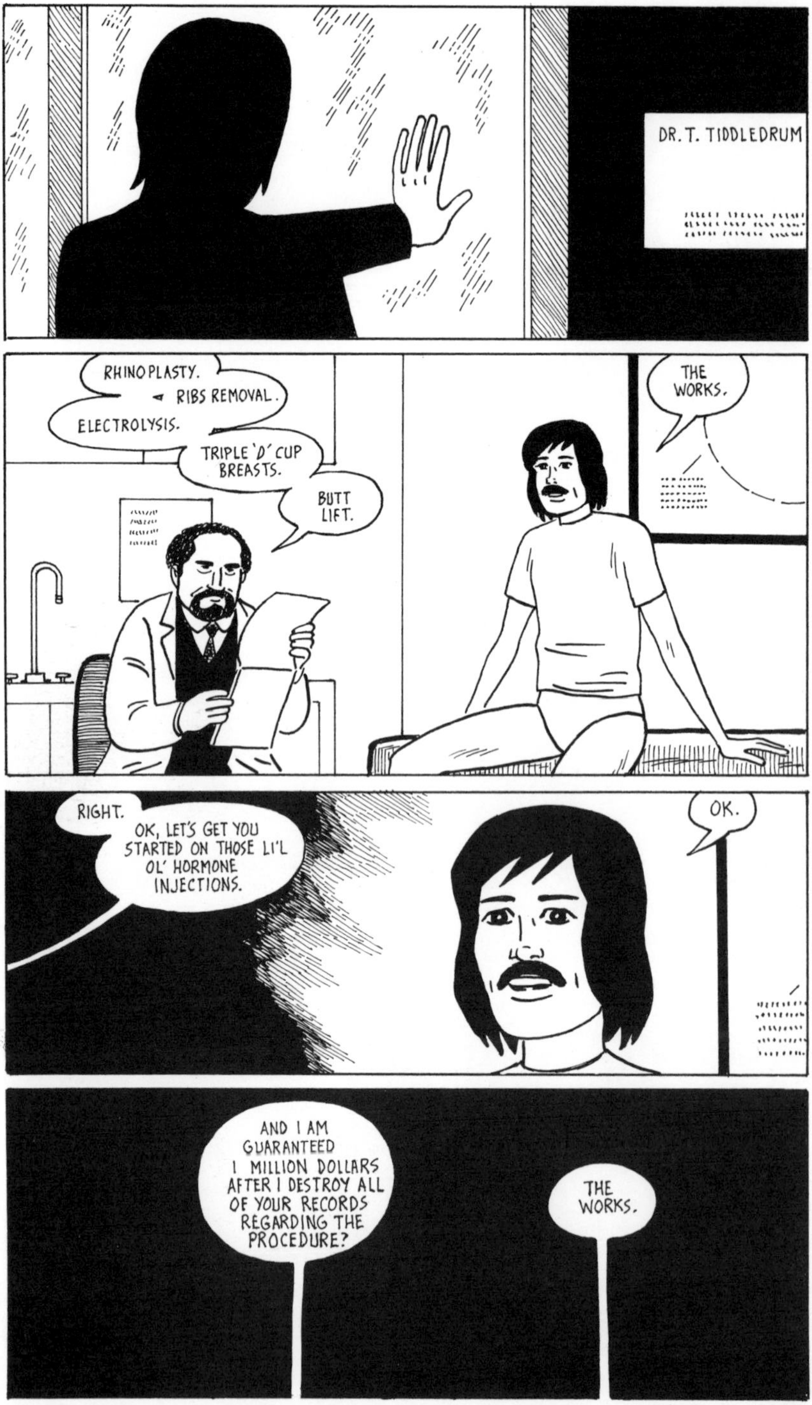
DR. T. TIDDLEDRUM
RHINOPLASTY.
RIBS REMOVAL.
ELECTROLYSIS.
TRIPLE 'D' CUP BREASTS.
BUTT LIFT.
THE WORKS.
RIGHT.
OK, LET'S GET YOU STARTED ON THOSE LI'L OL' HORMONE INJECTIONS.
OK.
AND I AM GUARANTEED 1 MILLION DOLLARS AFTER I DESTROY ALL OF YOUR RECORDS REGARDING THE PROCEDURE?
THE WORKS.

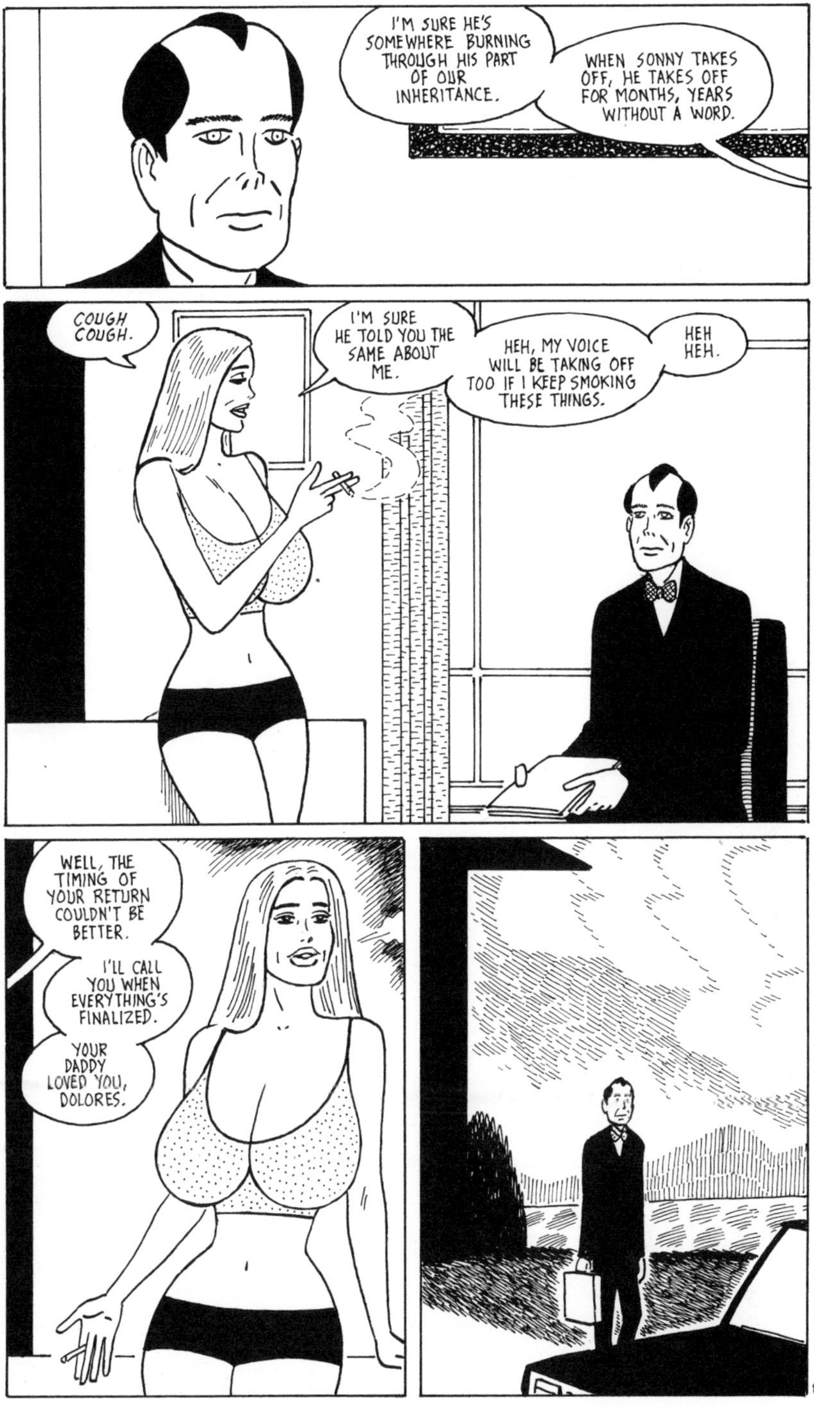
I'M SURE HE'S SOMEWHERE BURNING THROUGH HIS PART OF OUR INHERITANCE.
WHEN SONNY TAKES OFF, HE TAKES OFF FOR MONTHS, YEARS WITHOUT A WORD.
COUGH COUGH.
I'M SURE HE TOLD YOU THE SAME ABOUT ME.
HEH, MY VOICE WILL BE TAKING OFF TOO IF I KEEP SMOKING THESE THINGS.
HEH HEH.
WELL, THE TIMING OF YOUR RETURN COULDN'T BE BETTER.
I'LL CALL YOU WHEN EVERYTHING'S FINALIZED.
YOUR DADDY LOVED YOU, DOLORES.

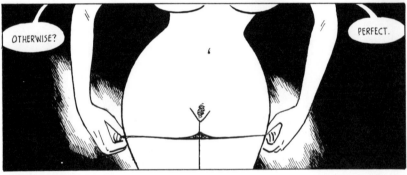

OTHERWISE?

PERFECT.

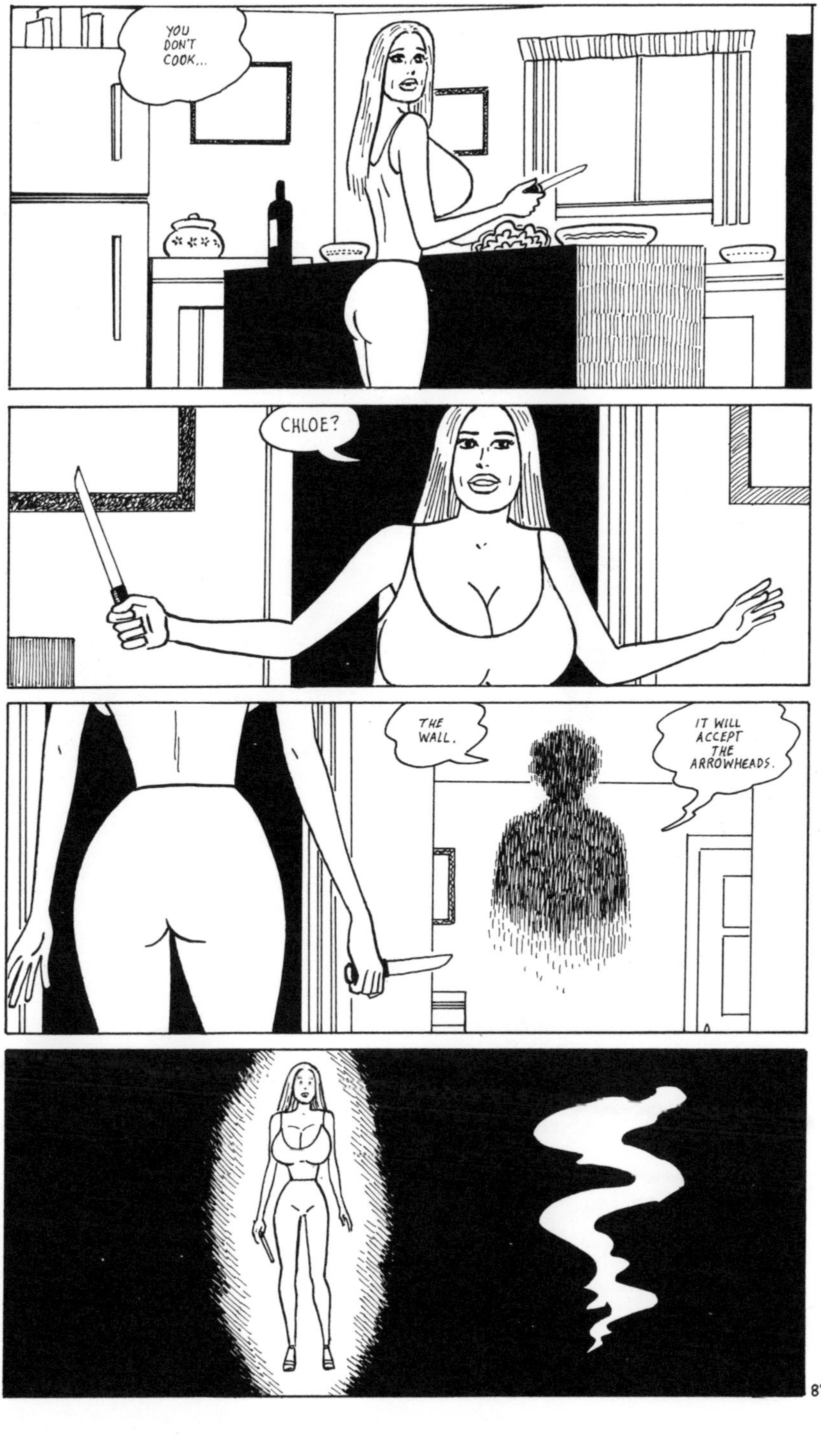
YOU DON'T COOK...
CHLOE?
THE WALL.
IT WILL ACCEPT THE ARROWHEADS.

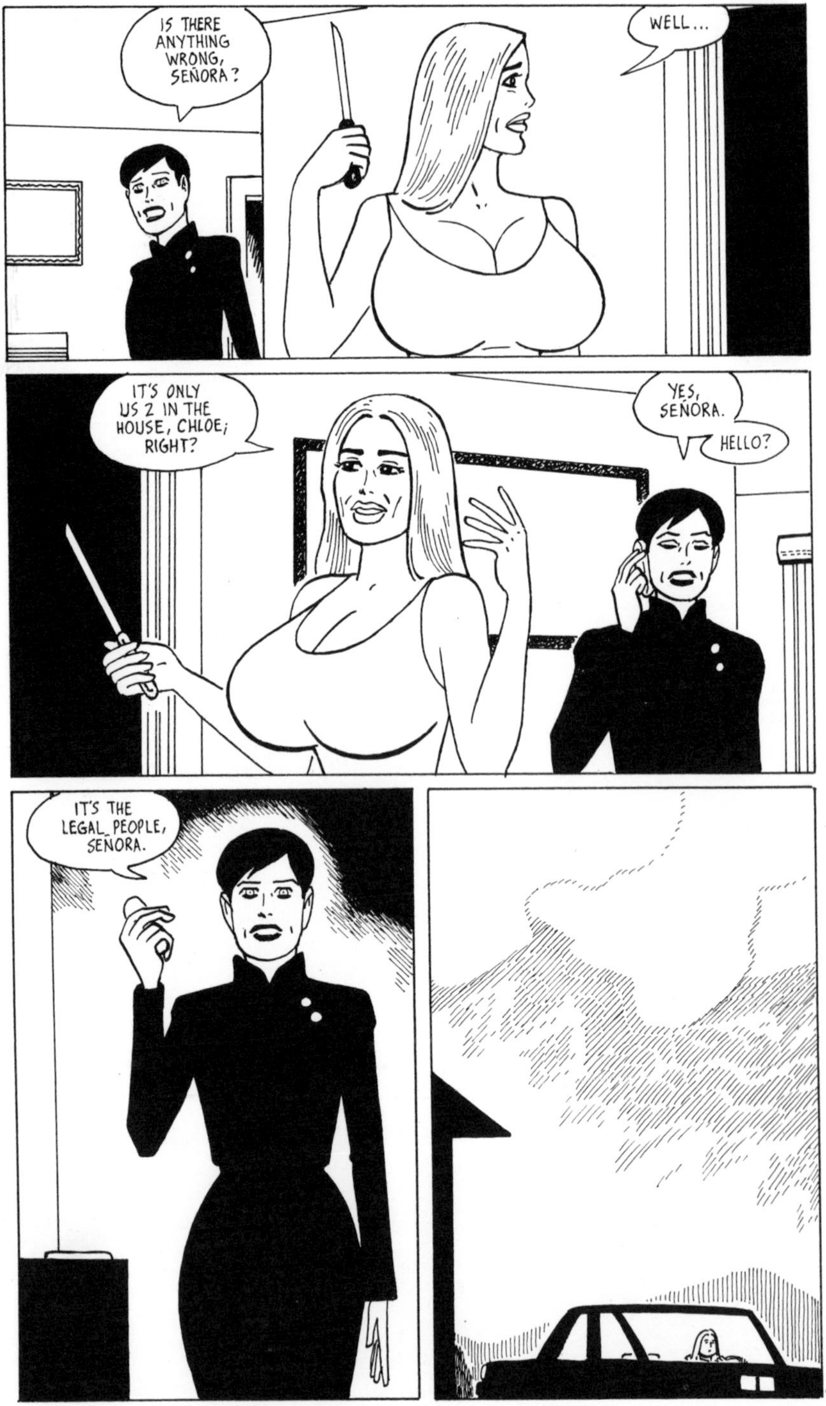
IS THERE ANYTHING WRONG, SEÑORA?
WELL...
IT'S ONLY US 2 IN THE HOUSE, CHLOE; RIGHT?
YES, SEÑORA.
HELLO?
IT'S THE LEGAL PEOPLE, SEÑORA.

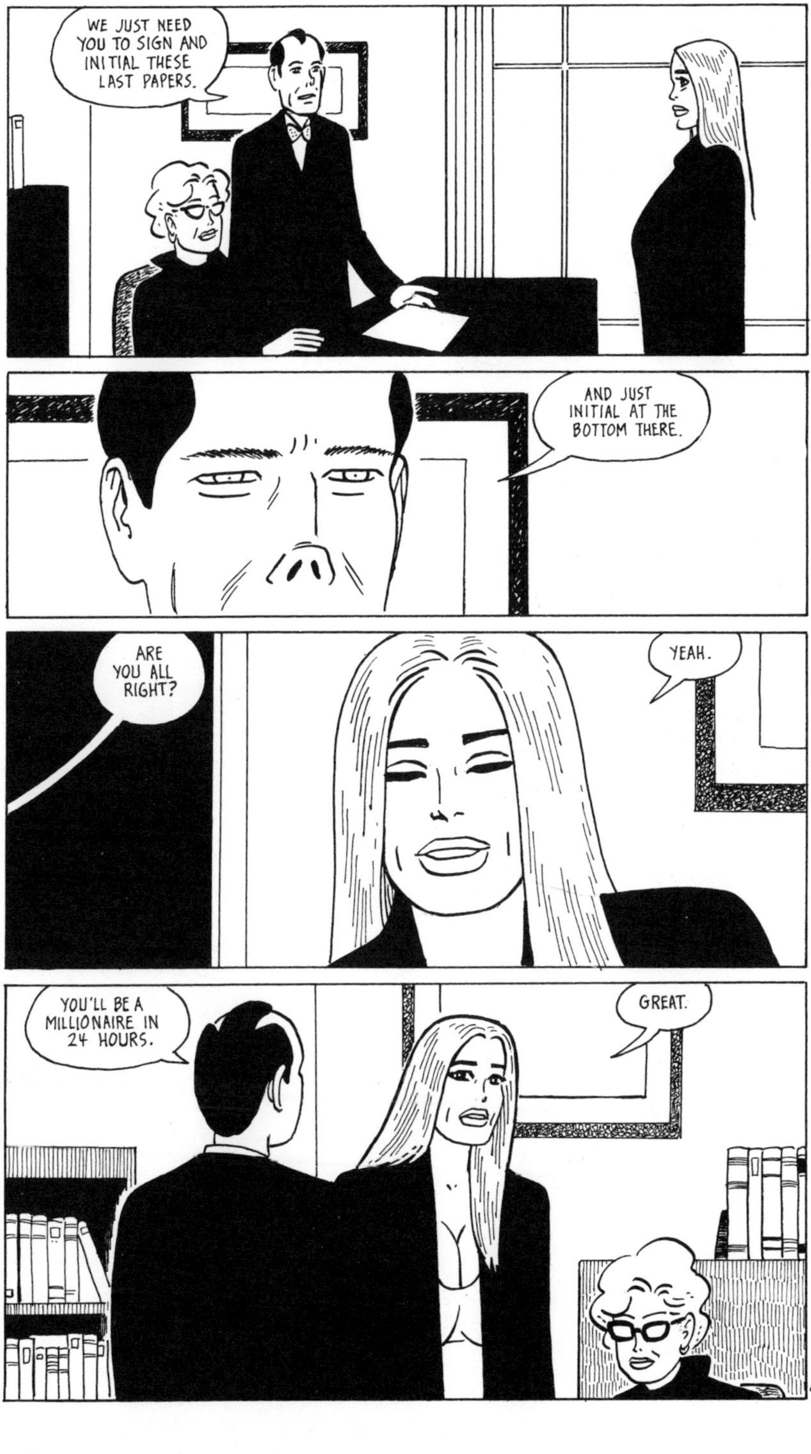
WE JUST NEED YOU TO SIGN AND INITIAL THESE LAST PAPERS.
AND JUST INITIAL AT THE BOTTOM THERE.
ARE YOU ALL RIGHT?
YEAH.
YOU'LL BE A MILLIONAIRE IN 24 HOURS.
GREAT.

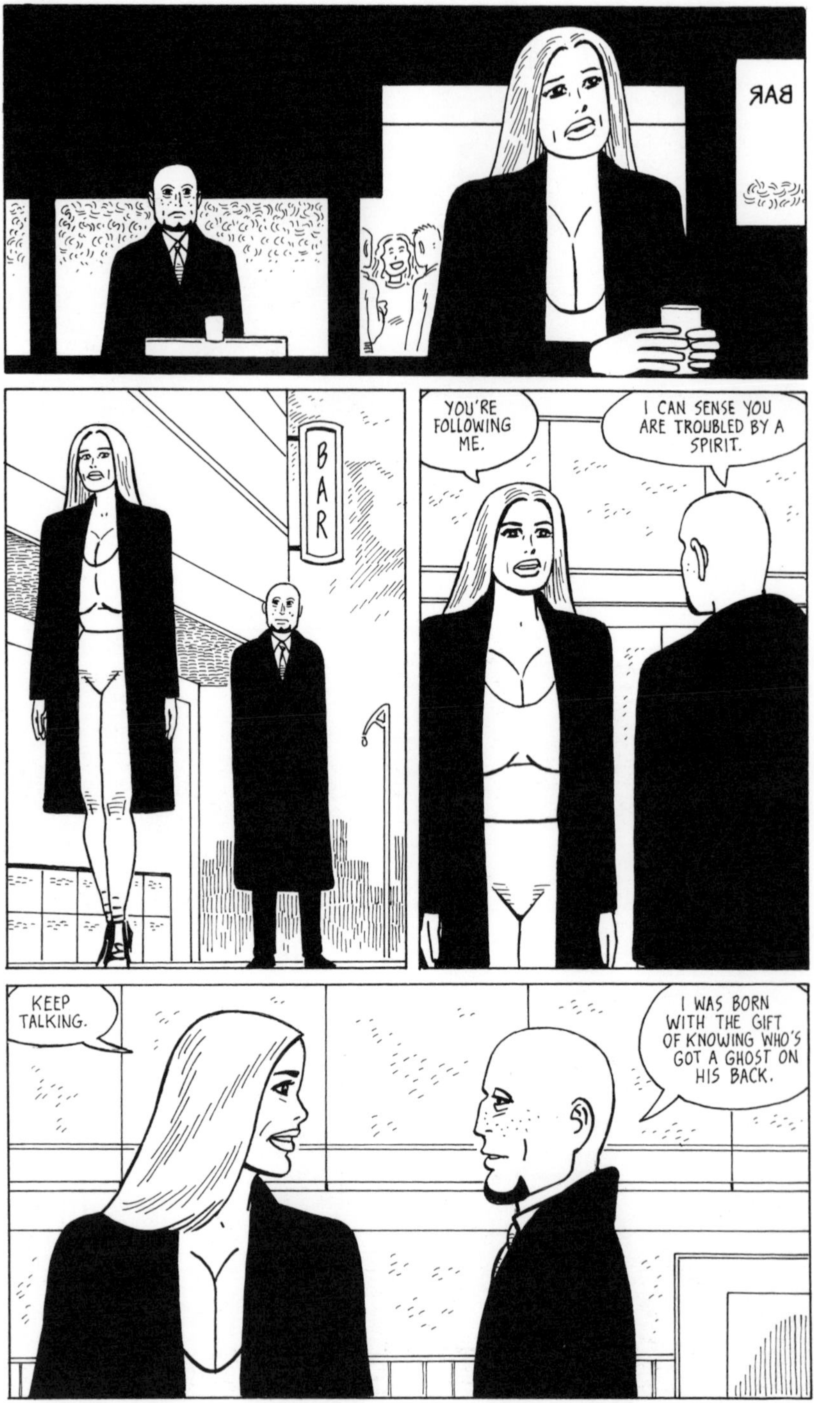
BAR
BAR
YOU'RE FOLLOWING ME.
I CAN SENSE YOU ARE TROUBLED BY A SPIRIT.
KEEP TALKING.
I WAS BORN WITH THE GIFT OF KNOWING WHO'S GOT A GHOST ON HIS BACK.

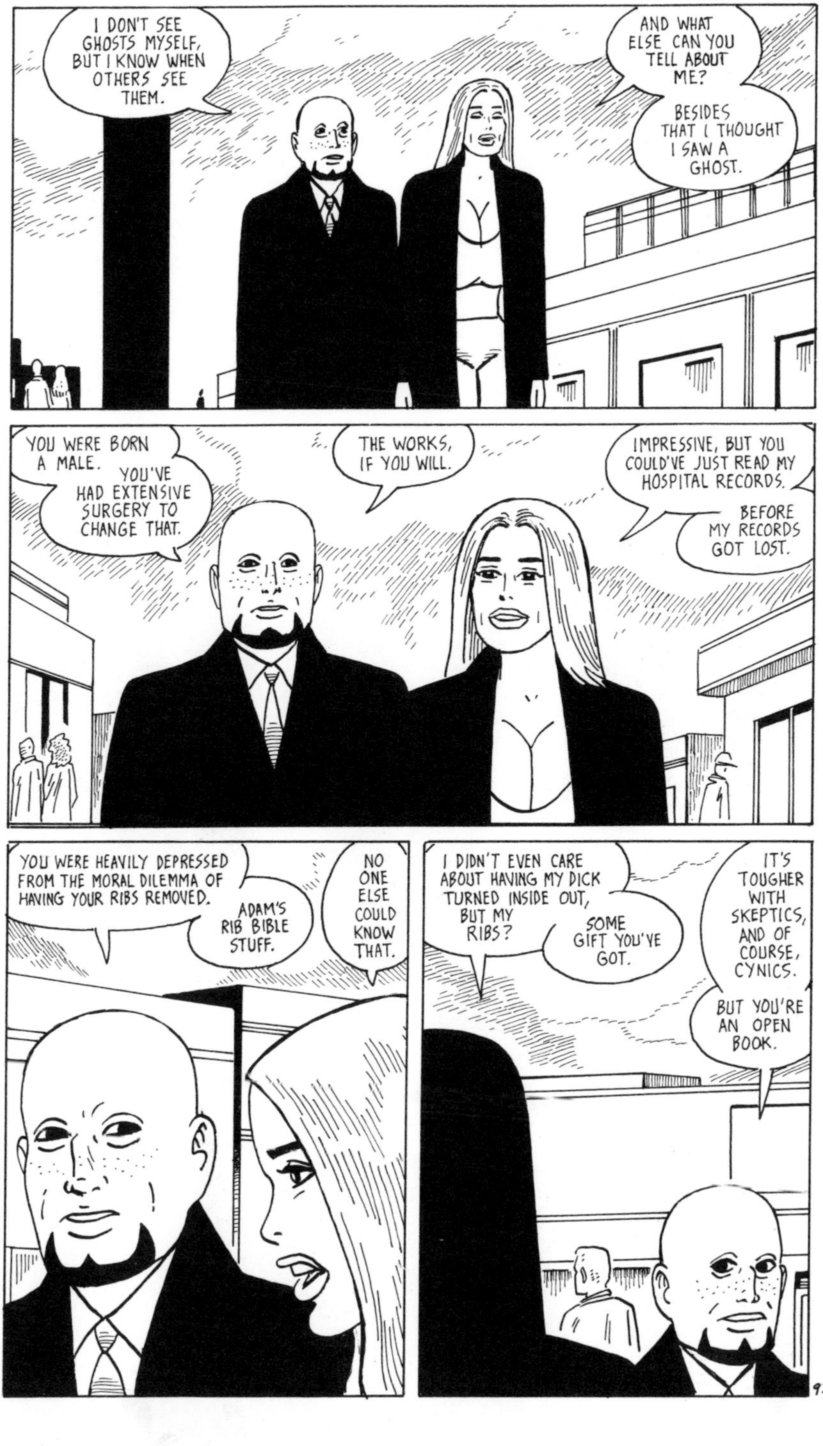
I DON'T SEE GHOSTS MYSELF, BUT I KNOW WHEN OTHERS SEE THEM.
AND WHAT ELSE CAN YOU TELL ABOUT ME?
BESIDES THAT I THOUGHT I SAW A GHOST.
YOU WERE BORN A MALE.
YOU'VE HAD EXTENSIVE SURGERY TO CHANGE THAT.
THE WORKS, IF YOU WILL.
IMPRESSIVE, BUT YOU COULD'VE JUST READ MY HOSPITAL RECORDS.
BEFORE MY RECORDS GOT LOST.
YOU WERE HEAVILY DEPRESSED FROM THE MORAL DILEMMA OF HAVING YOUR RIBS REMOVED.
ADAM'S RIB BIBLE STUFF.
NO ONE ELSE COULD KNOW THAT.
I DIDN'T EVEN CARE ABOUT HAVING MY DICK TURNED INSIDE OUT, BUT MY RIBS?
SOME GIFT YOU'VE GOT.
IT'S TOUGHER WITH SKEPTICS, AND OF COURSE, CYNICS.
BUT YOU'RE AN OPEN BOOK.

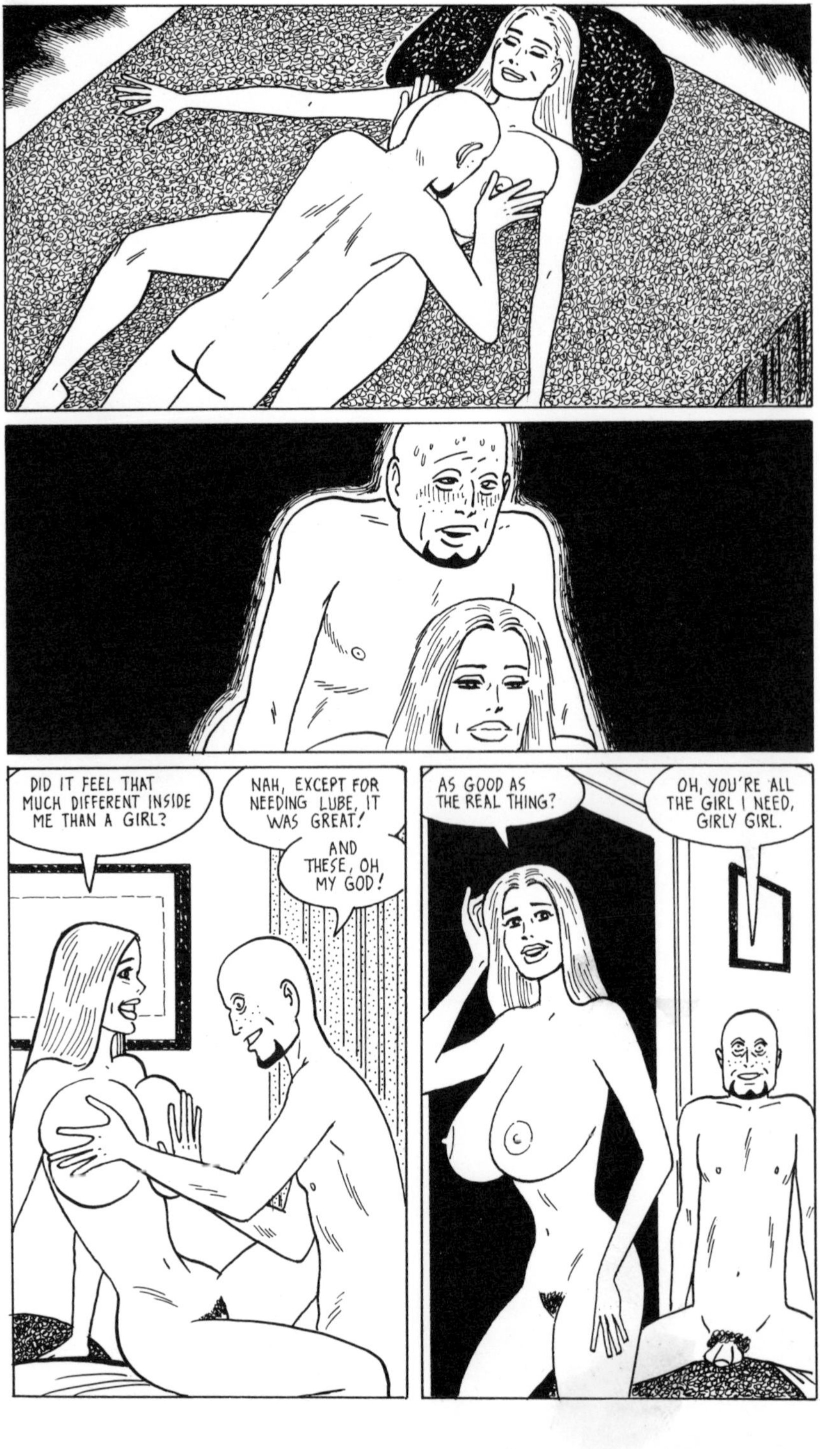
DID IT FEEL THAT MUCH DIFFERENT INSIDE ME THAN A GIRL?
NAH, EXCEPT FOR NEEDING LUBE, IT WAS GREAT!
AND THESE, OH MY GOD!
AS GOOD AS THE REAL THING?
OH, YOU'RE ALL THE GIRL I NEED, GIRLY GIRL.

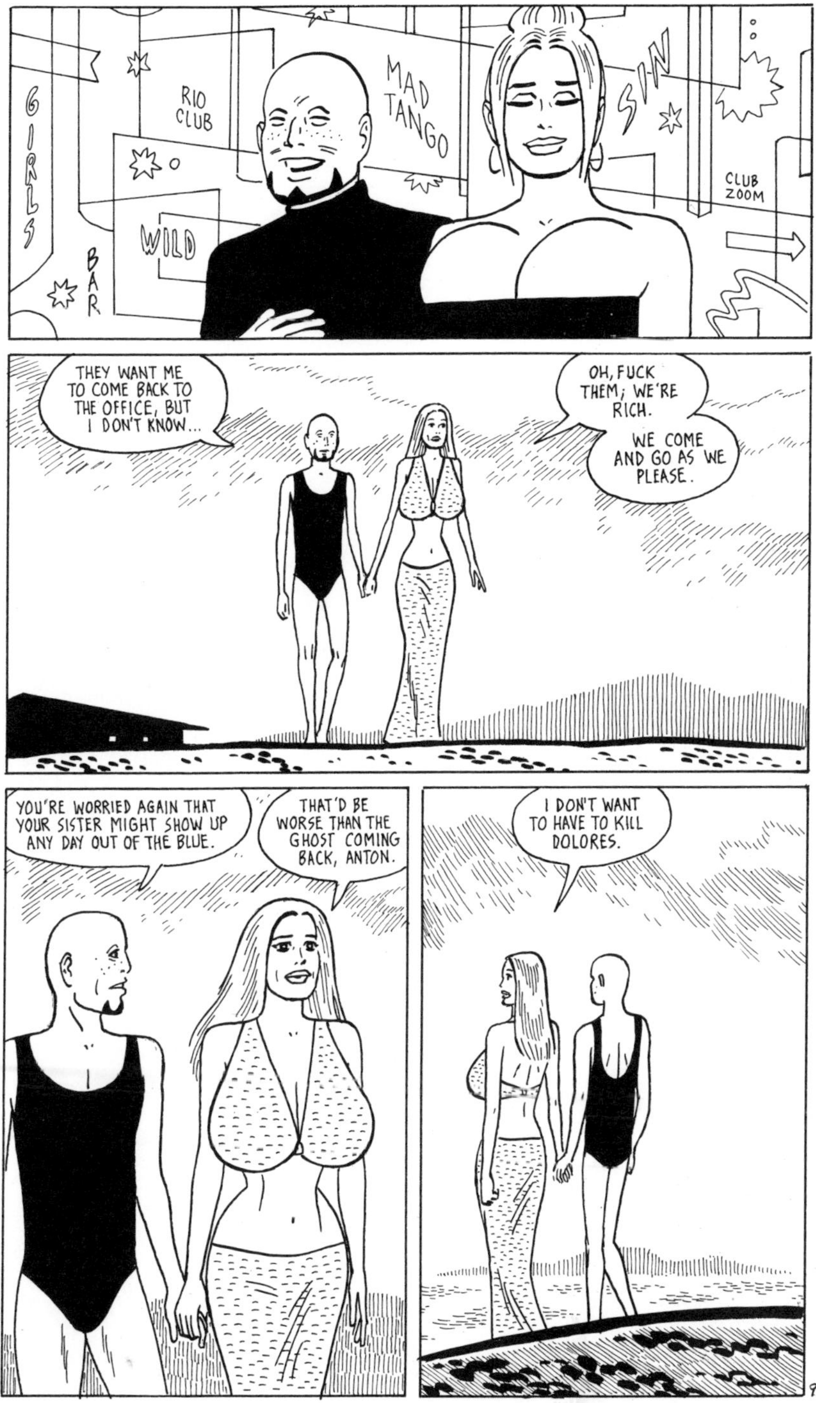
GIRLS
RIO CLUB
MAD TANGO
SIN
WILD
BAR
CLUB ZOOM
THEY WANT ME TO COME BACK TO THE OFFICE, BUT I DON'T KNOW...
OH, FUCK THEM; WE'RE RICH.
WE COME AND GO AS WE PLEASE.
YOU'RE WORRIED AGAIN THAT YOUR SISTER MIGHT SHOW UP ANY DAY OUT OF THE BLUE.
THAT'D BE WORSE THAN THE GHOST COMING BACK, ANTON.
I DON'T WANT TO HAVE TO KILL DOLORES.

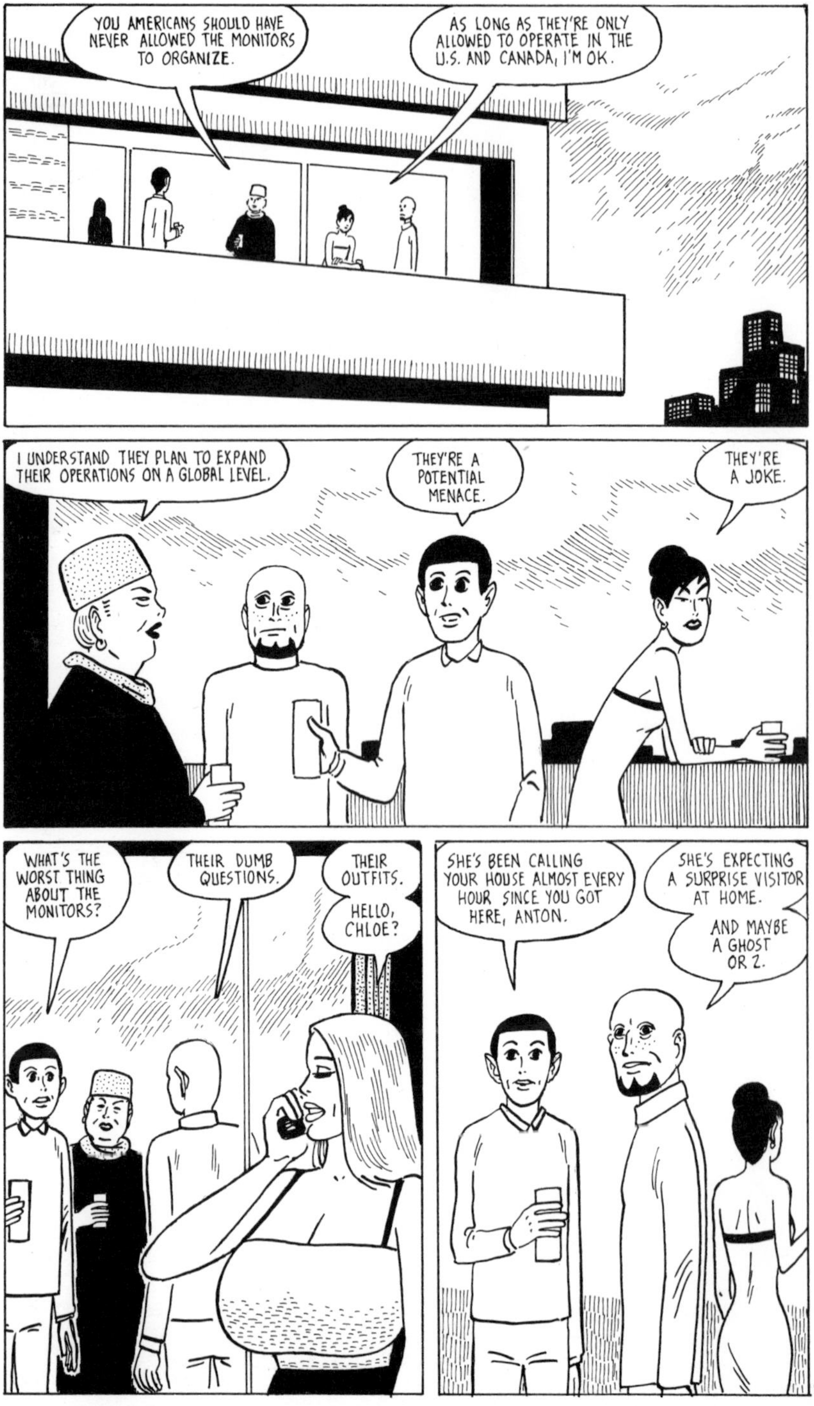
YOU AMERICANS SHOULD HAVE NEVER ALLOWED THE MONITORS TO ORGANIZE.
AS LONG AS THEY'RE ONLY ALLOWED TO OPERATE IN THE U.S. AND CANADA, I'M OK.
I UNDERSTAND THEY PLAN TO EXPAND THEIR OPERATIONS ON A GLOBAL LEVEL.
THEY'RE A POTENTIAL MENACE.
THEY'RE A JOKE.
WHAT'S THE WORST THING ABOUT THE MONITORS?
THEIR DUMB QUESTIONS.
THEIR OUTFITS.
HELLO, CHLOE?
SHE'S BEEN CALLING YOUR HOUSE ALMOST EVERY HOUR SINCE YOU GOT HERE, ANTON.
SHE'S EXPECTING A SURPRISE VISITOR AT HOME.
AND MAYBE A GHOST OR 2.

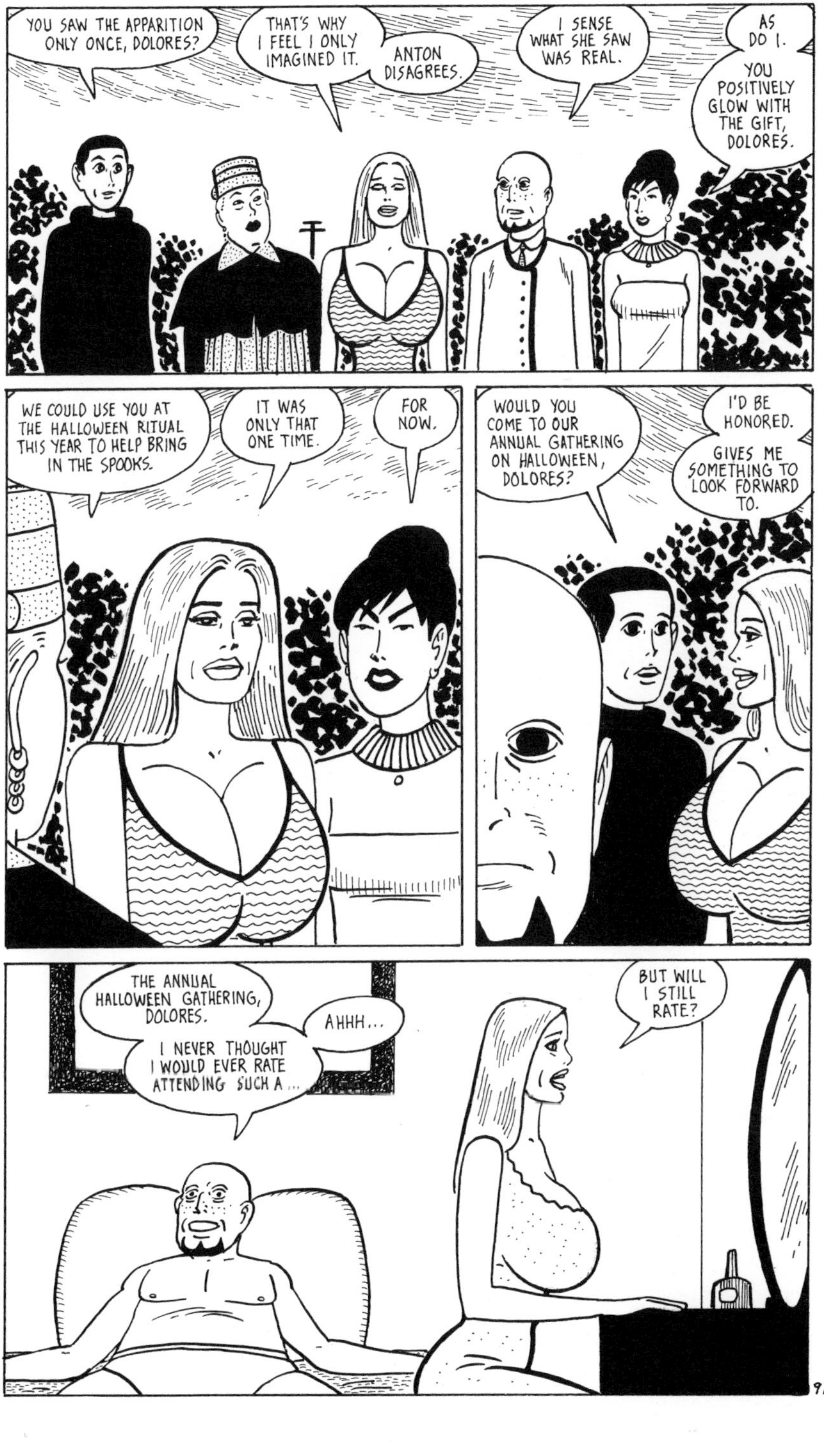
YOU SAW THE APPARITION ONLY ONCE, DOLORES?
THAT'S WHY I FEEL I ONLY IMAGINED IT.
ANTON DISAGREES.
I SENSE WHAT SHE SAW WAS REAL.
AS DO I.
YOU POSITIVELY GLOW WITH THE GIFT, DOLORES.
WE COULD USE YOU AT THE HALLOWEEN RITUAL THIS YEAR TO HELP BRING IN THE SPOOKS.
IT WAS ONLY THAT ONE TIME.
FOR NOW.
WOULD YOU COME TO OUR ANNUAL GATHERING ON HALLOWEEN, DOLORES?
I'D BE HONORED.
GIVES ME SOMETHING TO LOOK FORWARD TO.
THE ANNUAL HALLOWEEN GATHERING, DOLORES.
AHHH...
I NEVER THOUGHT I WOULD EVER RATE ATTENDING SUCH A...
BUT WILL I STILL RATE?

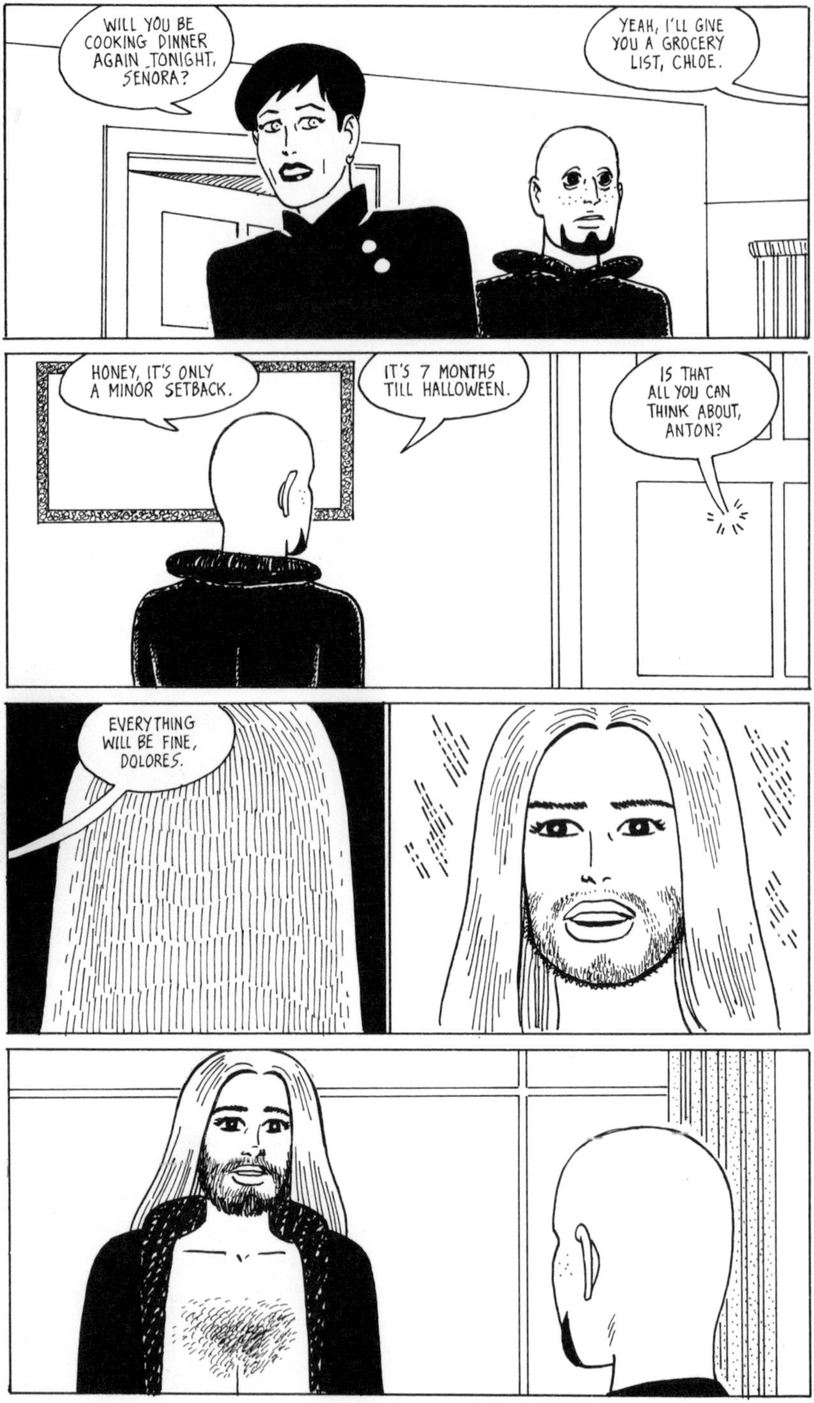
WILL YOU BE COOKING DINNER AGAIN TONIGHT, SEÑORA?
YEAH, I'LL GIVE YOU A GROCERY LIST, CHLOE.
HONEY, IT'S ONLY A MINOR SETBACK.
IT'S 7 MONTHS TILL HALLOWEEN.
IS THAT ALL YOU CAN THINK ABOUT, ANTON?
EVERYTHING WILL BE FINE, DOLORES.

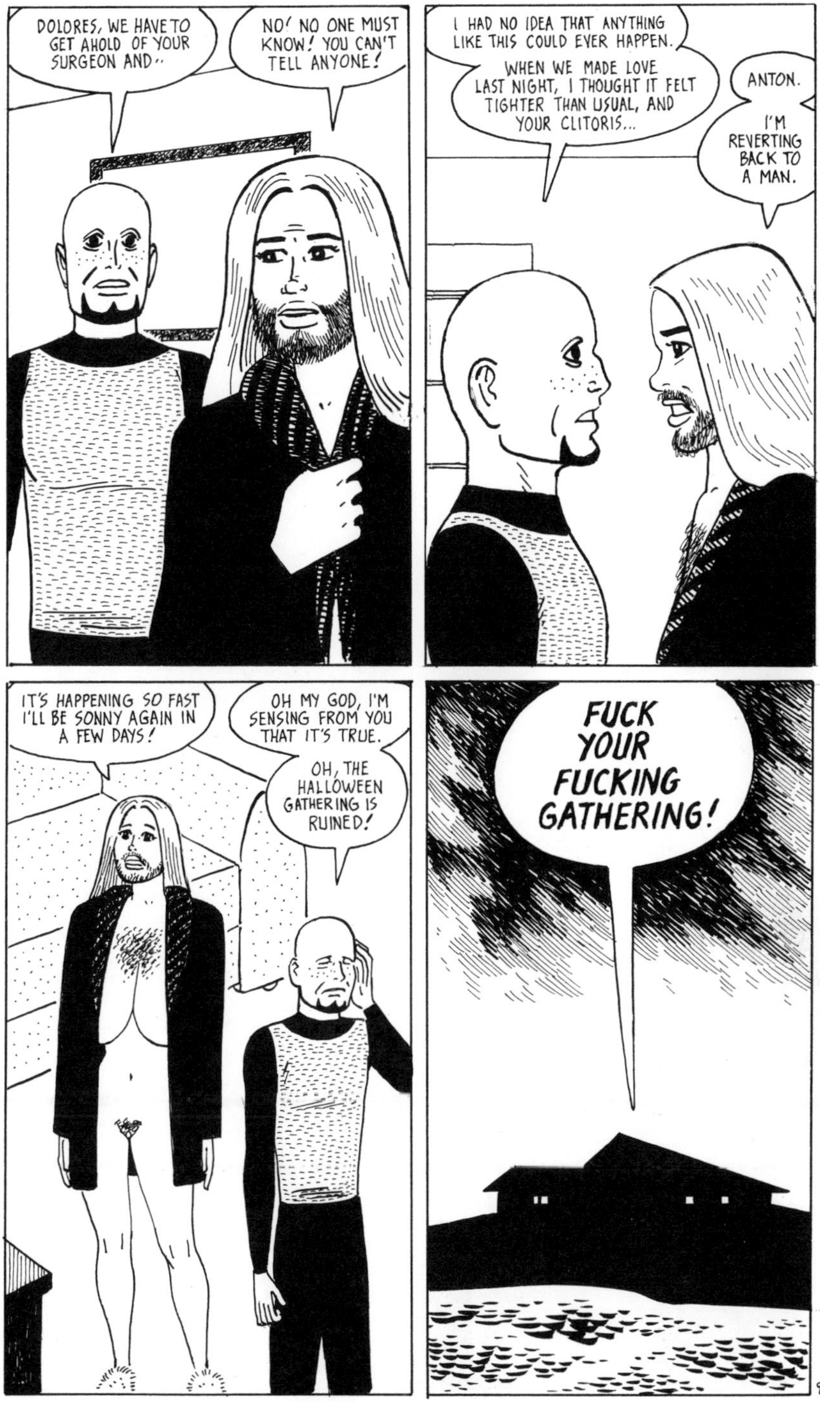
DOLORES, WE HAVE TO GET AHOLD OF YOUR SURGEON AND..
NO! NO ONE MUST KNOW! YOU CAN'T TELL ANYONE!
I HAD NO IDEA THAT ANYTHING LIKE THIS COULD EVER HAPPEN.
WHEN WE MADE LOVE LAST NIGHT, I THOUGHT IT FELT TIGHTER THAN USUAL, AND YOUR CLITORIS...
ANTON.
I'M REVERTING BACK TO A MAN.
IT'S HAPPENING SO FAST I'LL BE SONNY AGAIN IN A FEW DAYS!
OH MY GOD, I'M SENSING FROM YOU THAT IT'S TRUE.
OH, THE HALLOWEEN GATHERING IS RUINED!
FUCK YOUR FUCKING GATHERING!

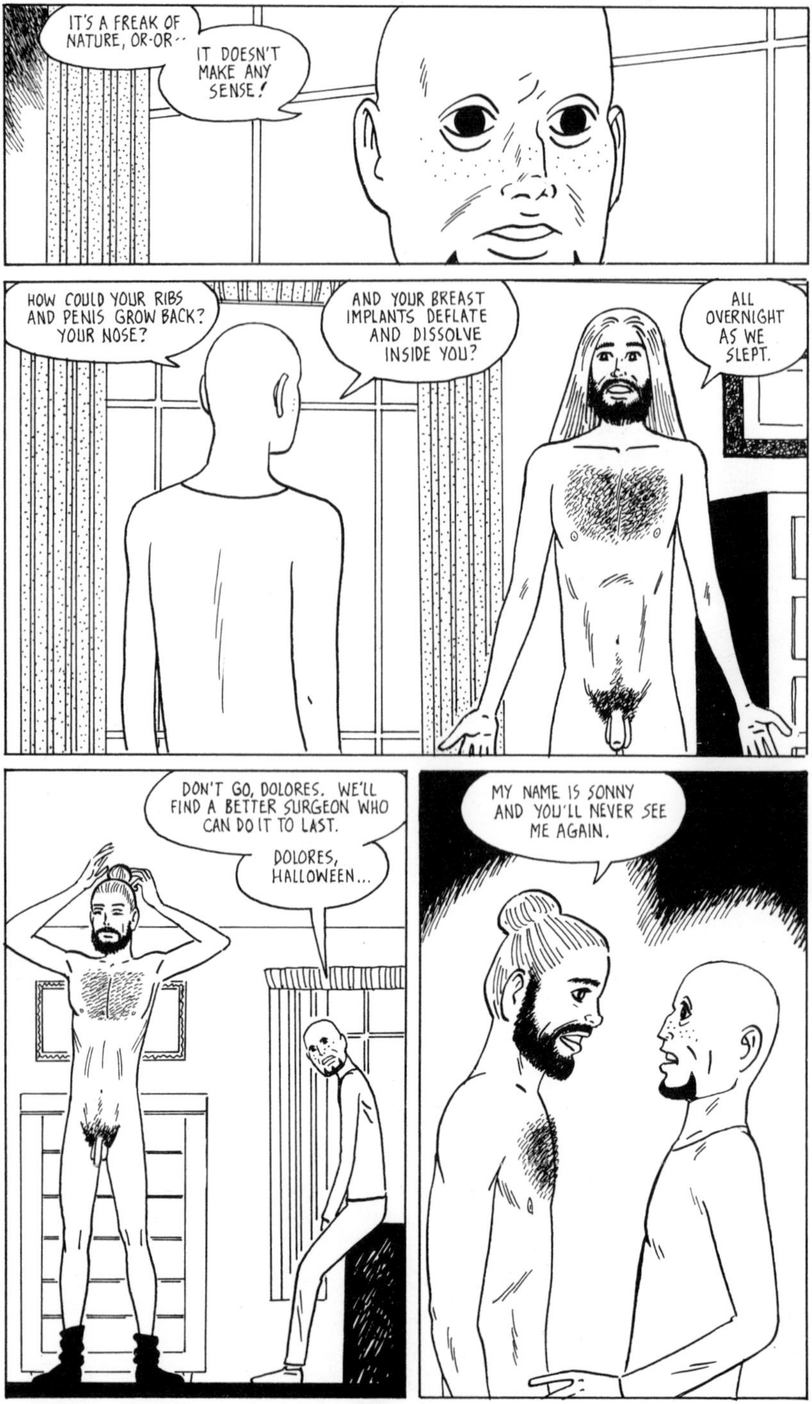
IT'S A FREAK OF NATURE, OR-OR--
IT DOESN'T MAKE ANY SENSE!
HOW COULD YOUR RIBS AND PENIS GROW BACK? YOUR NOSE?
AND YOUR BREAST IMPLANTS DEFLATE AND DISSOLVE INSIDE YOU?
ALL OVERNIGHT AS WE SLEPT.
DON'T GO, DOLORES. WE'LL FIND A BETTER SURGEON WHO CAN DO IT TO LAST.
DOLORES, HALLOWEEN...
MY NAME IS SONNY AND YOU'LL NEVER SEE ME AGAIN.

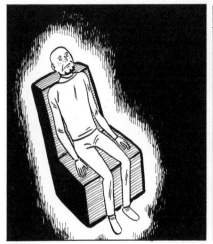

SOMEONE...
TO SEE YOU,
SEÑOR.

OH!
DID I FALL
ASLEEP...?

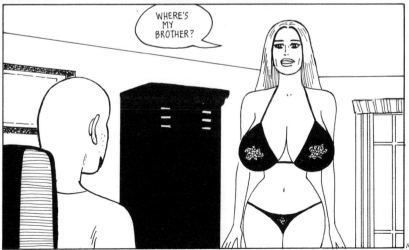

WHERE'S
MY
BROTHER?

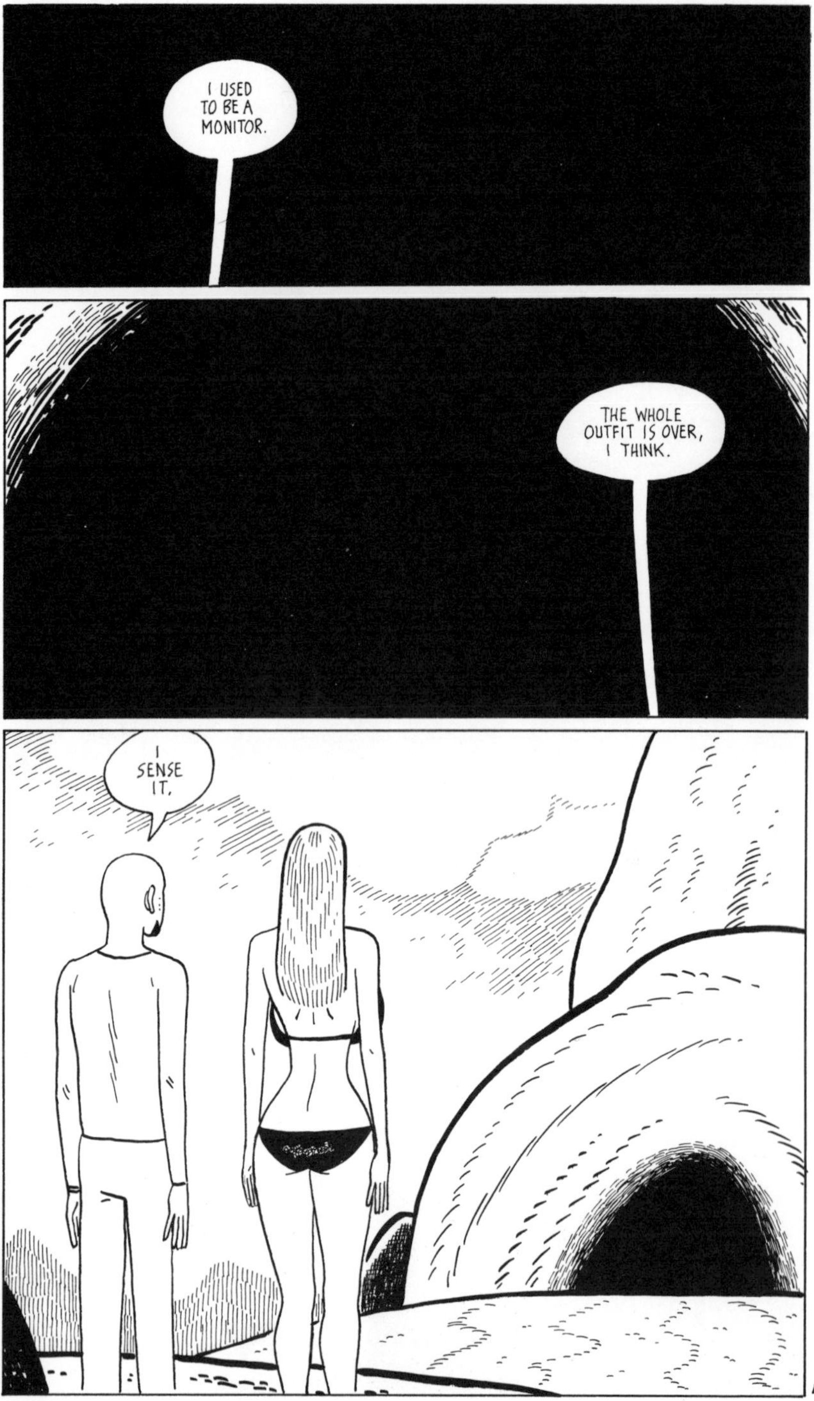
I USED TO BE A MONITOR.
THE WHOLE OUTFIT IS OVER, I THINK.
I SENSE IT.

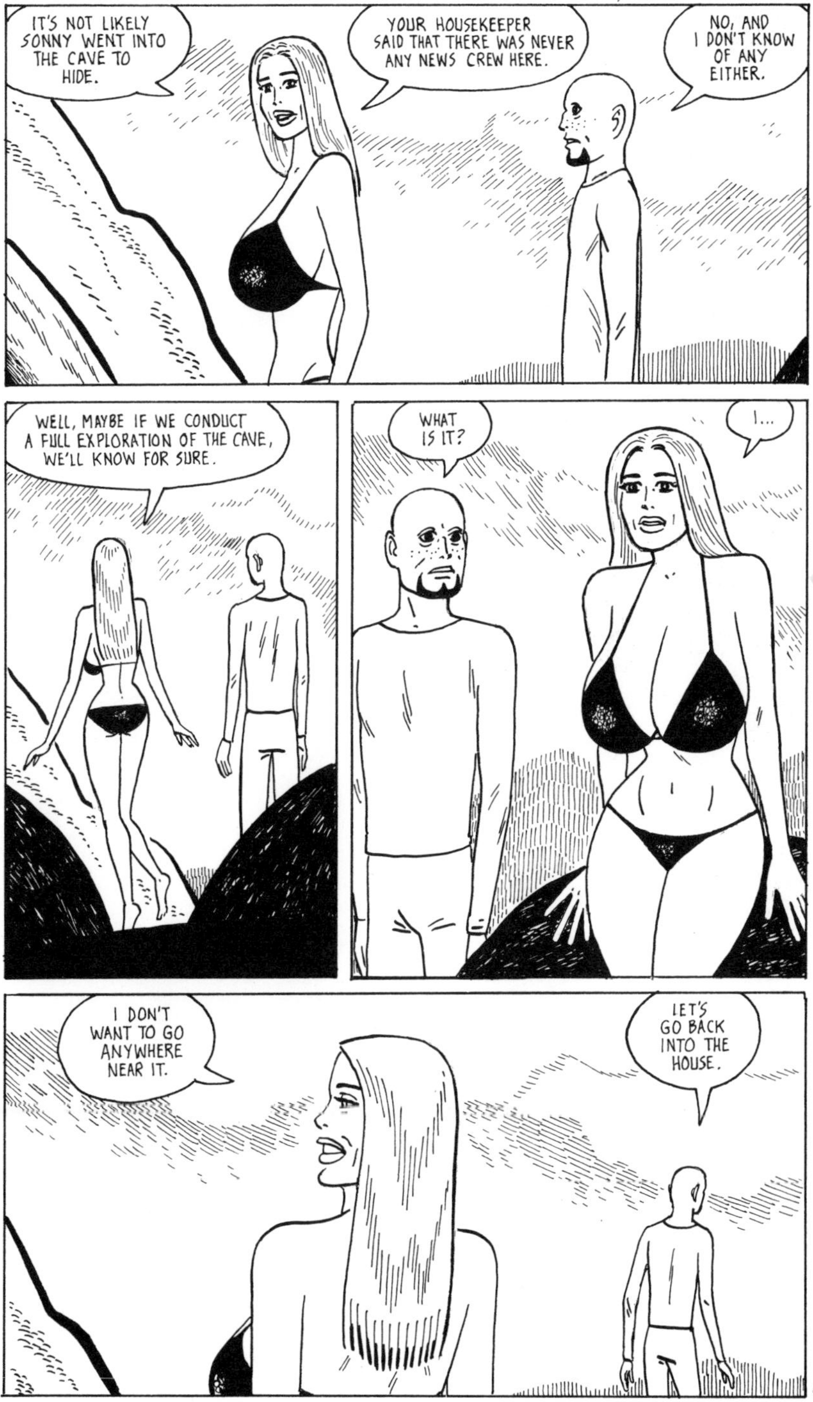
IT'S NOT LIKELY SONNY WENT INTO THE CAVE TO HIDE.
YOUR HOUSEKEEPER SAID THAT THERE WAS NEVER ANY NEWS CREW HERE.
NO, AND I DON'T KNOW OF ANY EITHER.
WELL, MAYBE IF WE CONDUCT A FULL EXPLORATION OF THE CAVE, WE'LL KNOW FOR SURE.
WHAT IS IT?
I...
I DON'T WANT TO GO ANYWHERE NEAR IT.
LET'S GO BACK INTO THE HOUSE.

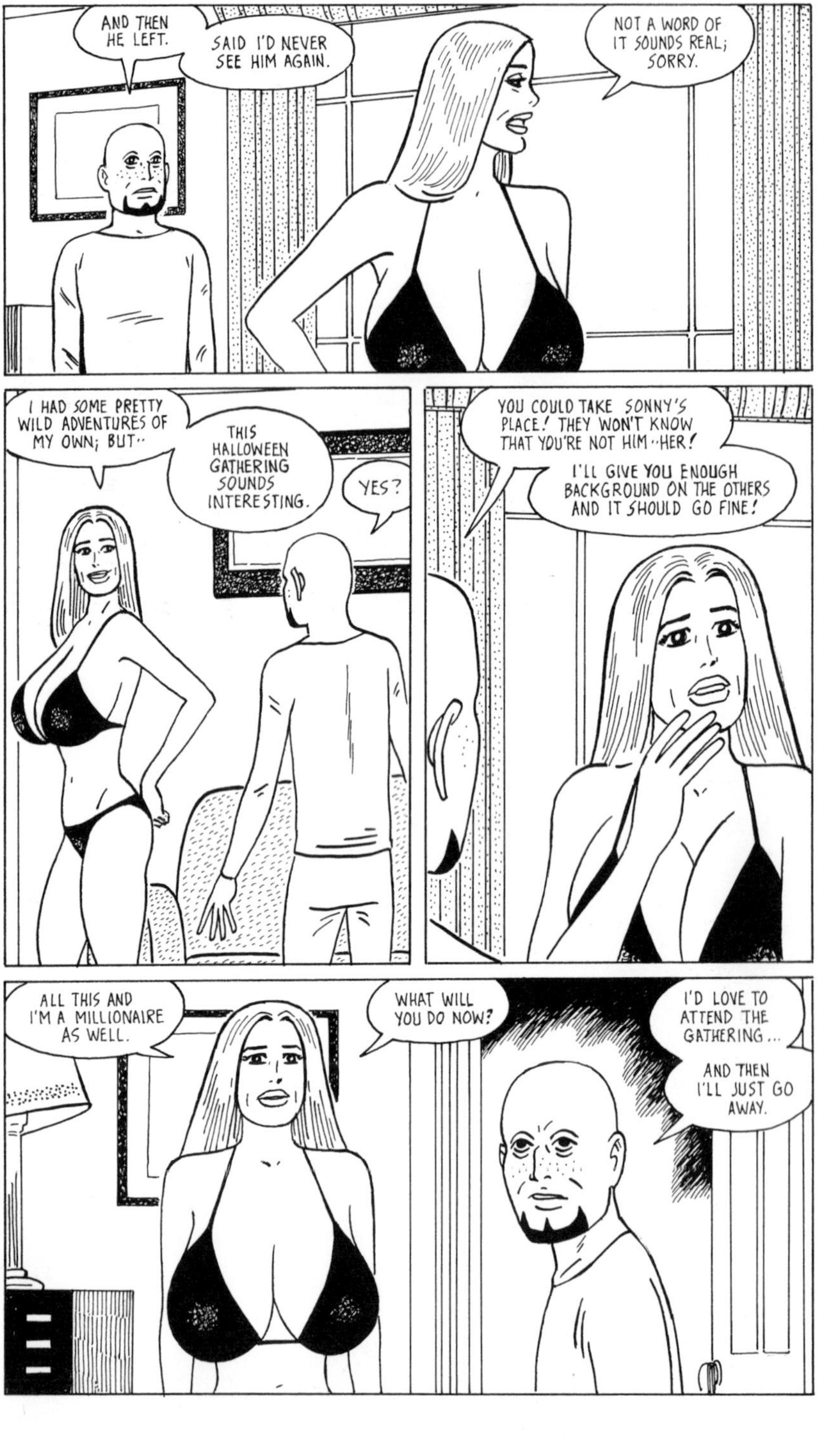
AND THEN HE LEFT.
SAID I'D NEVER SEE HIM AGAIN.
NOT A WORD OF IT SOUNDS REAL; SORRY.
I HAD SOME PRETTY WILD ADVENTURES OF MY OWN; BUT··
THIS HALLOWEEN GATHERING SOUNDS INTERESTING.
YES?
YOU COULD TAKE SONNY'S PLACE! THEY WON'T KNOW THAT YOU'RE NOT HIM··HER!
I'LL GIVE YOU ENOUGH BACKGROUND ON THE OTHERS AND IT SHOULD GO FINE!
ALL THIS AND I'M A MILLIONAIRE AS WELL.
WHAT WILL YOU DO NOW?
I'D LOVE TO ATTEND THE GATHERING...
AND THEN I'LL JUST GO AWAY.

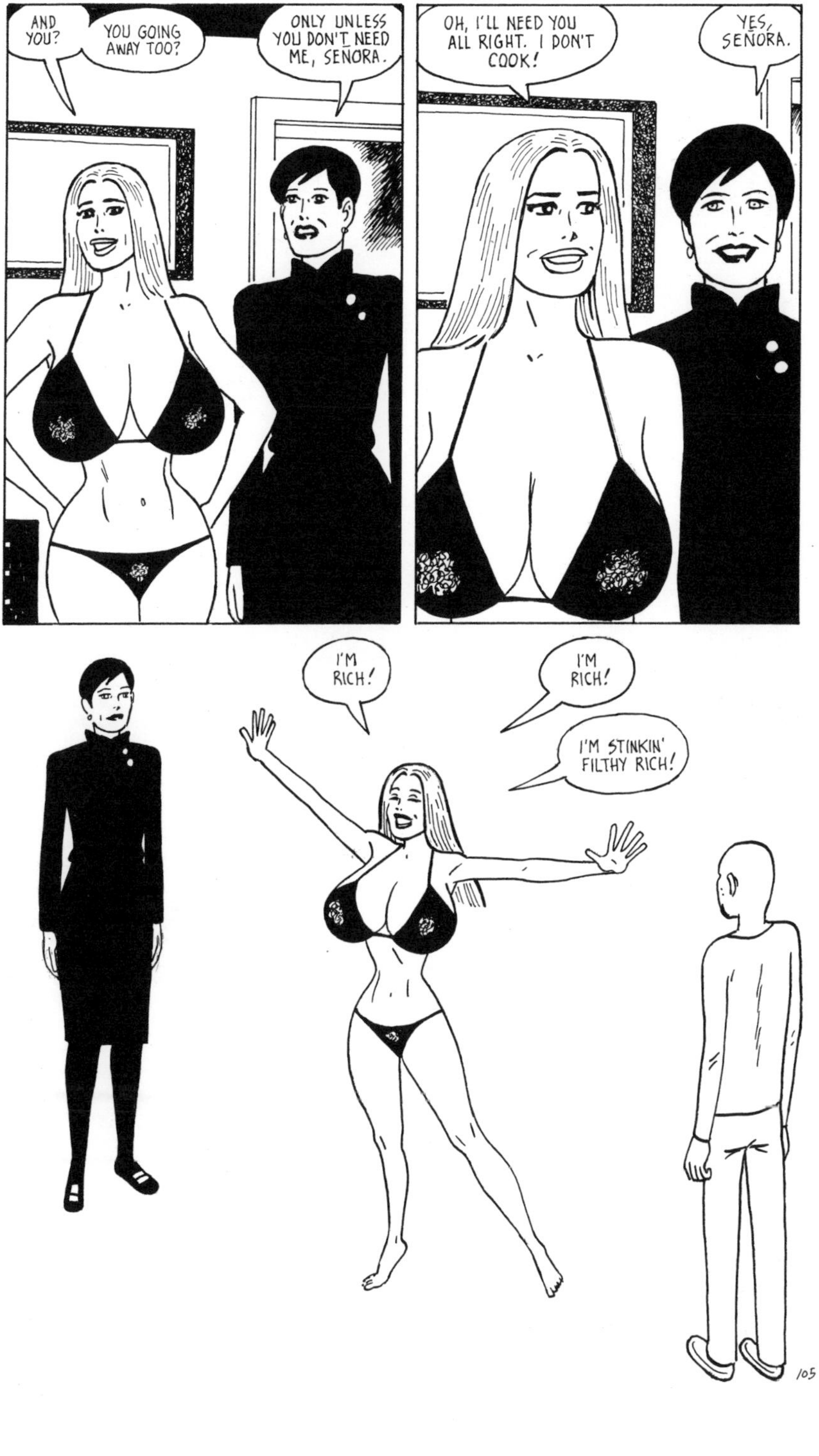
AND YOU?
YOU GOING AWAY TOO?
ONLY UNLESS YOU DON'T NEED ME, SEÑORA.
OH, I'LL NEED YOU ALL RIGHT. I DON'T COOK!
YES, SEÑORA.
I'M RICH!
I'M RICH!
I'M STINKIN' FILTHY RICH!

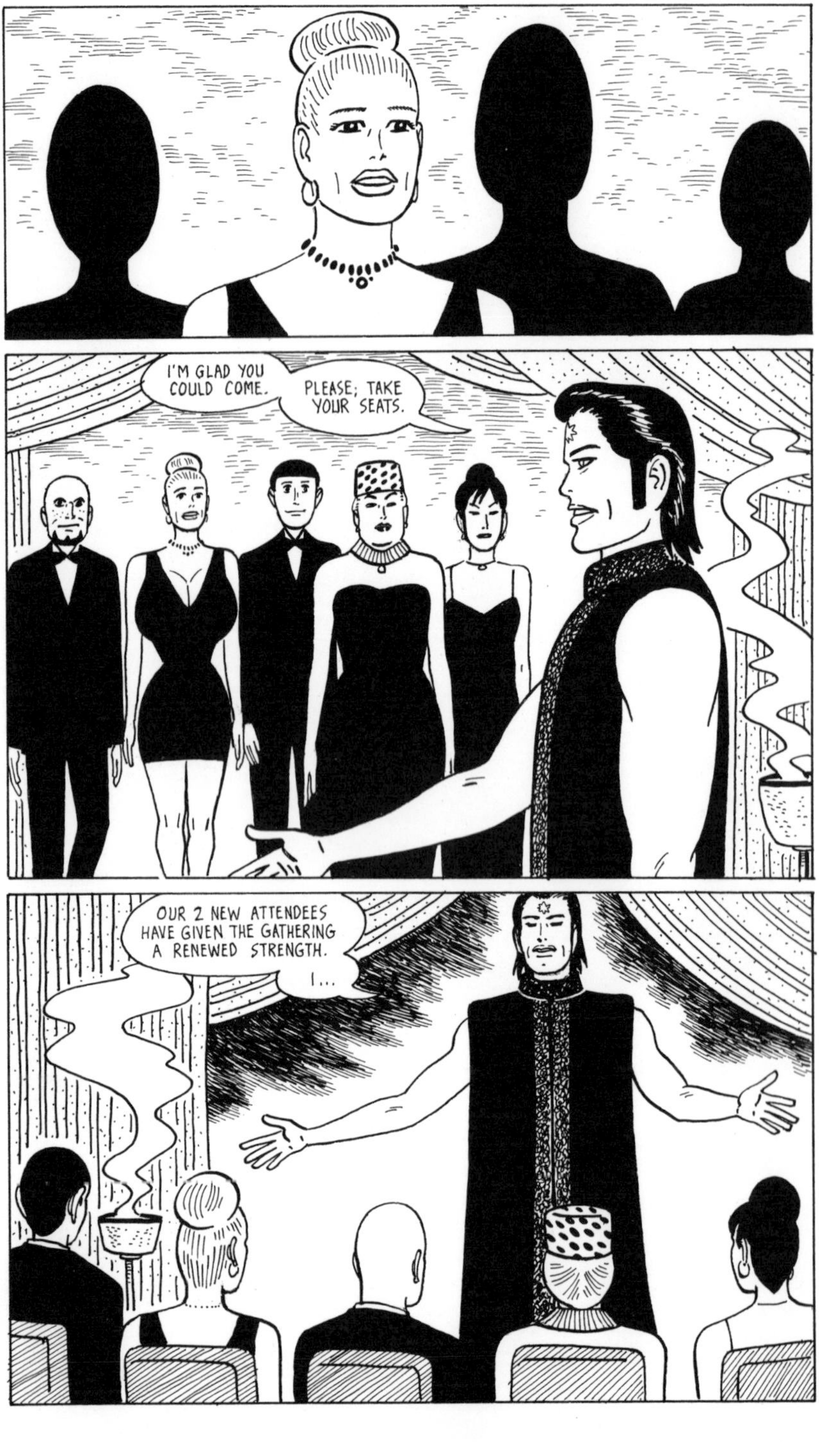
I'M GLAD YOU COULD COME.
PLEASE; TAKE YOUR SEATS.
OUR 2 NEW ATTENDEES HAVE GIVEN THE GATHERING A RENEWED STRENGTH.
I...

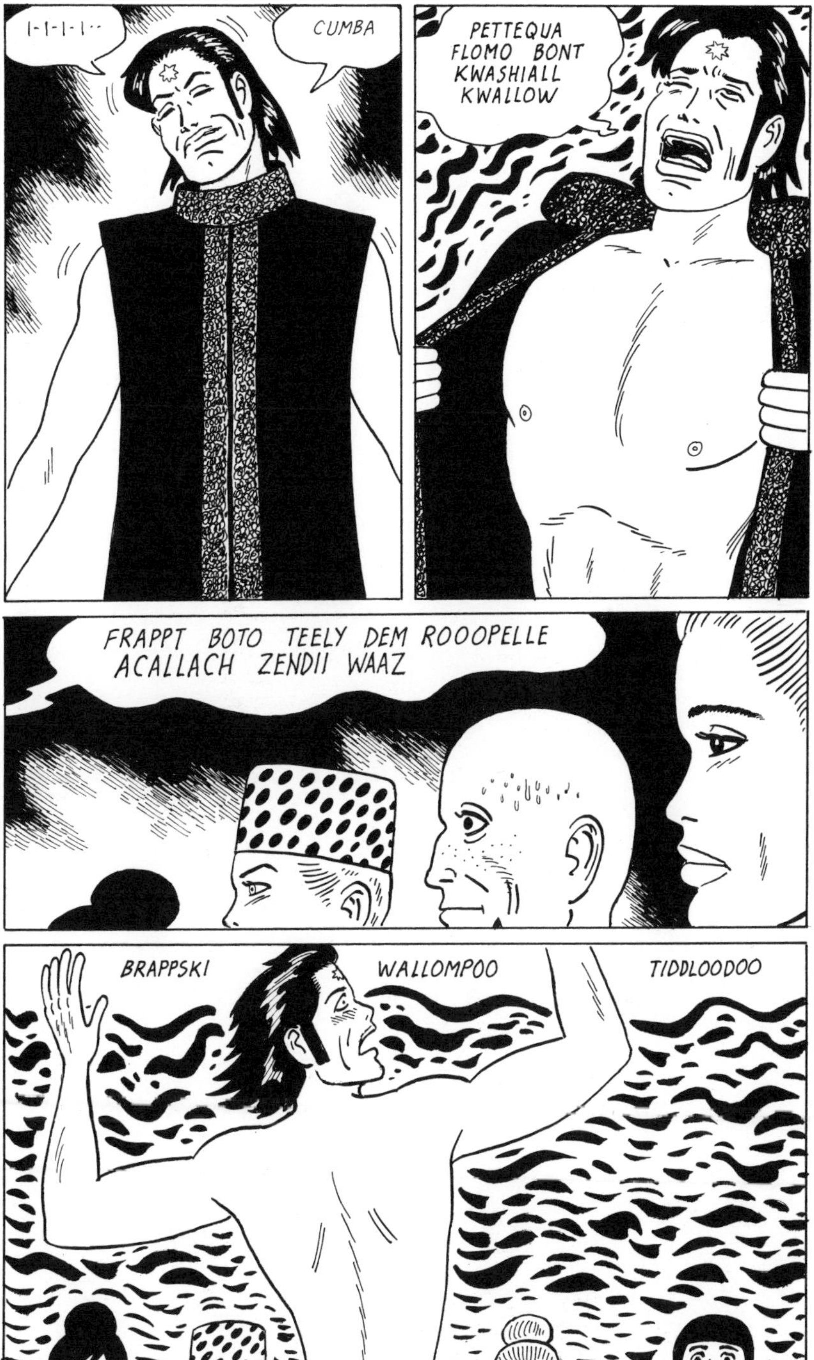
I-I-I-I..
CUMBA
PETTEQUA FLOMO BONT KWASHIALL KWALLOW
FRAPPT BOTO TEELY DEM ROOOPELLE ACALLACH ZENDII WAAZ
BRAPPSKI
WALLOMPOO
TIDDLOODOO

TENNTI TOONITE
PARTICLE IN THE
VEIN, VOSFO
EXPERIMENT: DIVIDED..! WAAAA..
PUHH...

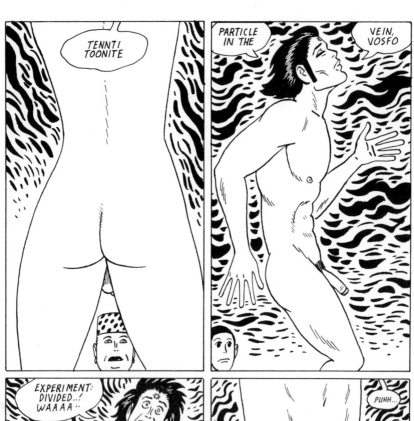

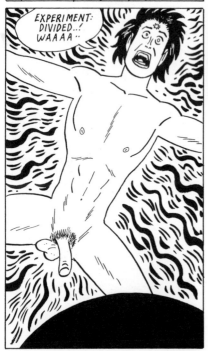

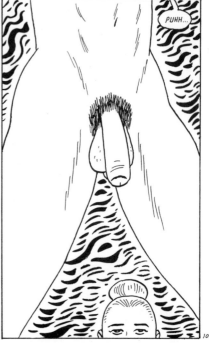

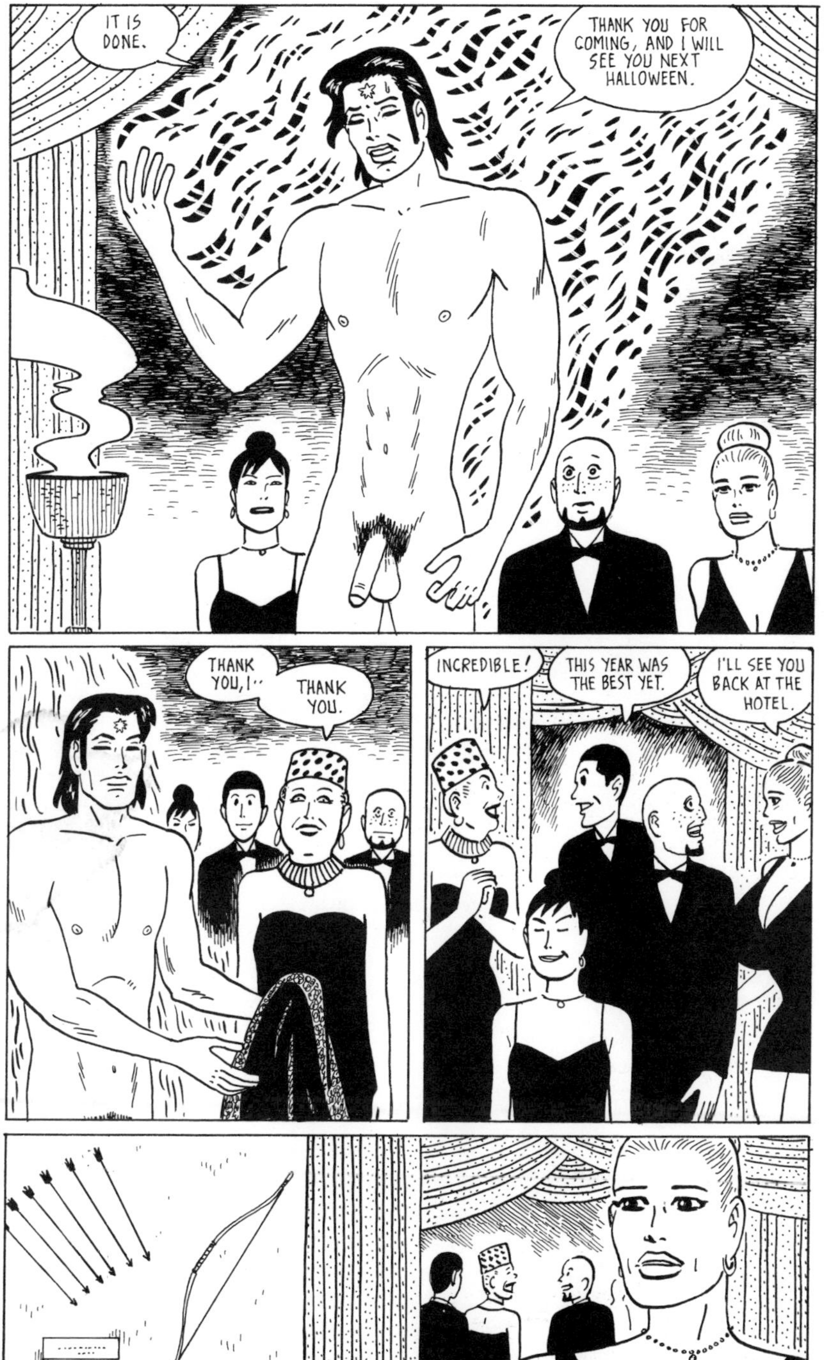
IT IS DONE.
THANK YOU FOR COMING, AND I WILL SEE YOU NEXT HALLOWEEN.
THANK YOU, I...
THANK YOU.
INCREDIBLE!
THIS YEAR WAS THE BEST YET.
I'LL SEE YOU BACK AT THE HOTEL.

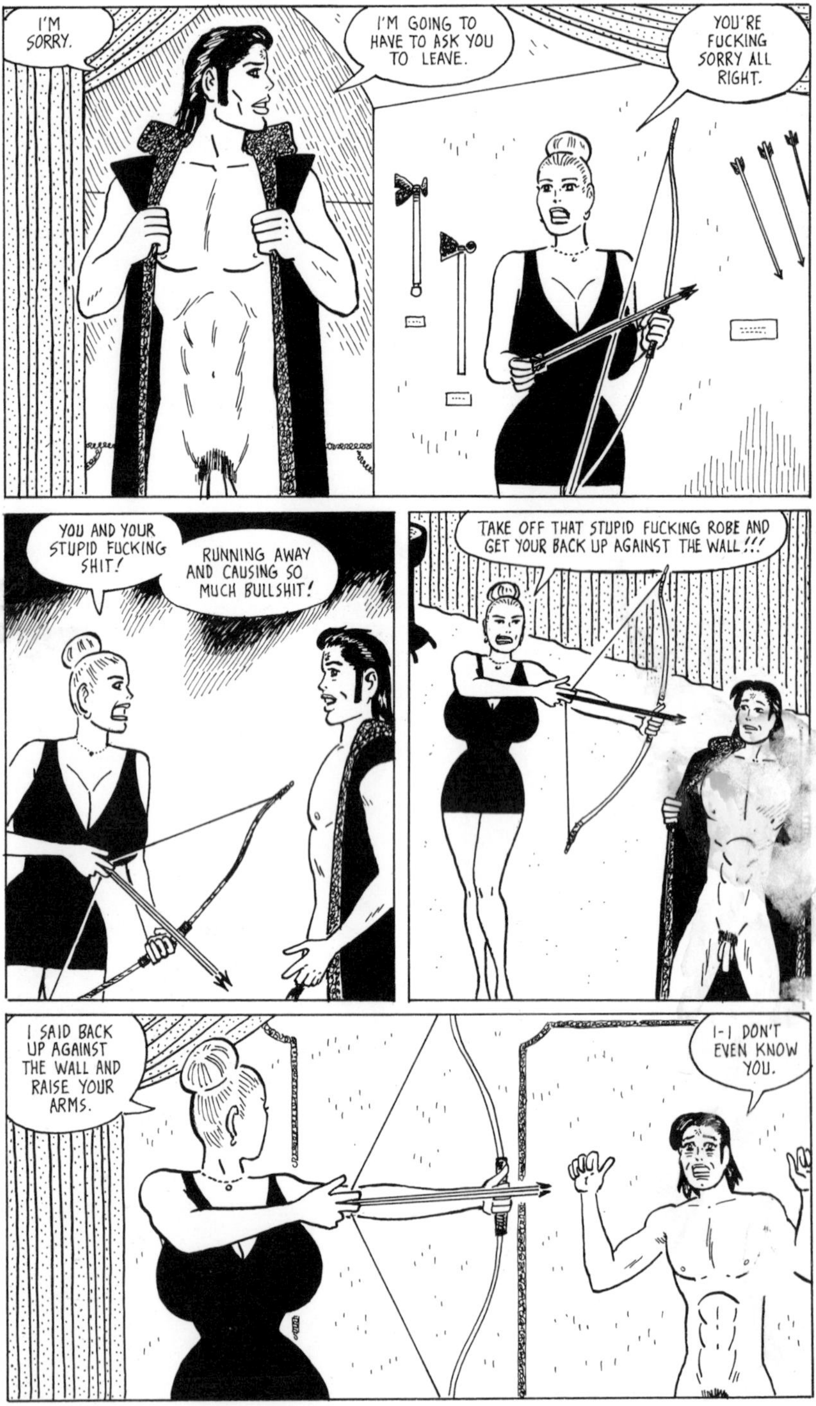
I'M SORRY.
I'M GOING TO HAVE TO ASK YOU TO LEAVE.
YOU'RE FUCKING SORRY ALL RIGHT.
YOU AND YOUR STUPID FUCKING SHIT!
RUNNING AWAY AND CAUSING SO MUCH BULLSHIT!
TAKE OFF THAT STUPID FUCKING ROBE AND GET YOUR BACK UP AGAINST THE WALL!!!
I SAID BACK UP AGAINST THE WALL AND RAISE YOUR ARMS.
I-I DON'T EVEN KNOW YOU.

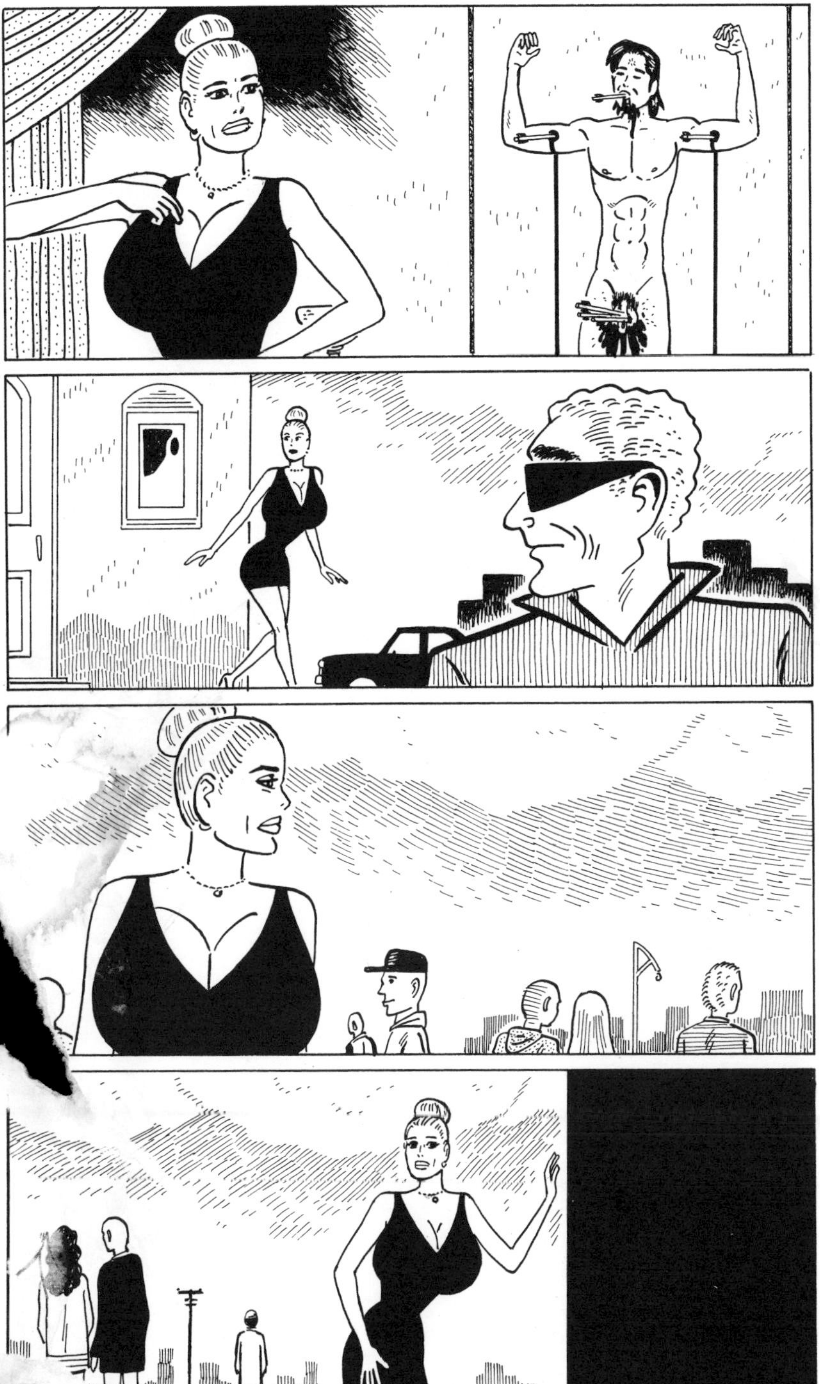

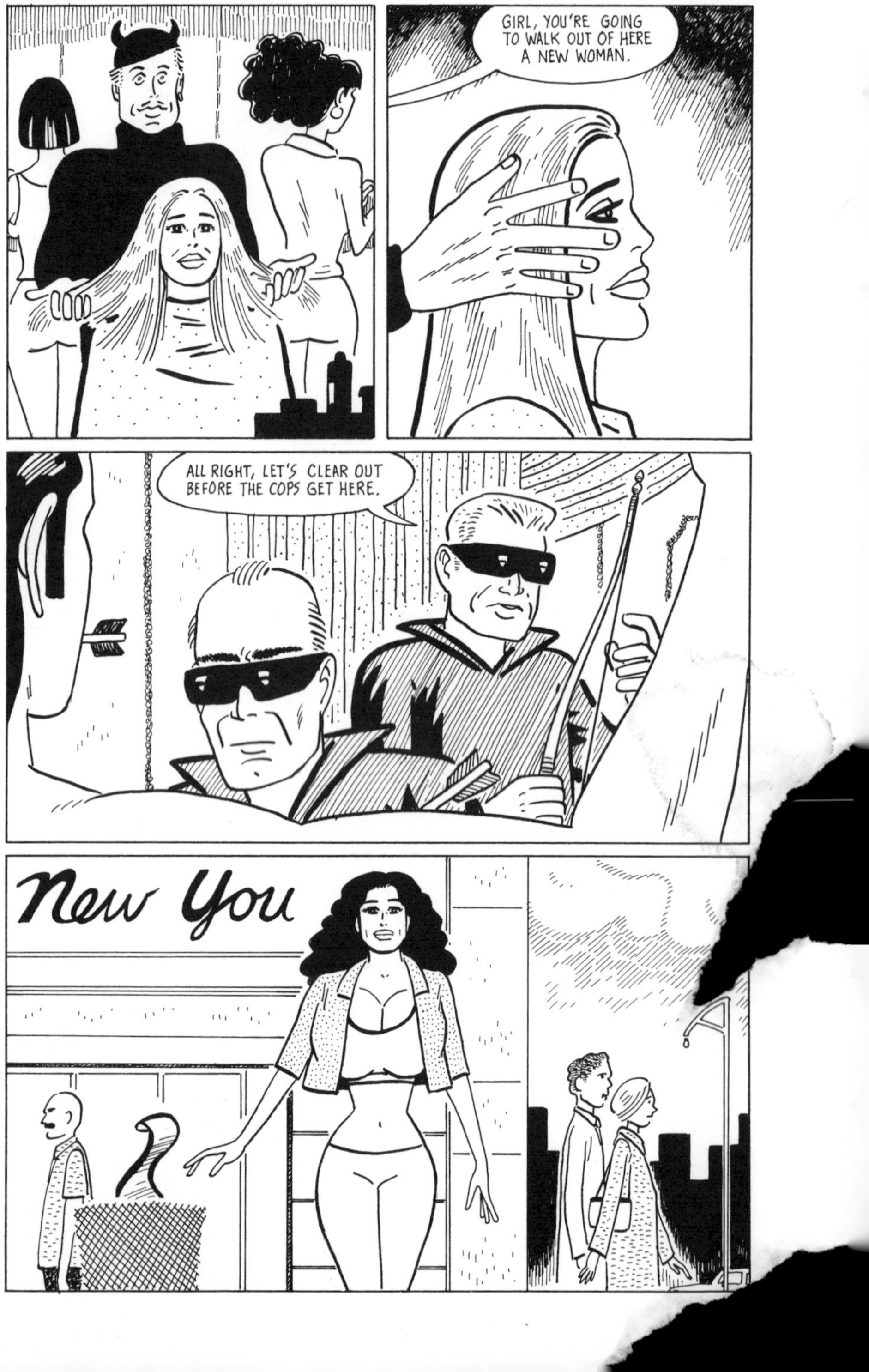
GIRL, YOU'RE GOING TO WALK OUT OF HERE A NEW WOMAN.
ALL RIGHT, LET'S CLEAR OUT BEFORE THE COPS GET HERE.
New You

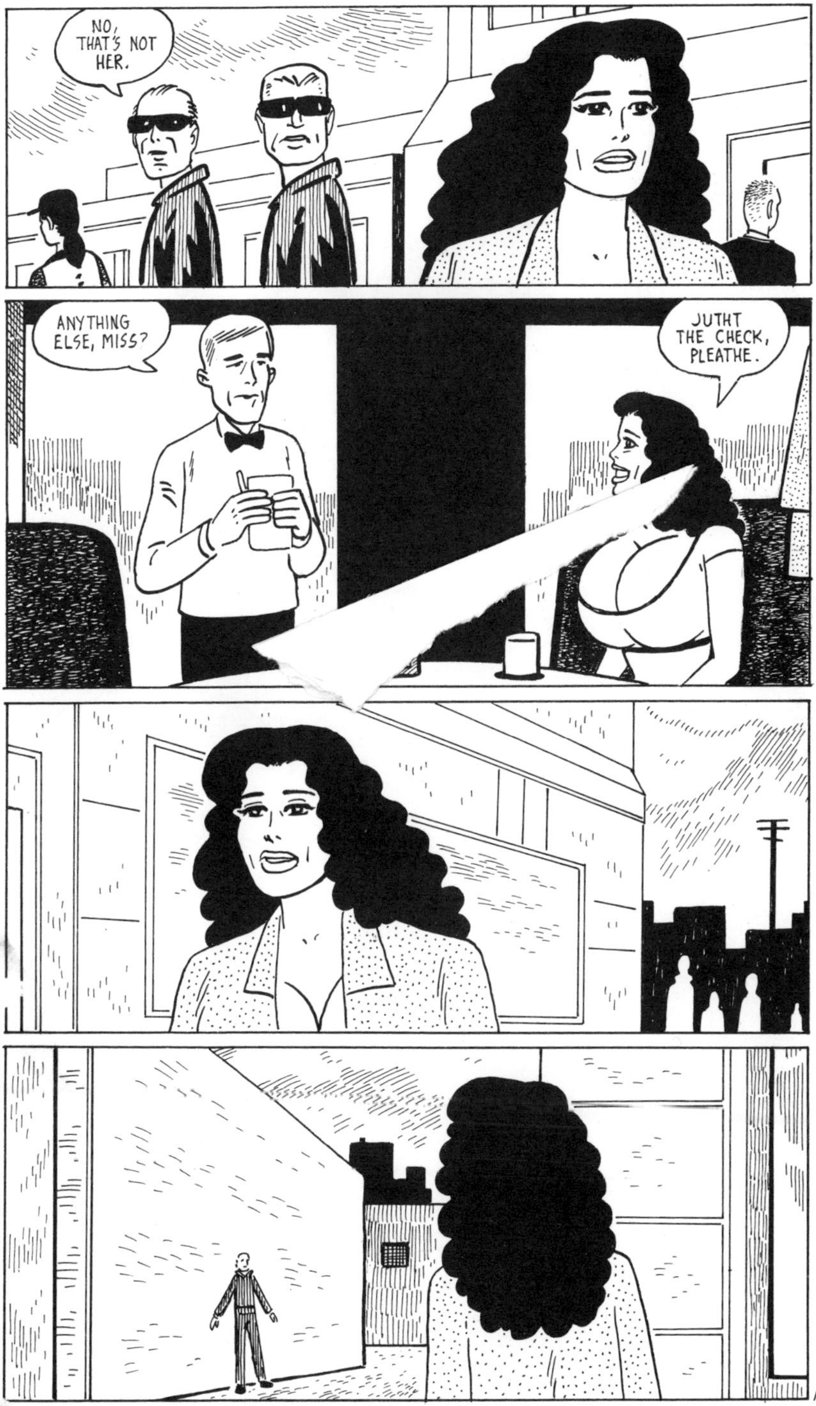
NO, THAT'S NOT HER.
ANYTHING ELSE, MISS?
JUTHT THE CHECK, PLEATHE.

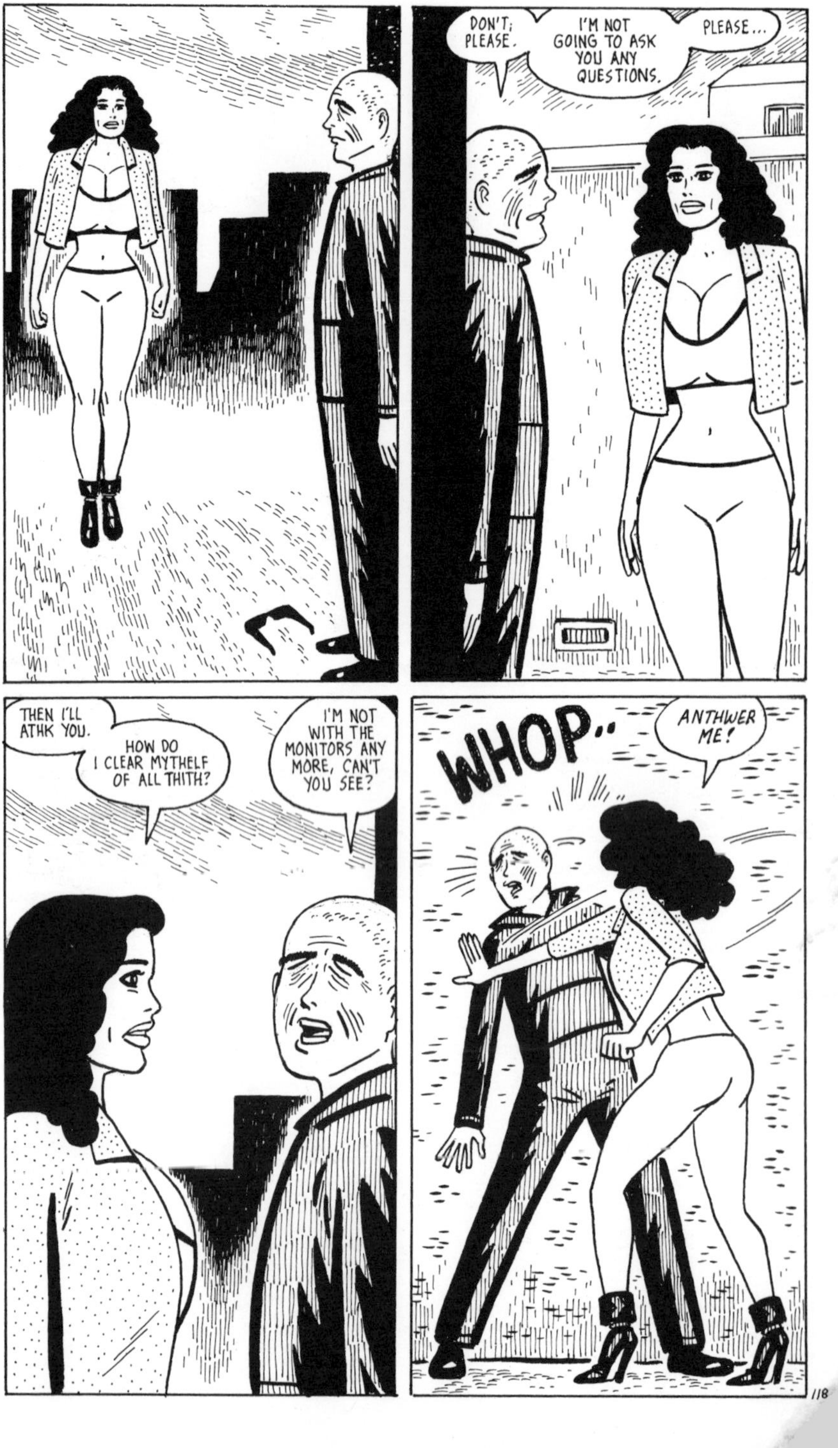
DON'T; PLEASE.
I'M NOT GOING TO ASK YOU ANY QUESTIONS.
PLEASE...
THEN I'LL ATHK YOU.
HOW DO I CLEAR MYTHELF OF ALL THITH?
I'M NOT WITH THE MONITORS ANY MORE, CAN'T YOU SEE?
WHOP..
ANTHWER ME!

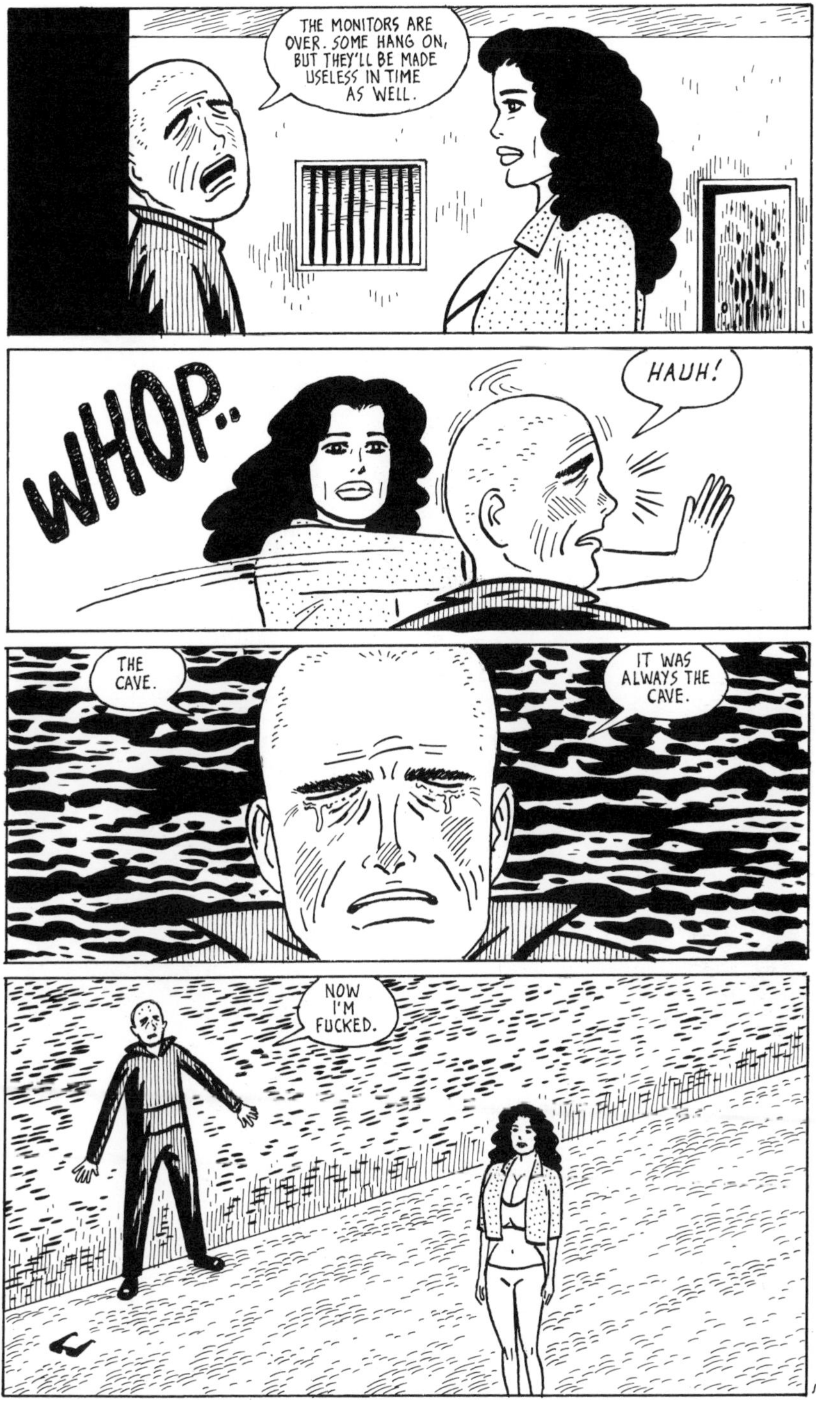
THE MONITORS ARE OVER. SOME HANG ON, BUT THEY'LL BE MADE USELESS IN TIME AS WELL.
WHOP..
HAUH!
THE CAVE.
IT WAS ALWAYS THE CAVE.
NOW I'M FUCKED.

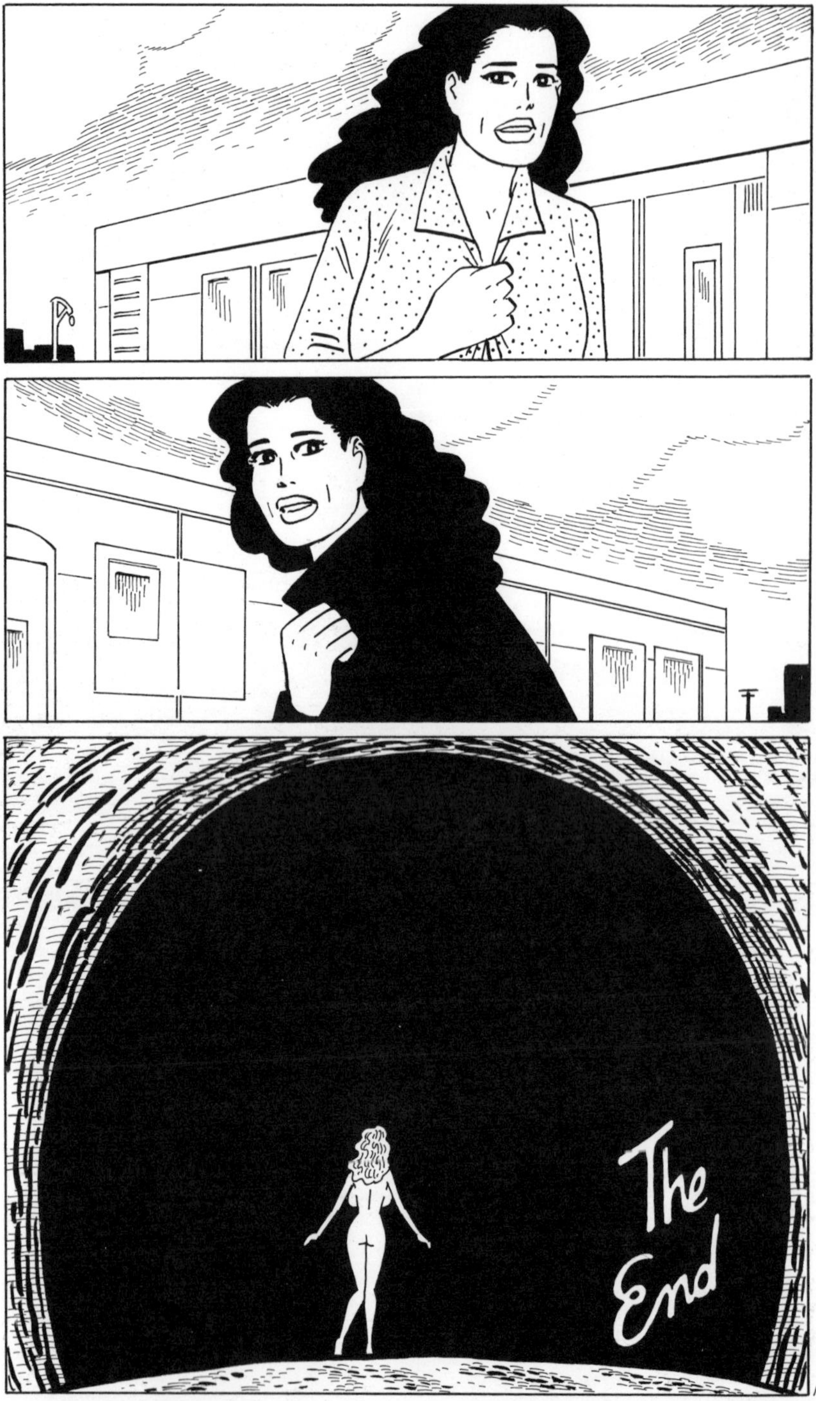
The End

OTHER GILBERT HERNANDEZ GRAPHIC
NOVELS FROM FANTAGRAPHICS BOOKS:

Fantagraphics has been publishing Jaime and Gilbert
Hernandez's LOVE AND ROCKETS since 1982. The following graphic novels by Gilbert Hernandez are currently available. All, with the exception of FEAR OF
COMICS and AMOR Y COHETES, are set in the world
of Palomar. PALOMAR: THE HEARTBREAK SOUP STORIES
(currently out of print but easily available on the web)
collects the two volumes of Palomar stories in a deluxe, oversized hardcover format; LUBA collects the
three volumes of post-Palomar Luba stories in a deluxe
hardcover format.

HEARTBREAK SOUP (Palomar stories Volume 1)
HUMAN DIASTROPHISM (Palomar stories Volume 2)
BEYOND PALOMAR (pre- and post-Palomar
    stories featuring Luba et al.)
AMOR Y COHETES (non-Palomar stories
    from Love and Rockets Vol. 1)
PALOMAR: THE HEARTBREAK SOUP STORIES (hardcover)
FEAR OF COMICS
LUBA IN AMERICA
LUBA: THE BOOK OF OFELIA
LUBA: THREE DAUGHTERS
THE HIGH SOFT LISP
LUBA (hardcover)
CHANCE IN HELL (hardcover)
THE TROUBLEMAKERS (hardcover)

Visit www.fantagraphics.com for
a complete listing, samples, etc.

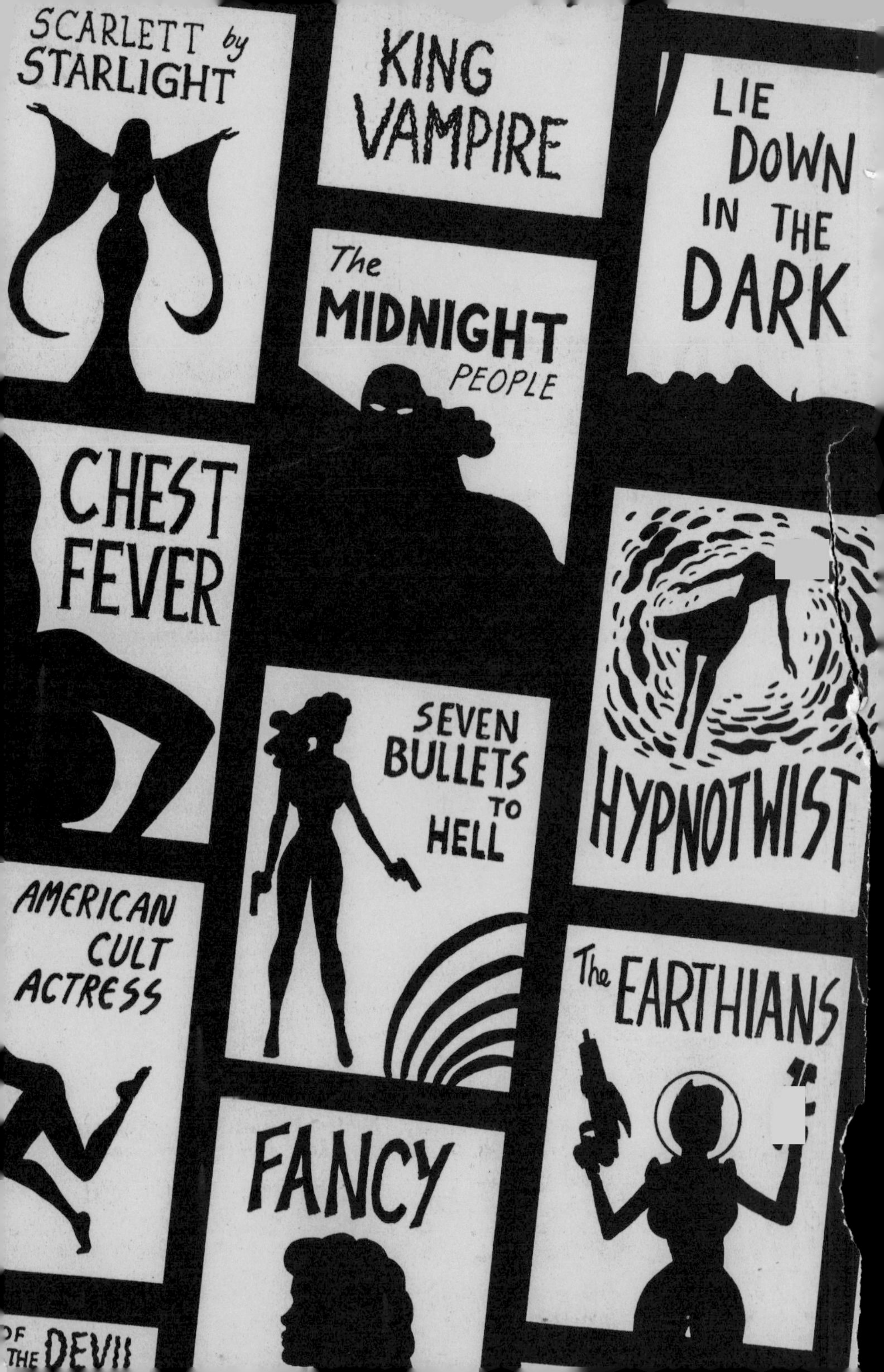
SCARLETT by STARLIGHT
KING VAMPIRE
LIE DOWN IN THE DARK
The MIDNIGHT PEOPLE
CHEST FEVER
SEVEN BULLETS TO HELL
HYPNOTWIST
AMERICAN CULT ACTRESS
The EARTHIANS
FANCY
OF THE DEVIL